BRICKS AND
MORTALS

BRICKS AND MORTALS

The dreams of the 80s and the nightmare of the 90s: the inside story of the property world

ALASTAIR ROSS GOOBEY

CENTURY
BUSINESS

First published in Great Britain in 1992 by
Century Business
An imprint of Random House UK Limited
20 Vauxhall Bridge Road, London SW1V 2SA

Random House Australia (Pty) Limited
20 Alfred Street, Milsons Point, Sydney
New South Wales 2061, Australia

Random House New Zealand Limited
18 Poland Road, Glenfield
Auckland 10, New Zealand

Random House South Africa (PTY) Limited
PO Box 337, Bergvlei, South Africa

Set in 10½ pt Garamond by Deltatype Ltd, Ellesmere Port
Printed and bound in Great Britain by
Mackays of Chatham PLC, Chatham, Kent

British Library Cataloguing in Publication Data
A catalogue record for this book is available from the British Library

ISBN 0–09–174768–6

Companies, institutions and other organizations wishing to make bulk purchases of this title or any other Century Business publication should contact:

Direct Sales Manager
Century Business
Random Century House
20 Vauxhall Bridge Road
London SW1V 2SA

Fax: 071-828 6681

Contents

———————

Introduction

So Foul and Fair a Day

THE WEATHER IN the first week of December 1991 had been resolutely dull and overcast above London. Together with the late sunrise and early sunset, it made an imperfect backdrop to an event which encapsulated all the excitement and change of the 1980s property boom and its consequent collapse. As Thursday 5 December progressed, the cloud began to break up and by the time the guests had begun to assemble in Exchange Square, Broadgate, on the northern fringes of the City of London, the sky had become dappled, although no sun penetrated into this new open space. The ceremony that was to be held marked the effective completion of the most striking piece of urban generation of the 1980s, Broadgate; over three million square feet of new offices spanning the tracks of Liverpool Street railway terminus, covering the site of the defunct Broad Street Station and running North along Bishopsgate.

At 3.45 p.m. the trumpeters of the Household Cavalry signalled the arrival of Her Majesty Queen Elizabeth II. To greet her, both wearing well-cut dark blue overcoats, were the two protagonists of the joint company set up to create this development: Stuart Lipton and Godfrey Bradman. The first cheerful, tall, and heavily built; the second a small, balding, bespectacled figure, every inch the accountant he had qualified as. It was symbolic of the state of the relationship between the two companies, Lipton's Stanhope and Bradman's Rosehaugh, that Lipton seemed to have taken on the role of the senior partner. He it was who escorted the Queen past the standing guests, among whom stood the Secretary of State for Northern Ireland, Peter Brooke, who was also the local MP, together with many luminaries of the British property industry: developers, agents and those precious beings, the tenants. Godfrey Bradman scuttled behind the towering Lipton and the tiny Monarch, unable to find space to walk on her other side.

Stuart Lipton made the first speech, typically praising 'good architecture' as 'good business'; Her Majesty the Queen then opened the development in two sentences, before Godfrey Bradman also spoke.

Then followed a spirited and professional representation of The Twelve Days of Christmas. To understand the flavour of this event you need to know only that it was compèred by singer/dancer Roy Castle and among the characterizations were can-can dancers as the 'three red hens', knees-up pearly queens as the 'four calling birds' and the Peggy Spencer Ballroom Dancers as the 'nine ladies dancing'; enough said. The climax of the entertainment came as fireworks rained silver confetti onto the audience and a giant star lit up the side of Exchange House.

So much for the fair part of the day, but what of the foul? For both Lipton and, particularly, Bradman, the inauguration of Broadgate was a bitter-sweet affair. Lipton knew that, the next day, Nigel Wilson, the 35-year-old managing director of his company, was to announce his departure to become chief executive of another interesting cash-flow critical business: GPA, the world's largest aircraft leasing company. Ironically one of that company's non-executive directors was Nigel Lawson, the Chancellor of the Exchequer who had created the conditions in which developments such as Broadgate had been possible; he has also, unfairly, become the scapegoat for the high inflation and recession which followed and pulled the rug from under both Rosehaugh, and to a lesser extent, Stanhope.

At least Lipton could look forward to a continuing future for his company. On 6 December it was reported that Rosehaugh had lost £226.6 million in the year to 30 June 1991, beating the £165.5 million loss reported in the previous year; the company was now in breach of some of its borrowing covenants and the auditors qualified the accounts. It was also announced that Godfrey Bradman, the symbol of finance-driven property development in the 1980s, was to step down as Rosehaugh's chairman, and it was widely believed to be only a matter of time before he relinquished his new post of vice chairman. On the same day it was reported that Greycoat, the development company headed by Geoffrey Wilson, an ex-colleague of Lipton's and another leading character of the 1980s property market, had also reported a loss. In this case it was only £5.8 million for the six months to 30 September 1991; the company's shares recovered marginally on the day, having fallen by two-thirds in the previous nine months.

If two days epitomize the 1980s property cycle, the 5th and 6th of December 1991 have a strong claim. As one who was present both at the ground-breaking of Broadgate by Margaret Thatcher in July 1985 and at the royal opening in 1991, I have been a witness and occasional participant. Like all good stories, the characters are as fascinating as the events. It is not too extreme to count the story as a tragedy. Tragedy involves people perhaps with heroic visions but certainly with fatal failings, and that is as good a definition of the property boom's participants as I can elicit. *Si monumentum requiris, circumspice*; Wren's epitaph will apply to most of these characters even when the companies they formed and deformed and they themselves have long passed into this history.

Property developers do not usually evoke the interest, still less the sympathy, of the average citizen. They tend to be faceless names behind companies with unknown names; they are thought to be slightly shady operators, foisting ugly buildings on our environment and walking away with unheard-of wealth. As with all caricatures, there are recognizable elements of the property market in this view. Yet the property men I have tried to describe, with the history of their companies over the past fifteen years or so, are a diverse and interesting group. Their activities infect our everyday life: where we work and what we see around us are dictated largely by their activities. For those reasons alone, they are worth study.

As a participant and observer of this area of activity over the past twenty years, I awaited with interest a chronicle of the 1980s to augment histories of previous property booms and busts, but 1990 arrived and no such volume had appeared. At that stage I mentioned this omission to Gill Coleridge of literary agents Rogers, Coleridge & White. She responded with a challenge to me to write a synopsis of what such a book would cover, and succeeded in interesting Lucy Shankleman of Century Business in such a project. Thus it has fallen to me to write what I had wanted to read – shades of Disraeli: 'when I want to read a good book, I write one'. As a result I have spent evenings and week-ends and the occasional holiday both researching and writing this book. That has required great forbearance on the part of my wife Sarah and my children Charlotte and George, for which I thank them.

I have felt reasonably well qualified to write these chapters. As an investment manager I have invested both in property directly and in the shares of many of the companies which are mentioned in these pages. As a result I have met most of the protagonists. They have proved very willing to share with me their thoughts and reflections about the events covered. I have quoted extensively from their interviews with me, and from contemporary newspaper and magazine interviews, but, where they have given their personal views of some of their contemporaries and competitors, I have allowed them a veil of anonymity. I thank them all for their kindness and patience. I hope they will feel that where I have been critical, at least I have been fair. To those whom I have left out, I apologize. A mercenary approach would have been to mention anyone who had participated in the market over the last twenty years, in the expectation that at least they would buy the book. My editors Lucy Shankleman and Martin Liu persuaded me not to create such a telephone directory.

Inevitably in an industry which is as large as property investment and development, I could not hope to cover all the events over a long period. I have concentrated on the particular attributes and outstanding participants of the 1980s property boom and its subsequent collapse. The giants of the industry, Land Securities, MEPC and Hammerson for instance, are mentioned only in passing, since they were already well established before the event and will emerge from the sector's recession bruised but unbowed.

As well as the interviews I have had with named participants, I have also spoken at length to other developers and investors, agents, investment analysts, corporate financiers and journalists. The industry's trade magazines, notably the *Estates Gazette*, the *Chartered Surveyor's Weekly* and the *Estates Times* have been important sources, as well as the prospectuses and annual reports and accounts of the companies covered. The published research of the agents, particularly that from Healey & Baker, Hillier Parker, Jones Lang Wootton, and Debenham Tewson has also proved a source which would have been unavailable twenty years ago.

I have not sought to embroider the story, since in my view it speaks for itself. There has been no need to seek an 'angle'; the varied character of both the men and their companies provides ample evidence of the collective myopia which affects all markets from time to time. Few indeed have been those who both invested at the bottom and sold at the top. Mistakes were made, not dissimilar in size and form to those made in previous cycles. I doubt whether this book will prevent similar mistakes being made in the future, even though the lessons and opportunities are clearly here to read. As always the opinions and errors are my own, and I must particularly emphasize that this work was entirely divorced from that of Her Majesty's Government and Treasury, for which I was working during a part of the time in which it was written.

1

THE ASCENT FROM THE ABYSS

THE BRITISH COMMERCIAL property collapse of 1974–76 came suddenly and late. The rest of the economy had already been sent into recession by the Heath government's introduction of a 'counter-inflation' policy in late 1972, compounded by the quadrupling of oil prices in the autumn of 1973, and the rise in the Minimum Lending Rate from seven and three quarters per cent in January 1973 to 13 per cent by November, but the property investment market seemed undisturbed by all these events until the very end of 1973. Even the standstill on business rents introduced on 6 November 1972, which had been part of the Heath measures, was not enough to calm the super-optimists. The Financial Times Property share index peaked at 357 in early November 1973; it fell 40 per cent in the following two months. Yet in February 1974 Town and City Properties was able to declare its profits for the six months to 30 September 1973 showing an increase to £3.4 million before tax and expectation of a 'very satisfactory' increase for the full year.

By March the problems were becoming apparent. Guardian Properties was admitting to 'liquidity problems' as its borrowings had risen from £10 million on 17 August 1973 to £48.5 million at the end of January 1974, and it simply did not have income to meet the interest payments on its burgeoning debt. The rent freeze together with rising interest rates and recession were combining to make it impossible for the ambitious developers to let their properties, and even if they were let, few pension funds or insurance companies were prepared to buy the resulting investments.

By May the Lyon Group was seeking support from its bankers following a 'technical default' on its loans, and by the end of the month, the most spectacular personal bankruptcy in British history began its inexorable progress when the property interests of William Stern had reached a state which necessitated talks with a committee of bankers to prepare 'a viable scheme for the orderly realisation of the group's assets as may be necessary to overcome its present liquidity problem'. At the beginning of June the new Labour government announced that the statutory rent freeze would be eased by March 1976, but meanwhile the property market was simply at a standstill. In June Guardian Properties had a receiver appointed and Wilstar, the key company in William Stern's empire, went into liquidation with borrowings of £212.5 million. It is not the purpose of this book to describe the progress of the 1974–76 property collapse and the consequent financial crisis, which seemed at one time to threaten the whole British financial structure; this has been well documented in Margaret Reid's book, *The Secondary Banking Crisis*. This brief introduction to that episode is included both to establish a starting point of this story, that of the recovery from disaster and the 1980s property boom and bust, and to point to some similarities and differences between the previous property boom and that of the 1980s. The 1970s collapse claimed many corporate victims and some individuals whose lives might have been prolonged but for the strain generated. Gabriel Harrison of Amalgamated Investment and Property died suddenly on 4 December 1974 aged 53, fifteen months before his firm finally went into compulsory liquidation, and a more dramatic passing was that of Sir Eric Miller, previously head of Peachey Property and a beneficiary of Harold Wilson's retirement honours list, who shot himself on 22 September 1977, as the affairs of his company were under legal investigation.

The seeds of the property crashes of both 1974 and 1990 were of a simple strain. In both cases several years of rising business rents, good demand for space, moderate buying of the completed properties by the long-term investors in the pension fund and insurance fields, and some spectacular fortunes being made had created a surge of building, only for demand for space to fall and interest rates to rise. What is extraordinary is that, so soon after the worst property collapse of the post-war period, a complete cycle of recovery, boom and disaster should have followed, with so many of the same mistakes being made by developers, bankers and investors. It is true that the mistakes were not exactly the same, and the differences are as instructive as the similarities.

The 1972 business rent freeze had not adversely affected the level of rents achieved on new lettings of recent developments, but many properties which had reached or were shortly to reach their rent review dates could not be sensibly valued by the property experts, since such 'reversionary' properties are usually bought and sold making allowance for the new higher rent anticipated, and the rent freeze had completely undermined this element of valuation. Companies found it impossible to sell properties with imminent reviews, and since many property companies were depending on these sales to fund the new developments which were eating capital, this caused problems throughout the property market. William Stern felt that the only way to have survived this financial blizzard was to have a 'tooth fairy' who could have told his group 'whatever your cash requirements are, don't worry, finish the buildings and as soon as the economy picks up, we'll wait until you rent it and let interest accumulate throughout the period. If that had happened, we would today be a very wealthy company. In the property world, Town and City is the only one I can think of [to which this happened].' (Quoted in *Minus Millionaires* by Jeffrey Robinson, Unwin, Hyman 1987).

The list of casualties in the property sector of the late 1970s is long, and would have been longer but for the Bank of England's lifeboat, launched to save the secondary banks who had been in the forefront of lending. Many companies came within a hairsbreadth of receivership, including some of today's giants. The other saviours of the system were the institutional investors, who both supported their development partners and, as the decade moved towards its close, bought substantial numbers of the properties which the property companies needed to realize to make repayments to the banks. Surprisingly enough the institutions began to buy fairly soon after the late-1973 collapse, and 1974 was not quite the black hole that William Stern later claimed: 'I challenge anyone to point to any deal done in 1974.' One of the most striking transactions in that year was the purchase of 36 per cent of the Commercial Union building in Great St. Helen's in the City of London by a consortium of the British Rail and Post Office pension funds with the Legal & General and the Commercial Union (CU) itself; in July CU sold its 44 per cent stake in the consortium to the Abu Dhabi Investment Authority. The CU building is perhaps the best example of the British-Miesian developments of the 1960s and 1970s. Some encouragement was taken from the statement by the new Labour government that after a continuation of the rent freeze there would be a gradual easing by March 1976, but this was not enough to revive the whole market. In the June 1974 edition of *Banker's Magazine* Gabriel Harrison, of Amalgamated Investment and Property, said it was imperative that rents be unfrozen as soon as possible. 'The pension funds and institutions will then be able to consider coming back into the market and purchase some of the £3 billion worth of property which is temporarily financed by the banking system.'

Most of the buying in 1974 came from the new sources of wealth, the oil producers, who could not absorb all the new-found income emanating from the quadrupling of the oil price in late 1973. The smaller nations particularly decided to invest their surplus funds in real assets in other countries, to provide income and capital when eventually the oil ran out. The Shah of Iran was thought to be the owner of a company named Evenrealm which bought two London office blocks and Blackfriars House in Manchester for a total of £15 million in September. The most spectacular example of this was the bid made by the Kuwaitis for the quoted property company St. Martins. In September 1974 the Kuwait Investment Office bid £91 million for St. Martins in cash, later raised to £107 million. St. Martins' largest asset was the Hays Wharf development on the south bank of the Thames between Tower and London Bridges.

Jeffrey Sterling, now Lord Sterling of Plaistow, whose career is more fully described in Chapter Six, describes how the valuation process was in abeyance during this period. 'The banks found that they had lent over three billion pounds [equivalent in 1991 pounds to nearly £15 billion], but they lost their nerve. When the big surveying firms started to value, they would go to an investment house, like a big insurance company, and say "what are you prepared to pay for this property?".' The response would be that the institution was not really prepared to buy at all, but if pressed, would quote some very low price. 'The valuer would then ask whether anyone else had sold anything in the area of late. In practice, about a quarter of a mile away some small property would have been sold as a forced sale. So they took that as an example, put the two pieces of evidence together and took the valuation back to the bank. The bank would say "bloody hell, our security is down; we want more security".'

'I got all the major agents together and told them we must have a more orderly basis of valuation. Horace Temple, the valuation partner of Healey and Baker, came up with the wording that valuations should reflect the price achievable between a "willing buyer, willing seller in an orderly market".' This was not enough because many investment and development companies, including Sterling's own, had currently low yielding portfolios which depended for their viability on the rents being adjusted at the leases review dates to current, much higher market rents. 'In early December 1974 I wrote a letter to Harold Lever [then Chancellor of the Duchy of Lancaster, a sort of Minister without Portfolio in Harold Wilson's Labour government], which was delivered by hand. I said unless something was done about the rent freeze, it was going to be extremely serious. People were worried about the banks.' The people brought together to make the decision on the rent freeze included Lever, Anthony Crosland, Wilson himself and, reportedly, the scourge of capitalism, Tony Benn.

The first sign that the property market might be able to make a real recovery was the announcement on 19 December 1974 by the Secretary of State for the Environment of the recently re-elected Labour government, Anthony Crosland, of the end to the rents standstill. 'The government have considered further the freeze on the business rents, which is now regarded as affecting parts of the economy in ways that even the previous government can hardly have envisaged when they imposed it. Much savings and pensions money, for example, depends on the income from commercial property, which also constitutes an important credit base for industry.' The second factor which underpinned that recovery was that the previous ten years of planning restriction in the south, particularly London, had in agents Chamberlain and Willows' words, 'created an underlying shortage of new space.' At the same time, rents on prime City offices had fallen back to ten pounds per square foot at the end of 1974 from the £20 level of the start of the year, while building costs had rocketed with the general inflation rate.

The economic recession, particularly in the stock market related industries, together with the completion of some developments started before the crisis, had increased the available office space in the City, where the greatest concentration of value was and is to be found, from some 637,000 square feet to 1,857,000 square feet in a year. By April Jones Lang Wootton was able to state in a report that 'there are signs that the confidence of the investor has been restored.' There was, as a consequence of both the high inflation rate and new pensions legislation, more money coming into the pension funds, and some of it continued to find its way into property investment.

The prime driving force in the recovery of the property market, as with all markets in 1975, was the fall in both short-term and long-term rates of interest. At this point it is vital that the practical functioning of the property market should be put in the context of its underlying economics. For those familiar with property investment, most of this will be only too well-known but it bears repeating none the less.

Many of the great fortunes of the twentieth century have been made where large capital projects and few people are involved. The Greek shipowners were famous for persuading some carrier to charter his unbuilt boat, ordering the ship from a yard on the back of the charter and only then raising the money from the banks on the security of the other two elements, putting up little or no money of their own. Banks like to lend money on large identifiable assets with an established second-hand market value; what they eschew, as one financier once put it to me, is lending on anything with wheels, as those assets have a nasty habit of disappearing if the bank tries to repossess. Commercial property is certainly one of the former types of asset; it is visible and unmovable and there is usually a second-hand market in it. As a result borrowing has always been the crucial feature of property development. If a developer builds a £20 million property and the sums are right, it is eminently possible for him to walk away with a two million pound profit; if the sums go wrong, the developer may have invested only a relatively small amount of capital in the project and it is the bank who ends up with egg on its face.

There are two elements to the mathematics of property: the world of the developer and that of the investor. The developer tends to be the person with whom this book is primarily concerned: he assembles a site, commissions an architect's design, obtains planning permission, finds the finance, employs the building contractor and lets the building. To cash in the profit made on his development and pay off the debts incurred in building it, the entrepreneur will need to sell the property to a long-term investment institution. This meeting of two rather distinct worlds is where the fortunes are made and lost. For the merchant developers, as they liked to be known in the 1980s, the costs may be divided into three broad parts: the land or existing building, the new building's direct construction costs and the interest cost of the whole. The investment institution will judge a completed development not on those criteria, but on the stream of income which it calculates will flow from the building's tenants over many years. The brutal truth of property investment is that the immediate income on a development will rarely if ever cover the cost of borrowing the money which has financed it. The developer made his money by selling the completed property on to the investors who did not need to borrow and could wait until the rise in rents gradually made the income return on cost higher than that available on other possible investments, the pension and insurance funds.

The purpose of investment for these giants of the financial world is to achieve the greatest long-term flow of income for their pensioners and policy holders. It is often thought that the capital value of an investment is the only relevant consideration for such funds, but the market value of investments is only a potential opportunity for increasing the income from a portfolio: if one of your investments suddenly rises in value and you can replace it with a similar asset with a higher immediate income, then the fund will benefit. If this thought is extended to cover a whole asset class, such as property or ordinary shares, then there is scope for increasing the long-term income of the fund through judicious adjustment of the portfolio between asset types. The institutions may perceive UK company shares to be the most attractive investment one year, foreign shares in another, property in a third and at certain times cash may be preferred to any other asset.

Property probably has the longest history as a portfolio investment. In earliest times the landlord was the Lord of the Manor or the church, but as savings became more institutionalized in the nineteenth century, so life assurance companies, and in the twentieth century, pension funds, came to be the major acquirors of investments. In the first 150 years of the history of modern investment, inflation was not a chronic affliction. Indeed, agricultural land prices in the UK peaked in the Napoleonic Wars at a level not seen again until just before the Second World War. Investment in commercial real estate was seen to be reasonably secure, but not without risks, since the income depended on the survival of the tenant. For this reason, most investing institutions either lent money to other property investors for long periods on a fixed interest rate basis, or let the property they owned on long leases with infrequent rent reviews; there was no history of inexorably rising rents, so the security of income was deemed more important than its increase. This factor, the absence of a trend of rising income, also dissuaded the same institutions from buying company shares, which looked risky in the light of the experience of the whole economy during the Depression of the 1930s.

The adoption of Keynesian economic management techniques in the years after the war changed all this. Inflation was deemed to be less of an enemy to society than mass unemployment, and prices started to rise without a break. Whereas the cost of living had not risen between December 1918 and the start of the war, between 1945 and 1965 the general price level doubled. For property investors this change was profound: building costs, like all other costs, rose, and it was uneconomic to build or refurbish a building at the old rental levels. As the economy expanded, demand for more commercial space, and of a better quality, also grew, but a combination of building controls and the unattractive economics of new building gradually drove rental levels higher. This cycle of the inter-relationship between building costs and rental levels is critical to an understanding of how the 1980s property boom both waxed and waned. New buildings can only be developed when rental levels are high enough to offer the entrepreneur the prospect of a profit when he comes to sell the completed project to an institution; the problem is that too much new development is then undertaken, outrunning the capacity of the potential tenants to absorb the new space. Rental growth slows, and may even reverse, leaving the developers with unlet buildings or lettings at rents which are not economic.

Since the investing institutions' main interest is long-term income flows, the critical variable from their point of view is the income yield on any investment. This is the annual income received from an asset expressed as a percentage of its capital costs or value. The various alternative investments open to the institutions have differing characteristics which are reflected in the yield basis on which they sell. Government securities, or 'gilts', have a fixed income but the ordinary shares of companies, equities, give an income which depends on the profitability of the underlying business. A diversified portfolio of equity shares will give a rising income over time, even if individual companies cut dividends or go bankrupt.

Similarly, a property portfolio's income will tend to rise, affected by building costs and the temporary shortages and gluts of space. An individual building may become vacant and non-income producing, but a well-spread stock of investment properties will not. As a consequence of this distinction between the profile of income between the different potential investments, the yield each sells on tends to be related, but usually in a clear order. Because the income of a pension fund is tax-free, it may be simply proved algebraically that a current annual yield of six per cent growing at six per cent per year forever is exactly equivalent in value to a fixed and perpetual initial yield of 12 per cent. For these reasons, gilts tend to sell on much higher initial yields than either equities or property, the latter two classes relying on income growth to make up the initial shortfall.

The important fact to recall which distinguishes the developer from the investor is that the former rarely has enough capital to finance a development without borrowing so much that the income available on the let investment does not cover the cash outflow on the debt; the investor will probably have no borrowings and may take the longer-term view that the growth of income over the years will more than compensate for the initial income he receives being lower than that on a fixed interest investment. The investing institutions carefully study the inter-relationships between the initial yields on all their potential investments, and, taking into account their assessment of the potential for income growth, adjust their portfolios accordingly. Unfortunately for both the institutions and the property developers the pension funds and insurance companies have not shown themselves to be adept at making these relative judgements, and too many times they have been buying asset classes at the zenith of their valuation levels and selling them at the bottom. This action is both cause and effect, since unanimous purchases by the institutions will cause peaks, as their selling will cause the troughs.

The fact that the suppliers and ultimate investors in property view the value of the assets in entirely different lights causes all the problems which lead to bankruptcies. The very reason why investment yields go up, primarily a rise in inflation, will increase the interest costs of a developer and slow the economy so that demand from tenants may diminish just at the time the development is completed. Such a change in yields will also cut the final value of the property on a sale to the investor. At this stage it is worth showing how this potential mismatch can develop.

A developer decides to build a state-of-the-art office block in the City of London of 100,000 gross square feet, which translates into about 85,000 square feet that would be lettable to a tenant. The 20,000 square foot site on which it is to be built has cost five million pounds and the building costs, including the basic fitting out of the client's space, might have been budgeted, for Central London and to the 1980's more demanding specifications, at £50 million. Professional fees, including architects and lawyers, would add another three million pounds and the interest on the bank borrowings would amount to a further five million, assuming ten per cent interest rates. The developer's total costs would then be:

	£ million
Site cost	5
Building costs	50
Professional fees	3
Interest @ 10%	5
Contingencies	5
TOTAL	68

Of this cost the developer may only be contributing only five million pounds, the rest being borrowed.

The letting market as the development starts suggests that the building may be let at £50 per square foot, giving an annual rental income of £4.25 million. Recent sales of such completed and let investments have been agreed on a yield of five per cent, which would give a sale price of £95 million and a profit to the developer of £27 million, a royal reward since only five million pounds of his money was at risk.

When things go wrong, they tend to go wrong together. Higher inflation will inflate the cost of building; it will drive up short-term interest rates, which in turn will create a slow-down in economic activity and may make letting the property much more difficult, and perhaps not at the rental level anticipated originally. At the same time, the institutional investor will be taking a more jaundiced view of the valuation yield on which it is prepared to buy the completed and let investment. Let us see the effect of all these factors on the original calculation:

	£ million
Site cost	5
Building costs	55
Professional fees	3
Interest @ 15%	8
Contingencies	7
TOTAL	78

With the rent achieved on letting now only £40 per square foot, the rent roll is £3.4 million a year, and because the institutional investor will only buy on a yield of seven per cent, this translates into a value of £48 million, leaving a loss on the project of £30 million, the developer bankrupt and the bank with a big loss on its loan.

These compounding changes in the environment can create huge wealth as well as bankruptcy. In the late 1960s, the Labour government had placed a general ban on office development which created an artificial shortage of office space. In *The Property Boom*, Oliver Marriott describes how Harry Hyams and other developers with those rare planning permissions for office developments benefited from rapidly rising rental values even though the developments themselves remained empty for one reason or another. The rise in rental values created an increase in capital values far ahead of the extra interest costs of leaving the buildings unlet. Planning restrictions have always stood in the way of the market finding an equilibrium between supply and demand of its own accord. This has only been relieved to a substantial degree during the 1980s, when first the previous Labour government's Development Gains Tax and Office Development Permits were removed and the Conservative government introduced Enterprise Zones which removed almost all restrictions in various designated depressed areas.

There are two measures of the health of the property market which will drive values of investments up or down: rents and investment yields. A £10,000,000 property which has an initial rental income of £600,000 per annum, thus yielding six per cent, may, on a review of its rent after five years, increase its income to £900,000; if the yield does not change then the value of the property will rise to £15,000,000. If however, despite the rise in rents, the investment yield, related as it is to yields on other securities, rises to ten per cent, then the capital value of the investment will have fallen to £9,000,000 (£900,000 income gives a ten per cent return on £9,000,000). It is this interplay between rents and yields which causes the cycles of investment interest emanating from the institutions.

As a consequence of the property crash of 1974–76 there had been scarcely any new development in the 1976–79 period, and as the British economy began to revive from the 1974–76 recession a shortage of space became apparent. This had the effect of driving up rents in all areas of the economy, first in retailing, then offices and industrial properties. As described in the next chapter there was simultaneously a great change in the type of property demanded by the tenants, technology friendly offices, out of town shopping centres and high-tech industrial units, and these were not readily available. For those who had developed such space the early 1980s were a period of great advance despite the onset of the worst recession since the 1930s, following the second oil shock and the new Conservative government's policy of withdrawal from the direct control of industry. As the economy began to recover from this second recession, by the end of 1981, overall demand for space began to rise, and this time the developers were in a position to provide the buildings now in demand. The financial institutions had recovered from the shocks of the 1970s and were again prepared to back entrepreneurial property developers. The institutions had made tremendous returns on the properties which they had bought while the cost of money was coming down and the planners were becoming more amenable to new development, especially in the City of London and with retail parks. There was also an important technical change in the planning environment, in the classification of buildings, which again we shall examine in the next chapter.

There is one other peculiarity about the English commercial property market which distinguishes it from almost all others around the world and has made it much more popular to investors, both domestic and foreign, than might otherwise have been; (Welsh law is the same but Scottish law is slightly different). The standard lease to a tenant is for 25 years, with no provision for the tenant to cease paying rent; furthermore the lease will provide for periodic reviews of the rent to current market values, but *upwards only*. In the pre-war and immediate post-war periods the major properties were let on 99-year leases with no provision for a review of the rent; grandually, as inflation took hold, landlords began to shorten the length of fixed rent they would grant.

A further feature of English leases is what is known as 'privity of contract'. If you, as a tenant company, decide to move offices and sell your lease to a new tenant, which the landlord cannot 'unreasonably' prevent, and if the new tenant cannot pay the rent, the landlord may pursue you in the courts, even if you no longer have any connection at all with the property. These factors make English commercial property leases very valuable to long-term investors. The *cliché* three rules of property investment are 'location, location, location', suggesting that a well-located building will always have a premium value, and that should be the prime consideration when weighing up a purchase. The English investor may be confident of achieving his income for the length of the lease from even the worst located property provided that the covenant of the original lessee is undoubted. If the landlord is lucky, the rent of a badly-located property will be dragged up by better properties in the vicinity. The owners of those well-located properties will certainly have bought their investment on a much lower initial yield than the badly located one and if the tenant happens to go broke in a recession, they may be left with an empty building with no income. Even if the tenant of the badly-located property no longer occupies the building and it is empty, he is liable for the rent as long as the lease runs.

We left the property market in 1975 showing the first signs of recovery in capital values. That recovery was a consequence of yields on properties falling, but was soon augmented by a rise in rents as the recovery in the economy met a dearth of supply. It was the large pension funds and insurance companies who invested heavily in 1975/76. The Prudential, Legal & General, and Norwich Union insurance companies; the Post Office, Coal Board, Electricity Supply, ICI and Combined Petroleum (Shell) pension funds, these were the names that recurred as buyers of property from the distressed sellers. Institutions invested £800 million net in property in 1975 and a further £530 million in 1986.

The relatively better financed companies had also been able to raise some finance from the Stock Exchange in 1975. Law Land, English Property and Land Securities had all raised convertible loans in the year, totalling £40 million. In the first two cases the financial institutions had been very unwilling to put new money up and the stockbrokers who placed the underwritings had a very hard task, as I can personally vouch, since I risked the wrath of the mighty stockbrokers, Cazenove, by refusing to underwrite the English Property convertible.

By early 1976 investment yields had fallen sharply from the peaks of early 1975. According to Healey & Baker's graph, the yield on shops and offices had fallen from the peak of eight and a quarter per cent to six per cent by the end of 1975, a rise in capital value of 37.5 per cent for a property being valued on these 'prime' investment rates. There was even some sign that the developers were beginning to regain their confidence. MEPC announced the £20 million scheme that was to become the West One development over Bond Street tube station in Oxford Street. One of the biggest projected developments of this time was that on the Trocadero site just off Piccadilly Circus, which the Electricity industry pension fund, Electricity Supply Nominees, (ESN), bought advised by the agents Richard Ellis. As the economy began to recover from its oil trauma the schemes of the previous booms opened: Brent Cross and Eldon Square shopping centres, in North London and Newcastle respectively, both opened early in 1976.

The agony of the property developers was not yet over. In March 1976 the shares of Amalgamated Investment and Property (AIP) were suspended from dealing on the Stock Exchange and a week later the company was put into compulsory liquidation, despite the fact it owned £209 million of first class property. The receiver appointed was the firm of Hacker Young, the eponymous Young in question being the accountant who became Chairman of the BBC before his premature death, Stuart Young. His brother David Young had sold his property business, Eldonwall, in the early 1970s to Town & City, on whose board he sat as a director; he was later to become a peer and Cabinet Minister under Margaret Thatcher.

Other property companies which were having to sell to stay afloat were beginning to find buyers more active. In May 1976 English Property sold 39 properties to Eagle Star for £55.5 million, eliminating the company's short and medium term UK debt. The price achieved was still below that the portfolio was carried at in the books (£62.5 million at 31 October 1975) but was above the directors' estimate on the 31 March 1976 of £51.8 million. In May 1976 Berkeley Hambro sold its green-windowed tower at 99 Bishopsgate to the HongKong Bank for £32.4 million. Today the building is worth well over £120 million. Greater detail of how some of the notable survivors of the 1970s property crash managed to survive are given in a later chapter, but the next change in the economic climate almost killed off those companies which had thought the worst was past.

In October 1976, Denis Healey, the Chancellor of the Exchequer, arrived at Heathrow Airport to take a plane to the Commonwealth finance minister's conference. He was greeted with the news that there had been a serious run on the pound and that the foreign currency reserves were not sufficient to stem the tide. On his immediate return to Downing Street the Labour government had to abandon much it held dear, and was forced to apply for an emergency loan from the International Monetary Fund to tide it and the currency over. The conditions for that loan were painful: higher interest rates, including a Minimum Lending Rate of an unprecedented 15 per cent and swingeing cuts in public expenditure, particularly on capital projects. The Financial Times property share index fell to 95.95 on 27 October, a level only one quarter of that reached in late 1973, as investors feared that this new blow would finally put paid to the weaker companies. For Town & Commercial Properties, October 1976 did mark the end, as the company was put into liquidation that month. Unlike the previous crisis however the institutions did not withdraw altogether from markets. By the end of 1976 the Financial Times property share index had recovered to 142.69.

1977 was described by the *Estates Gazette* as 'the year when property as an investment medium came back from the dead.' The combination of a dramatic fall in short-term interest rates from 15 per cent in early December 1976 to seven per cent in December 1987, and a resumption of economic growth, drove rents higher and investment yields lower, a powerful combination for property values: the Jones Lang Wootton

Index of overall property performance gave a total return of 27 per cent between June 1977 and June 1978. The clearance sale continued for those companies which were still too highly geared, but the whole atmosphere had changed. The institutional buyers of property were strongly influenced by the small number of firms of agents who dominated the investment field: Jones Lang, Healey & Baker, Richard Ellis and Hillier Parker made sure that their clients were aware of this change and encouraged them to build up their property portfolios. One of the peculiarities of institutional property investment is that, apart from the very biggest institutions, such as the Prudential, Legal & General or the Coal Board pension fund, the fund managers might have no experience in the property world, and almost certainly would have no professional qualification in the field. As news of the property market's recovery became more widely understood, many institutions decided that they too should participate. The first act of such funds would often be to appoint one of the large agents as their property advisor. The agents would not normally be paid a fee based on the capital value of the property portfolio but would be remunerated through the commissions he would earn on buying and selling property for their clients. The agents thus had a vested interest in persuading as many funds as possible to buy property. Most of them used their position responsibly but it was very difficult for them actively to try to dissuade the clients from investing since their livelihood depended on such activity.

One of the great *canards* of property investment over the period between 1978 and the early 1980s was the pursuit of 'prime'. A prime property is one which, for the time being, meets exactly the requirements for the majority of the property investors: usually well located, let to one 100 per cent safe tenant, it would be a modern building with a modern lease pattern of five-year upward-only reviews of rent, and a covenant in the lease forcing the tenant to keep the property fully repaired and insured. The most modern leases even had the further imposition on the tenant that he would pay for the day-to-day management of the property, the upkeep of the common parts and so on, which would actually be the responsibility of the landlord. Such properties represented coin of the realm for the average property investor. It is on such properties that the yield charts and performance indicators are usually based, because they represent the nearest thing the property sector has as standard investments. They will be expected to achieve the fastest rental growth and therefore they sell on the lowest investment yields. The trap is that today's prime can soon become tomorrow's secondary property. A secondary, or even non-institutional property, will be valued on a higher yield, to reflect the absence of one or more of the characteristics which define the prime investment. Few agents will recommend their clients to buy a property in a poor location with a multitude of poor quality tenants let on a lease with one or more defects from the point of view of the landlord.

A prime property can become secondary and a secondary property can become prime, which leaves the risk/reward equation all in favour of the buyer of the property currently out of favour, but this was rarely acknowledged in the late 1970s. Most institutions wanted to participate in the property market and, since many of them knew little about it, they preferred to buy what everyone else told them was the best bet. The major deals of 1977 and 1978 still involved the companies trying to rebuild their balance sheets and deals were done on first-class properties at less than prime prices as the sellers were weakly placed.

By 1977 and 1978 rents on shop properties had recovered sharply from the recession lows as the economy, particularly in the South, began to grow again, and the lack of new development since 1973, especially in the office market, had begun to exacerbate the shortages of space to let. The more farsighted of a new generation of developers began to put together the deals with which this book is mainly concerned. Tim Simon of agents Savills said 'the attractions of office property as an investment are based more on restrictions of supply than weight of demand.' At this time the combination of rising demand for space from tenants, which was pushing up rents, and the burgeoning demand from investing institutions, which was driving down yields, was forcing property values rapidly higher. A sharp rise in short-term interest rates from the middle of the year, with the Minimum Lending Rate surging from six and a half per cent to 12.5 per cent by the end of 1978, seemed not to deter investors, who saw this as a natural response to the recovery in activity.

It was at this point that property yields began to lose contact with the normal relationships to which they had adhered for most of the past 25 years, since the modern property lease became commonplace. Why this happened, and its consequences for the 1980s, is important to the understanding of what happened later. Investment institutions are very strongly influenced by the recent performance of the various investment classes in which they may invest. If equity shares have done well in the last two years, many institutions will want to increase their investment in those assets; if property has been the best performing asset class, then it is to property that new attention and money is given. You might think that the job of the institutional investor is to forecast which of the assets will perform best in the future rather than simply reflect the past, but the pressures investment managers are subject to makes them relatively cowardly when it comes to taking an independent stance. This began to be apparent in 1978, as property was perceived by institutions as the most certain of assets to hold in the pursuit of high returns. 1977 had been an *annus mirabilis* for equities, bonds and property, average portfolios of which had all risen in value by around 40 per cent, but in both 1978 and 1979 it was property which rose in value while other assets were adversely affected by the rise in interest rates. The WM Company has been measuring the returns achieved by Britain's pension funds for the past 20 years, and the table for the 1975–80 period shows how property suddenly seemed, in 1978–79, to be the answer to investors' prayers (Fig 1).

Figure 1 Rate of Return on Investments 1975–80						
£%	*1975*	*1976*	*1977*	*1978*	*1979*	*1980*
UK Equities	151.2	2.2	49.0	8.5	10.5	35.2
Overseas Equities	34.1	36.3	− 18.8	18.4	−31.2	17.2
UK Gilts	39.0	13.2	50.9	−3.4	4.6	21.4
Cash	11.0	12.3	8.4	9.2	14.7	18.5
Property Unit Trusts	18.0	27.1	34.4	17.7	24.7	18.5

Source: WM Company

The rise in property rents alone could not account for this sudden enthusiasm for pension fund investment in property. Two other factors were at work: disillusion with fixed interest securities and an absence of opportunity elsewhere. Fixed interest stocks are only attractive if the investor can be sure that his interest return is not going to be totally undermined by a high level of inflation. Having had one shock during the 1973/74 oil-exacerbated inflation, and with no certainty that the then Labour government had determined to make beating inflation its priority, the institutions were abandoning their long-held commitment to bonds. However, many funds felt that they held enough UK equity shares, and foreign investment was constrained by the controls on foreign investment which existed until 1979. Property became the obvious answer.

The more cynical view of why property suddenly became the desirable asset to hold for the institutions is that the managers and trustees of such funds were most influenced by recent experience. Because property values did not collapse in the spectacular way equity prices did in 1973/74, falling by two-thirds at the worst point, but had recovered well in the period between 1975 and 1979, many investors felt pressured to increase their exposure to the sector. Almost inevitably, as soon as the last institution woke to this proposition, the picture changed again.

The 1980/81 UK recession was a serious blow to property investors. Not only did inflation and interest rates rise sharply again but the economy suffered its most severe set-back since the 1930s depression. Retail rental values had risen by three quarters in the three years between June 1977 and June 1980, according to the figures published by Healey & Baker, twice as fast as retail prices. In 1980 rental growth came to a grinding halt. It was five years before rents caught up with the rise in retail prices again. For industrial property the picture was even worse; as factories closed, rental growth stagnated completely for the next five years, rising only ten per cent while prices in the shops rose by a half. Offices were much the most resilient sector of the property market, benefiting from the absence of new development during the mid-1970s, the Labour Party's new taxation on development gains and the continued expansion of service industries, even while the industrial recession was at its depth.

Unlike the 1970s recession, this combination of high interest rates and low growth in rents did not cause a collapse in property values. Although short-term interest rates were about 14 per cent from mid-way through 1979 until early 1981, yields on property did not rise at all. In fact Healey & Baker reported prime yields on shops continuing to fall throughout the period. The institutions continued to commit between one and a half and two billion pounds a year to property during this period. The relative stagnation in rental values was hidden by the falls in yields and the continuous round of rent reviews, which gave the erroneous impression that property was still doing well.

As the economy revived from 1982 onwards, the outlook improved again for rents as demand for property from tenants rose. By the second half of the decade, as the economy's growth rate averaged an unsustainable four per cent and more, rents began to rise very rapidly, driving up values and encouraging new development. Unfortunately, at the same time, investment yields were actually rising as the institutions abandoned their earlier enthusiasm for property. Why should this happen when the yields on all other financial assets were falling? The answer lies again in the unfortunate timing of the major institutions: having suffered the poor relative performance of property in the early 1980s, which had done even worse than stodgy gilt-edged government stocks, many institutions were actively reducing their exposure to the sector. Net investment by the institutions was lower in money terms in each of the years 1981 to 1986, by the end of which year there was barely any net investment by them in the area at all.

The classic case of an institution suffering from its exposure to property was the giant Legal & General insurance company. In the late 1970s the Legal & General had been a leader in the pensions market in both size and the performance of its pension fund unit trust. Much of the credit for this was attributable to the bold purchases that Legals had made of property at the nadir of the property bust of 1975. Unfortunately that very high exposure to property had been a serious handicap to performance in the 1980s and their clients were complaining, or worse, taking their money elsewhere. Legals could have battled on in the expectation that property would prove its value in due course, but the needs of running a business meant that the company simply couldn't take the risk of that not happening soon enough to keep sufficient clients.

Because most pension funds and insurance companies had sufficient new money to invest for most of the 1980s, the shunning of property did not necessitate large-scale selling. It was more that almost no-one put new money into the sector. The WM Company, which monitors where the pension funds put their money as well as how well they perform, publishes a table which demonstrates the effect of this on the average fund's holding of property in the 1980s, starting at the peak levels of 21 per cent of the average portfolio at the end of 1979 and falling away to the derisory level of eight per cent by the end of 1990.

If it was not the investing institutions which financed the major investment projects of the 1980s, who provided the money? The answer, as it was in the 1970s boom, was the banks. This time however, it was the major clearing banks and foreign banks who supplied funds directly, rather than through their own clients, the fringe banks of the 1970s. The ability of banks to read investment cycles makes institutional investment managers appear to be relatively clairvoyant, and the banks' enthusiasm to lend to exactly the same areas as their rivals makes investment managers look like free-thinkers; by comparison to both lemmings seem positively rational. The American banks in the 1970s and early 1980s were drawn into a succession of lending crazes: oil, third-world governments and real-estate all took their toll. In the UK, the past twenty years has seen two booms in bank lending to property developers. The equivalent figure of £15 billion of lending to property companies which marked the peak of the 1970s credit boom in 1974, has been left behind by the £40 billion lent to property companies by early 1991, three times the level in real terms of the last peak. Fortunately the absolute size of the lending does not pose as great a threat to the system as the relatively smaller sum of the last boom. In that instance, the lending made up 20 per cent of total commercial lending; today the figure is about 12 per cent of the total.

Lord Sterling identified the potential danger of the late 1980s lending boom in 1987, telling the then Prime Minister and Chancellor: 'I sniff the same as happened before.' When he conveyed his suspicions to the Bank of England he judged that the Bank was unable to gauge the size of the potential problem because so much was being offered by foreign banks, off the balance sheets of the companies. This was the subtle difference between the 1970s and 1980s. In the more recent boom, the foreign banks were much more aggressive, accounting for about half the net lending to UK property borrowers according to research done by agents Debenham Tewson. Japanese banks increased their share of property lending from two per cent in 1987 to the current 26 per cent, often lent to the UK developments or joint ventures of Japanese companies.

The 'off-balance sheet' factor was also important. In the United States, it has been the rule that property borrowings are secured on individual buildings, rather than the assets of the company as a whole. In the 1980s, corporate structures were developed whereby the parent property developer might only show its interest in its biggest development in its balance sheet as a small equity investment in a joint-venture company. The advantage of this was that the borrowing associated with the property would not appear. If the parent company did not have any responsibility for the borrowings of its subsidiary, there was an argument which suggested that the shareholders need not know the full extent of the borrowing. This 'non-recourse' lending was a phenomenon of the 1980s. As we shall see, the idea that a really substantial investment company could in practice walk away from the debts of its subsidiaries has not been seriously tested, and, if the principals involved wish to continue in the property business, they are unlikely to see whether they can or not. Nevertheless, the off-balance sheet lending gave both the lender and borrower a feeling of greater security about the debt: the borrower because such borrowing could not bring down his whole company; the lender because his security was specific and unable to be interfered with by any other borrowing that the group might have.

By the middle of the 1980s, the scene had been set for a property boom on a scale which exceeded that of the 1970s and probably surpassed that of the 1960s. In that boom the restrictions on development meant that relatively few companies made enormous amounts of money. In the 1980s everyone seemed to be developing property, and the cranes were looming over every city. The tale of the boom cannot cover all the participants, but the following chapters chart the rise, and sometimes fall, of the most active developers and investors of the 1980s property boom. The last chapter will try to identify what went wrong and what the prospects are for the future.

2

CHANGING THE FACE OF THE CITIES

THE HEAD OFFICES of some of the world's greatest companies are over-crowded, have no air-conditioning and are situated in narrow back streets; but this is not New York or London, it is more likely to be Toyko or Osaka. In Japan there are relatively few modern offices and even though the industrial economy of Japan has strengthened dramatically over the past 20 years, the factories in which some of the most advanced equipment is made can often seem as dilapidated as any of the relics of the Industrial Revolution in Britain.

In the 1980s the UK property world suddenly woke up to the fact that much of the accommodation for all aspects of commercial life had been made obsolete by the new demands of technology on both offices and factories and the trend away from the High Street in retailing. At the same time there has been a reaction against the concrete brutalism which characterized much of property development during the first boom of the 1960s, when the cities of Britain rose from the ashes of the Blitz. The pre-war face of the office, shop and factory was that of the late Victorians and Edwardians: Dickensian gloom on the inside of monumental exteriors; from the multi-storey Lancashire cotton mills to the curved double shopfronts of the High Streets and the labyrinthine and sometimes rat-infested offices of the average worker, there had been relatively little new development in the Depression years, and the immediate post-war period had been constrained by building licences, which were not finally removed until 1958, supply shortages and confiscatory taxes on new buildings.

As always the City of London presents the most obvious continuum of changing styles. Such buildings as the GPO headquarters in St. Martin's-le-Grand, constructed between 1890–95 to designs by Sir Henry Tanner, although using reinforced concrete, retained the classic lines of the past. Relatively little had changed in the style of building by the time Sir Henry's son, another Henry Tanner, designed 8–10 Moorgate in 1922. There were innovative buildings, such as Adelaide House on the approach to London Bridge, which, built in 1924–25 to a design of Sir John Burnet and Thomas Tait, contains such improvements to the life of the City office worker as electic lifts, central heating and an internal mailing network, but real change had to wait until after 1945 and the introduction of both American ideas and more modern materials.

The first City office block in the style which became synonymous with the first post-war property boom was Fountain House, 125–135 Fenchurch Street, developed by the City of London Real Property Company, now a subsidiary of Land Securities, to a design by W. H. Rogers in 1954–57. Planning controls in the City of London have traditionally included a restriction on the amount of lettable space allowed to be built for every square foot of land covered by the underlying plot. This so-called plot ratio had varied at different times between three and five and in the 1950s the former figure applied. Fountain House did not simply cover the site on which it was built to a limited number of floors along the line of the street; instead it followed the New York idea of a low-built podium with a highrise tower covering only one end of the plot. According to Sir Nikolaus Pevsner in the volume of his *Buildings of England* covering the City, the development's design is derived from the Lever Brothers headquarters in Manhattan, which has now been declared a 'landmark building', equivalent to a British 'listing'. One of the other distinctive features of Fountain House is that it was built with curtain walls. In this building method the external walls are hung like curtains from the concrete floors; in most cases the curtain is made up of glass and some hard-wearing but lightweight material between the glazing. This was the commonest building method of the 1960s, in both senses of that word, since it was both prevalent and low quality; many of the curtain wall buildings of the period have either seen major rebuilding or demolition, and those remaining no longer fit into the category of building desired by the investing institutions.

For most of the next 20 years, these curtain-walled tower blocks were the norm in office design all over the United Kingdom. The name of Colonel Richard Seifert became synonymous with office developments in London, partly through his close association with Harry Hyams of Oldham Estates, one of the most prolific of the period's developers. Colonel Seifert's partnership designed its first City tower block in Drapers' Gardens (1962–65), the era culminating with their design for the National Westminster Bank's new headquarters between Old Broad Street and Bishopsgate; this is the apotheosis of the 1960s–1970s tower. Built between 1977 and 1981, at 600 feet it was, until the advent of Canary Wharf, the tallest in Britain, and is the highest building in the world with floors hung from the top of the building down, by cantilever. Most of these 1960s office blocks were developed piecemeal taking advantage of rarely gained planning consents, but there were some attempts to establish more thorough-going order to this redevelopment. The prime sites for these wholesale changes to the cityscape were those most badly affected by the Blitz, notably the area just north of London Wall, known as the Barbican, and the neighbourhood to the north of St. Pauls.

On the former site the City Corporation, with encouragement from the London County Council, drove a dual carriageway road, dubbed Route 11 rather ominously since it suggested at least another ten of these urban motorways were planned. It runs between Moorgate and Aldersgate, flanked on either side by a total of six tower office blocks, all built by different developers and looking like two lines of dominoes ready to be toppled. This vision of Le Corbusian breadth was tied in with the Barbican residential and arts development to the north of London Wall, with its 412-foot towers of apartments challenging the offices along Route 11; the comprehensive redevelopment took 17 years from 1962 to 1979 to reach fulfilment, just before the original buildings on London Wall themselves became obsolete. The Barbican development with its elevated walkway connections to and over Route 11 was described by the ex-President of the Royal Institute of British Architects Lionel Esher in 1981 as 'a credit to the boldness of the City's notoriously conservative establishment ... the spaciousness and the achievement, after the claustrophobia of the inner City, after all the makeshifts and accidents along Gresham Street, are exhilarating.' Lord Esher admitted ruefully however that 'there is never enough traffic below ... and never enough humanity above.' Most residents of the City and workers in it are glad that such total planned environments never replaced the chaotic juxtaposition of buildings which still makes the City resonate its earlier street plan. That such offices as were built along Route 11 have not taken over the whole area is accounted for by the change in demand for the type of space needed by the occupier, not just by a change in aesthetic taste.

Beside St Pauls, plans for the Paternoster Square development were finalized in 1961, but the precinct was not finished until 1967. The designs, co-ordinated by master-planner Lord Holford, were praised by Pevsner as an 'outstandingly well-conceived precinct', but these mostly low-rise buildings clustered around a notoriously windswept open space never met with public approval, especially Juxon House, the most westerly of the buildings which intrudes into the view up Ludgate Hill to the cathedral.

Probably the most Miesian building erected in this period was the solid black Commercial Union building in Great St. Helens. This, like the later National Westminster tower, has a central core and the floors were built downwards from the top level with a service floor halfway down. Designed by the Gollins, Melvin, Ward Partnership, it has survived better than many of the buildings of its time, even the IRA bomb of April 1992, despite inflicting on the inhabitants of the City another gale-blown paved area around its base. The Kleinwort Benson building in Fenchurch Street, completed in 1969, was another building designed with a central core and hanging floors. This building became notorious in the late 1960s as the 'leaning tower of Fenchurch Street' as structural problems held up work on the site for many months. This was no disadvantage to Kleinworts since part of the space they had pre-let from the developers was surplus to their requirements, and while they waited for completion, the rental value of the building, under the influence of the Brown ban on office development, rose sharply, much as keeping Centre Point empty suited Harry Hyams' Oldham Estates for some time.

One of the most controversial proposals for the City which proved to be an idea whose time had passed was the Palumbo scheme for Mansion House Square, a development of a site bounded by Queen Victoria Street, Poultry and Bucklersbury pieced together over many years by the late Rudolph Palumbo and his son Peter, now Lord Palumbo and Chairman of the Arts Council. Their private property company, City Acre, is based in a Georgian annexe to St. Stephens Church, Walbroook; Peter Palumbo has endowed this church, the original home of The Samaritans and its founder the Rev. Chad Varah, with a massive altar sculpted by Henry Moore, confirming his aptitude for challenging classical form with modernism.

The Palumbo plan involved the building a 290-foot tall block designed by one of the fathers of modern architecture, Mies van der Rohe. The site is one of the most sensitive in the whole of London, facing as it does the junction of streets onto which the Bank of England, the Royal Exchange and the Mansion House all face. The proposed development was described by the Prince of Wales as a 'stump' and that prevailing, probably unjust, sentiment was reflected in the refusal of planning permission in 1985 after a public inquiry. Palumbo then accepted that such a stark development would not meet with approval and has achieved permission for an alternative development on most of the site, designed by James Stirling in the current genre which mixes the appearance of the old Cunard liners and Odeon cinemas. The Prince of Wales described the design as looking 'like an old 1930s wireless', and went on to ask 'why pull down one of the few remaining bits of the Victorian City, including no fewer than eight listed buildings?' Those who wish to maintain the existing buildings, including 2–10 Queen Victoria Street, designed by J&J Belcher in 1870 and long occupied at street level by Mappin & Webb, have to accept that such properties no longer meet the needs of the modern world, and mere refurbishment would not suffice to turn them into desirable offices.

The end of the 1970s marked the culmination of the rash of pre-Brown ban developments, typically in the tall, plain curtain-wall style, and by the end of the decade there had been a sea-change in architectural ideas. Perhaps the most striking of these new ideas was the property designed by Arup Associates in 1976, known as Bush Lane House, 80 Cannon Street. Suddenly a building appeared to have been turned inside-out, with a lattice of structural stainless steel supporting a curtain-wall on its inside. The idea was to provide more clear interior space without obstructing pillars.

In May 1978 Frank Duffy, senior partner of architects Duffy Eley Giffone Worthington, now known simply as DEGW, wrote an article entitled 'The Thinner the Better' criticizing the traditional design of British speculative office developments. These, he said, were both 'difficult to utilise effectively . . . avoiding columns' being 'too narrow or too deep – or both', and were 'by no means superior in environmental performance to pre-war offices'. Duffy pointed out that most British office developments, while copying many of the design features of US blocks, had one fatal difference: most of them, such as Fountain House or the buildings strung along London Wall, had been built as wings protruding off a core containing central services such as lifts and plumbing. They were only 45 feet deep, about the worst depth for configuring useful office space. This depth dictated two rows of cellular offices about 20 feet deep and a central corridor; as Duffy pointed out in *The Changing City*, (by Francis Duffy and Alex Henney, published by Bulstrode Press, 1989), unless the standard window width is great and the central core can be used, this produces long, narrow offices with tremendous waste of space. Closed offices need be no deeper than 16 feet, whereas in an open plan office, each workspace needs to be about six feet in diameter.

This critique was not the final death-knell for the post-war standard building. It was the work done by Duffy and others on the demands of changing Information Technology usage which caused the shape of new offices to change and brought premature obsolescence to so many of the 1960s buildings. Although the Duffy criticism of the shape of these office blocks was damaging to their long-term viability, it was the advance of technology which condemned them to the demolisher's swinging concrete ball.

DEGW was commissioned by far-sighted developers such as Godfrey Bradman of Rosehaugh and Stuart Lipton of Greycoat and, later, Stanhope, to look at the changing needs of likely office users. In the 1970s the conventional wisdom was that, with the advance of telecommunications and technology, there was likely to be a fall in the number of office workers needed in the centre of cities, and the amount of space required would be reduced overall. This argument was adduced particularly by those who opposed new office developments, such as Coin Street on the south bank of the Thames between Waterloo and Blackfriars Bridges. An article in 1979 by Richard Barras, principal scientific officer of the Centre for Environmental Research, pointed out presciently that whether the burgeoning property boom he identified would turn into a renewed bust would depend largely on final user demand and the financial conditions under which the new developments were funded. However he also predicted that the trend of the recent past would not be broken and that 'declining growth in office employment can be expected to continue' despite the fact that there would be 'a continued growth of the financial service sector relative to the national economy as a whole'. Barras concluded that 'with less redevelopment of secondary offices and only selective growth in user demand, the pressure of institutional investment funds and the competition for development profits therefore seem certain to create a new phase of over-supply in the early 1980s, resulting in falling capital values and sharply reduced profits'.

The Inspector in the Coin Street inquiry seemed to accept the claim that technological advances would reduce office employment. It was certainly true that between 1961 and 1981 there had been a dramatic fall in the numbers of workers in the geographical confines of the City of London, from 385,000 to 300,000; it is estimated that office employment in the City rose by 20 per cent in the 1980s, while the new areas of office activity, the southern tips of Hackney and Islington, the western extremity of Tower Hamlets and the Thames boundary of Southwark have seen much greater increases. The reasons for this turn-around in demand for space are manifold and no single one takes precedent, but the developments unforeseen by the planners included the growing internationalization of financial activity, particularly after the removal of capital controls in most of the world, the liberalization of access to the markets, particularly 'Big Bang' in the Stock Exchange in 1986, and the growth on the other hand of more regulation covering these newly liberalized markets.

At the same time the demand for space per employee has risen markedly, partly as a response to demands for a better working environment but mostly as a consequence of the increased space taken up by technology and environmental equipment. Even between 1971–1981, when office employment in the City fell by 15 per cent, office space occupied rose by ten per cent, so that the average floor space per employee rose from 118 sq. ft. to 150 sq. ft., by roughly a quarter.

In 1981 Stuart Lipton argued that there would be a demand for large units over 100,000 sq. ft., that new office technology was generating a demand for new flexible office building and that deep plan office space would prove inefficient in the energy-conscious 1980s. Most of these views were contained in the publication Orbit 1 by Francis Duffy and Maryanne Chandor, published by DEGW and EOSYS in April 1983. ORBIT was an acronym for Office Research on Buildings and Information Technology. This view was widely ridiculed at the time and many developers and investment companies have paid a heavy price for ignoring the research. 1 Finsbury Avenue, developed by Rosehaugh and Greycoat, is generally accepted as the first of the new generation of buildings created for the new environment.

The change in the requirements of tenants coincided with a growing disillusionment among both architects and, more obviously, the general public, with the Modernist school of architecture. In the 1960s and 1970s the major commissions tended to come from the public sector. The building of new universities, leisure and educational facilities, from Leicester University to the National Theatre and the Knightsbridge Barracks, were more adventurous than the standard product of the commercial developer. By 1976, when the IMF insisted on cuts in the capital expenditure programme of the Labour government and, in the words of Anthony Crosland 'the party is over' for local government spending, these commissions suddenly became scarce.

It was not until 1980 that the Department of the Environment listed the Jubilee Hall, one of the last critical sites in Covent Garden, in response to a strong conservation movement to save the old market buildings. The resulting development of the area into a copy of Faneuil Hall and the Quincey Market in Boston has been a popular transformation with the public and tourists and marks a clear break from the certainty of the 1970s that new development was necessarily an improvement. This feeling of certainty about schools of architecture has existed for some time, although in different eras various schools have been championed. For Pugin and Ruskin the revealed truth was the Gothic style, but by the 1960s Mies and le Corbusier had triumphed. Modernism brooked no opposition, and followed the Miesian stricture that 'less is more'. A consequence of this view was that buildings should not hide their purpose with superfluous ornamentation, and concrete should be seen and not screened. Public housing was perhaps the worst sufferer from this dogma, since the ultimate consumers, the council tenants, were not consulted on their preferences at all. No matter that the city dwellers liked their own front doors and a patch of garden; acres of small, and undoubtedly substandard, Georgian and Victorian housing were swept away in the name of le Corbusier and blocks of high-rise flats built in their place.

By the end of the 1970s, the taste of the consumer was turning against the new brutalism in architecture and some were bold enough to suggest that Modernism was not the only possible way forward. The revolutionary idea that there was no such thing as a morally correct school of architecture was promoted by David Watkin in his book *Morality and Architecture* published in 1977; this was an idea whose time had come.

During the period of Modernist supremacy there were some architects who persevered with the unfashionable. Quinlan Terry was one such. Terry had briefly worked with James Stirling, the architect of such classic public sector Modernist buildings as the Engineering Faculty at Leicester University, the History Faculty on the Sidgwick Avenue site in Cambridge and, more recently and in a more eclectic style, the Staatsgalerie in Stuttgart. The major part of Terry's career was with the idiosyncratic Raymond Erith, whom he joined in 1962. Erith acted as though Modernism had never been invented; he continued to design new private houses in the classical tradition. After Erith's death in 1973, Terry carried this torch alone. Terry's new gates for the Cutlers Gardens development was his first foray into the City of London. The first major urban design was for the well-known conservation-minded developers, Haslemere Estates, in Dufours Place, Soho. This is a seven-storey conversion in brick with Classical detail. Terry believes, with as much enthusiasm and conviction as the Modernists had pursued their credo, that the classical architectural rules are absolute and inviolable. His most widely discussed development is that on the riverside in Richmond. This group of buildings has mixed new and old buildings cemented by strict adherence to classical tradition, at least on the outside. One architect told me that he thought this development was 'sad; you look through the windows and you see mile after mile of fluorescent lights. It is not truly classical.' Whatever the sneers of the architectural profession, the new buildings are popular with the locals, although it may well be that in 100 years no-one will be able to tell from what period they date. Cabra Estates has a Terry plan for the Fulham football ground site which is redolent of the Crystal Palace.

Terry is a tall, conservative Christian in his fifties, who looks oddly like the comedian Bob Monkhouse. His rebellion against the modernist orthodoxies started while he was a student at the Architectural Association. In an extensive interview with the *Evening Standard*, he claimed 'I started doing traditional classical Gothic buildings and I was told that, if I continued, not only would I fail my exams but I would undermine the foundations of the modern movement.' He dismisses modernism and post-modernism, willing to criticize openly his architectural contemporaries. 'You've got to realise that you have an architectural establishment which has a stranglehold on the taste of the profession. It is like Eastern Europe was. They put you through a five-year training course, and if anyone can come through that and think straight, they are pretty remarkable. They give awards and gold medals to all their sycophants and good boys. So someone who designs a building in oil-refinery style in the City of London gets a gold medal because he is abiding by their rules, he is a good boy.' The recent reaction in architectural taste has meant that Terry is now among the first names considered for commissions, with a new Roman Catholic cathedral in Brentwood and part of the most recent Paternoster plan benefiting from his idiosyncratic adherence to the classical forms.

The reaction from Modernism did not necessarily mean a rediscovery of the Classical. The two other major 'schools' which were defined in the 1980s were those of 'High-Tech' and 'Post-Modernism'. The former allowed the design of buildings to be dictated by their purpose; this followed the Modernist precept that things should not pretend to be something else, but the technology itself ensured that the buildings could not be the pure cubes and towers of Miesian modernism. Two examples already mentioned (Bush Lane House and 1, Finsbury Avenue) were both designed by notable proponents of the 'High-Tech' school, Arup Associates. Other well-known buildings of this type are the Lloyds of London building in Lime Street London, and the Pompidou Centre in Paris, both designed by Richard Rogers, and the HongKong Bank building built in that territory by Norman Foster. One commentator has dubbed these buildings as belonging to the 'bowellist' school of architecture, since so many of their vital organs are revealed on the outside. Pipework and lifts both expose themselves to the public gaze. Another version of this school has been seen in the work of Michael Hopkins, who designed the Schlumberger Research Centre in Cambridge, which looks like a circus tent pitched on the Fens, the new Mound Stand at Lords and Ohbayashi Gumi's redevelopment of Bracken House behind its listed façade in Cannon Street. It is in buildings like these last two that modern architecture has been able to bridge the gap between the professional purists and the lay consumer. It is difficult to imagine a more conservative body of men than the members of the Marylebone Cricket Club, but the stand, again with a tented-style roof, is looked upon with general favour.

Perhaps the most influential voice raised in the debate about architectural styles was that of the Prince of Wales. Using his many public platforms and access to the media, Prince Charles led a layman's crusade against modern architectural orthodoxy. To some architects this smacked of a privileged amateur abusing his position to make ill-informed criticism of their profession. To the vast majority of the consumers of architecture, the general public, the Prince of Wales seemed to be expressing what they themselves felt, but were too intimidated to say: the modernist Emperors had no clothes. The problem of such a viewpoint is that contemporaries cannot be the best judges of what will last in architecture. If no daring experimentation or development of style can be allowed, then design will stagnate. Nevertheless, the Prince of Wales was a critical voice in determining the fate of at least three important developments.

As early as 30 May 1984 he made a dramatic intervention into the world of design in a speech to the Royal Institute of British Architects calling the winning design for the National Gallery extension on the so-called Hampton Site on the north-west corner of Trafalgar Square 'a monstrous carbuncle on the face of a much-loved and elegant friend'. The Hampton site, formerly occupied by a furniture store of that name, burned down in the Blitz, had been the object of many plans for a National Gallery extension since before the First World War. In the 1950s, the government acquired the site and the *Sunday Times* ran a competition to select a design for the new wing. Even the most avid supporter of modern design would be hard-pressed to support the brutalist winner of that competition, but fortunately it was never built. In 1981 Michael Heseltine, then, for the first time, Environment Secretary, commissioned designs which would enable commercial developers to provide gallery space in exchange for permission to build offices on part of the site. The competition was beset by disagreements and cries of 'foul' from the losing architects, but in December 1982 Heseltine announced that the design by Ahrends, Burton and Koralek, in association with developer Nigel Broakes' Trafalgar House, was the winner. After a year of further compromise and change, the new extension's design was unveiled and a public enquiry began in April 1984.

By this time, so much had been subject to compromise that scarcely anyone was happy. The Prince of Wales' speech was a general critique of modern architecture, but he singled out the National Gallery extension, feeling that, as one of its Trustees, he had a locus in the case. He described the design as being like a 'kind of vast municipal fire station complete with the sort of tower that contains the siren.' This first public intervention into the world of architecture was greeted with headlines and a rush of agreement from architectural reactionaries who had been reluctant hitherto to express their reservations about trends in the profession.

By September 1984 the design of Ahrends, Burton and Koralek had been abandoned and a new building commissioned. It comes from the practice of Robert Venturi and his wife Denise Scott-Brown. Venturi, an American architect, has had the gall to challenge the wisdom of Mies van der Rohe that 'less is more' by countering that 'less is a bore'. The extension has been greeted with almost universal damnation by the architectural critics; for instance the architectural historian Gavin Stamp has called it 'a camp joke, pretentious architectural rubbish and an insult to London.' While the building is well-mannered, complementing both Wilkins' National Gallery and Canada House on the west side of Trafalgar Square, it does look as though a cardboard pseudo-classical facade has been erected like a film set to hide a more modern building. The Prince of Wales believes it to be 'a building of which London can be proud'; at least it is a building for which London does not have to apologize.

The Prince later intervened in the long saga of the Palumbo attempt to redevelop the Poultry site. His public utterances culminated in a television programme and accompanying book called *Visions of Britain* in which he roundly criticized much recent development as being out of sympathy with its surroundings. In this he was in harmony with the mood of the times and the public, and Modernism has continued its general retreat.

In its place there has developed an eclectic style which picks the acceptable parts of Modernism and blends with it the style and decoration of many previous eras of architecture. The term 'Post-Modernism' encompasses designs by many different architects, some of whom seem to have a sense of humour. Terry Farrell is perhaps the best-known of this group. His first substantial commission, in 1982, was the TV-AM building backing onto the Regent's Canal in Camden. This 1930s garage was dressed up in Art-Deco outerwear and topped by egg-cups to signify its use. Farrell, a beetle-browed man with a passing resemblance to the French actor Michel Lonsdale, has gone on to be one of the most prolific of the 1980s commercial architects. Among his larger buildings is Embankment Place, which rises like a cinema organ above Charing Cross Station, overlooking the Thames. This is the most complete example of the Cunard/Odeon school of architecture which has come to dominate the end of the 1980s. Multi-coloured polished granite and a broken pattern of roofs has replaced the bland orderliness of concrete and glass in straight lines which characterized the earlier decades. Farrell is also responsible for the much less successful Alban Gate, built for MEPC astride Route 11, replacing one of the earlier 1960s dominoes, Lee House. Alban Gate has little of the panache which imbues much of Farrell's work. The development of the Vauxhall Cross building, for so long the subject of planning blight, is also a Farrell building. In May 1991, Farrell unveiled his revised plans for rebuilding the South Bank Arts complex between Waterloo and Westminster Bridges.

The return to the 'well-mannered' building, which sits easily with its neighbours, is the result of the pendulum swinging violently away from the conventions of the Modernist period. The third major project, in which the Prince of Wales' interest has led to at least a partial loss of nerve on the part of the developers, is the Paternoster Square redevelopment. The original owners, Stockley, in partnership with two pension funds and British Land, appointed Arup Associates as the master planners after a competition; among the designs rejected for this prime site were uncompromising suggestions from Norman Foster and James Stirling, which in the Prince's view 'demonstrated how wrong the original brief was.' When the Prince 'saw the developer's initial concept for a replacement, I must confess that I was deeply depressed . . . Paternoster Square was something that I felt I had to speak up about.' In a speech in the Mansion House on 1 December 1987, the Prince of Wales challenged the developers: 'Surely here, if anywhere, was the time to sacrifice some profit, if need be, for generosity of vision, for elegance, for dignity; for buildings which would raise our spirits and our faith in commercial enterprise, and prove that capitalism can have a human face.'

By this time, the ownership of Stockley, the leading partners in the Paternoster consortium, had changed hands with Tony Clegg's Mountleigh now in control. The Arup plans of 1987 were displayed in public, accompanied by an alternative scheme commissioned by the *Evening Standard* from the classic-revivalist John Simpson. Arup's scheme was taken away for re-thinking and re-presented for public scrutiny in November 1988. 'The new Arup scheme' says Jonathon Glancey, 'showed a more traditional approach to urban planning in its use of squares and crescents, stone and brick. Sensitive architects such as Michael Hopkins and Richard MacCormac were invited to design some of the individual buildings on the site.' Unfortunately for everyone concerned, the ownership of Paternoster had changed again. In October 1988, Mountleigh announced the sale of the site to the Venezuelan-based Cisneros group. The potential development moved no further forward until, in October 1989, the site was sold again.

Greycoat, which bought the site in partnership with American and Japanese investors, was initially reluctant to display its new plans, and brought in several architects, most of whom wished the site to return to a medieval road plan. The result was unveiled in May 1991. The Masterplan, drawn up by Terry Farrell, Thomas Beeby, Dean of the Yale

University School of Architecture, and John Simpson, has employed the talents of five other architects, all exponents of the classical tradition: Robert Adam; Paul Gibson, whose partnership Sidell Gibson has rebuilt Grand Buildings on the south-east corner of Trafalgar Square behind a reproduction of the previous facade; the American Allan Greenberg; Quinlan Terry and Demetri Porphyrios. The Royal Fine Art Commission has likened part of the development to Disneyland, but it is likely that something akin to the plans will be built in due course. Even the proprietors of those properties not owned by the Paternoster Consortium, notably Standard Life, which owns Juxon House, and Nuclear Electric which owns Sudbury House, currently the tallest building, have indicated their general support, although they still have reservations about the detail. In the words of *Sunday Times* journalist Hugh Pearman, the artists' impressions of the new design 'suggest the kind of Utopian enclave where philosophers might hold forth to audiences, and where merry laughter and tinkling fountains are heard from crystal dawn to wine-dark dusk. Stuff and nonsense. These are office blocks. Very big office blocks.' The Porphyrios building has an Italianate tower on the corner looking into the new Square; Beeby's building at the western end of the Square resembles the Bank of England building without Soane's enclosing wall. There is a problem of matching the commercial requirements of lettable space and a pleasing environment, but this plan is more likely to command the support and eventual affection of the users than previous plans. Like Richmond Riverside or the Covent Garden Market, the lack of dramatic new initiatives will disappoint the profession, but may create another frequented space, rather than one which has only been used to scurry across for the past 30 years. Although the downturn in the property cycle has postponed the likely date of the new proposal getting under way, the Paternoster Partnership has now applied for planning permission on the buildings it owns itself.

On the south bank of the Thames the plan for the downstream stage of London Bridge City is also likely to be postponed. The Kuwaiti owners have other uses for funds over the foreseeable future and the prospect of seeing a London version of St. Mark's Square, Venice, designed again by John Simpson, has retreated.

Two of the largest district redevelopment schemes are also going slow. Both Spitalfields and Kings Cross were the subjects of bitter competition for the privilege of redevelopment. The winners, London and Edinburgh, now owned by a Swedish pension fund, and the London Regeneration Consortium, owned by Rosehaugh Stanhope and National Freight, are not likely to be committing scarce funds to grandiose projects until the economy has recovered. In May 1991 the Spitalfields Development Group appointed the American based architects, Benjamin Thompson and Associates, as master planners. Thompson was responsible for the pioneering regeneration work in Boston and Baltimore for the Rouse Company, where they used the existing old buildings as the keystone of the development. Among the architects chosen to design the individual buildings of the scheme is Sir Norman Foster.

The 1980s were marked not only by a reaction in architecture but also a revolution in planning. For all the post-war period, planning had been a prize, anxiously sought and jealously given. The very award of a planning permission gave the developer the opportunity to turn it into a fat bank balance. The new Conservative administration was driven by a desire to deregulate and planning was one area in which it put its policy to work. Indeed, some inner city areas were designated Enterprise Zones in which all the traditional planning restraints were to be removed. At the same time it became apparent that, even if the new technology was not destroying office jobs or distributing them into smaller and smaller units, there was no need for these offices to be as close to one another as they had been. The traditional need for banks and brokers to be clustered around the skirts of the Bank of England and the Stock Exchange had been obviated by electronic communications. These factors had a marked effect on the attitude of the existing planning authorities. Faced with new competitors for new development, the City of London abandoned its previous development plan. In March 1986, the Corporation, by increasing the permitted plot ratios and relaxing some of their conservation measures, increased the allowable office space in the City by 11 million square feet. Since the City's existing stock of offices at that time was around 40 million square feet, this was a revolution in potential supply. It did not even include some of the large developments already under way on the City's fringes, such as Broadgate (in Hackney), London Bridge City (in Southwark), or in the west extremities of Tower Hamlets, let alone the 10 million square feet planned for Canary Wharf in Docklands.

For many Londoners of a certain age, the funeral of Sir Winston Churchill in 1965 marked a rite of passage. As the coffin was borne up river on a barge, the cranes of the Pool of London dipped in homage; it was their last public act. Even then London as a working port had almost disappeared as containerization took the trade downstream to Tilbury, and the old docks and wharves of London were falling into disuse and dereliction. The Pool itself, between London and Tower Bridges, and St. Katherine's Dock by the Tower soon drew the attention of the developers, but the downstream docks, from the Isle of Dogs onwards, were left to rot. In July 1981 the government established the London Docklands Development Corporation, (LDDC), charged with the overall rejuvenation of the docks on both sides of the Thames: on the north bank from Tower Bridge through Wapping, Shadwell and Limehouse to the Isle of Dogs then on to the South from London Bridge through Bermondsey to the peninsula of Rotherhithe. Here the writ of the now-abolished Greater London Council and the Borough councils did not run. Instead the LDDC was the planning authority, and on the Isle of Dogs itself, a peninsula jutting into a loop of the Thames and serviced by only two bridges, the government went one step further: in 1982 it made the Isle into an Enterprise Zone. In this area, as in several other derelict city centre sites around Britain, there were to be no planning controls, no local taxes for ten years and tax allowances against the cost of the buildings.

The architectural writer Stephanie Williams, in her book *Docklands*, describes the result: 'London's Docklands contains one of the worst collections of late 20th century buildings to be seen anywhere in the world. It is a marvel, if it were not so embarrassing, that so many very bad buildings from the same period can be found in such a comparatively small area of the city, massed so closely, and so incongruously together . . . And yet it is to Docklands that you must go to find some of the best British architecture of the 1980s.' Whatever the doubtful qualities of the buildings, it is incontrovertible that the kick-start given to the Docklands has revived the area more rapidly than years of careful strategic planning could ever have done. Developments of over 25 million square feet of commercial space have been planned and a substantial amount of that has been or is being built. A centre half the size of the City of London is being built in a commercial desert.

One of the early pioneers of the move east was Rupert Murdoch's News Corporation. As part of a carefully planned coup, News had taken a long lease of 13 acres in Pennington Street from Tower Hamlets council as early as November 1979. Its plans were to build nearly one million square feet of commercial space on the site, just south of The Highway in Wapping, no more than a mile from Tower Bridge. What was not apparent at that time was the intention to move all its production facilities for *The Times*, *News of the World* and *Sun* to the site from their traditional positions in and around Fleet Street. Not only would this prove to be the secret ingredient for unlocking the vice-like grip of the print unions, but the Fleet Street sites then became available for redevelopment. In March 1980, the Daily Telegraph paid £2 million for a similar site in Wapping Lane. Both these sites had previously been leased jointly by Town and City Properties, still selling non-income producing investments, and the Port of London Authority.

In 1984 construction began on the Docklands Light Railway (DLR). One of the greatest problems with the whole of the Docklands area, both north and south of the river, was the fact that there was relatively poor provision of public transport; the DLR was an attempt to create some in a hurry. Built with the latest driver-less technology, it was not planned to carry the volumes of passengers on its short, and unreliable, trains that subsequent events have suggested will be needed. In July 1991 the crucial extension to Bank underground station was opened; at last the Docklands transport system was linked directly with the rest of London's Tube. The government has also announced that the Jubilee Line is to be extended from Embankment across the river to London Bridge and then back again to Canary Wharf. Part of the capital cost of this project is to be borne by the developers of that vast project on the Isle of Dogs, if they can find the money.

The transformation of the Isle of Dogs is the result of the dream of one man, G. Ware Travelstead. This American developer, backed by the leading American investment banks of First Boston and Morgan Stanley, produced a plan in 1985 for a development on the 71-acre site of Canary Wharf of 10 million square feet of commercial property, mostly in Brobdignagian office blocks. Although the two banks agreed to take space in the scheme, Travelstead was unable to secure sufficient pre-lettings to finance it. It was taken over in 1988 by the Canadian Reichmann family company, Olympia & York (O&Y). Their other successful schemes in North America were thought to be sufficient to see this new project through to completion. It was said that the developers had written into their financial plan the expectation of two economic recessions; they have certainly now experienced the first. The idea behind Canary Wharf is to create a critical mass of tenants that will themselves attract others to the site. This is to be done by providing both the desired size of building, or of individual floors, with all the state-of-the-art technology, unavailable elsewhere and at a lower rental than that asked in Central London.

At the centre of the development is the 800-foot high pyramid-topped tower designed by Cesar Pelli. This is the tallest building in the United Kingdom, and can be seen from as far away as the elevated section of the A40 passing the White City in west London. Unfortunately, it is also right in the line of sight when looking down the hill towards the Royal Naval College at Greenwich. The overall plan is under the control of Skidmore, Owings and Merrill, (SOM), who are also responsible for the later stages of the Broadgate development on the north edge of the City. By the summer of 1992 the developers had managed to let only 60 per cent of the first two stages, which were occupied in early 1992. The first contracted tenants were the investment bank backers, but O&Y has made a decision to try to create a media colony in the area. Several advertising agencies have agreed to give up their West End offices and relocate to Docklands, although attempts to attract Saatchi & Saatchi proved unsuccessful. This was despite the fact that O&Y were prepared to offer substantial financial inducements to prospective tenants. These would include buying their existing property or taking over their tenancies. Among the companies which have relocated to Canary Wharf is the *Daily Telegraph*. The newspaper's offices had previously moved from Fleet Street to the Isle of Dogs, but to South Quay Plaza, a Richard Seifert designed office development further into the island. O&Y agreed to buy that *Telegraph* office.

The success of Canary Wharf will not be clear for some years. It is likely that the amount of space let before the buildings were completed proved disappointing to O&Y, since the property slump has been at least partly a consequence of overbuilding in the City, where new lettings are taking place at well below the £60 per square foot peak of 1989/90. At that time, Canary Wharf's rents offered a 50 per cent saving on equivalent space elsewhere, but today with City space being let at well under £40 a square foot, the differential has not proved sufficient. On the Isle of Dogs one of the offices on South Quay Plaza was being offered at a rent of ten pounds per square foot in early 1991. Since O&Y cannot achieve three times that rent, the first phase of the development has proved an economic disaster in the short term, and further phases will be postponed. Fortunately for the developers, such property can also turn into a great success in the longer term. Their hopes of surviving as others of the buildings rest in the hands of their bankers. In May 1992 the Canadian parent applied for protection from its creditors, and O&Y's continued involvement in Canary Wharf hung in the balance.

The speed of development of such projects as Canary Wharf or Broadgate is in marked contrast to the traditional snail-like pace of British construction. The introduction of American methods of building has brought about major changes in the industry. Stuart Lipton of Stanhope, who has done as much as anyone to change the perception of British building methods and city architecture, keeps a copy of a book in his office sidelined in the margin by Peter Rogers, Stanhope director, project manager of the Broadgate development and brother of architect Richard Rogers. While this may not be a surprise, the fact that the book was published in 1934 and written by the English MP for Maidstone and architect Alfred Bossom, certainly is. (Apart from this book, Bossom is chiefly remembered for the remark Winston Churchill made of him on learning his name: 'I see, neither one thing nor the other.')

The reason for the presence of this arcane and long out-of-print book in Lipton's office is that it foreshadows many of the changes to British building practices which the 1980s developers introduced. Bossom had spent many years in the early part of the century working on the construction of skyscrapers, such as the 20-storey Chesapeake and Ohio Building in Richmond, Virginia. His book, *Building to the Skies*, drew attention to the differences between the planning, achitectural and, particularly, building methods of the Americans and the British; these differences persisted into the 1970s. The skyscrapers were designed down to the last detail before construction commenced; the architect's drawings were comprehensive: 'They show everything – every steel column, girder and plate, every pipe, every vent duct, every push button, every groove or chase for wiring or piping – everything.' The construction process too drew acute observations from the future Member for Maidstone. He noted that the building of a skyscraper was almost entirely a matter of on-site assembly of prefabricated components, organized minutely. 'It is thanks almost wholly to this scheduling of everything in advance and working to an agreed time-table that buildings in America cost no more to erect than in England, are completed far more quickly, yield larger profits both to the owner and the contractor, and at the same time enable the operatives to be paid from three to five times the wages that they receive in Great Britain.' The result was that the Empire State Building went from the first upright steel member being put in place in April 1930 to completion before May 1931. Those of us who watched the hesitant progress of so many 20-storey buildings of the 1960s find it difficult to believe that the bricklayers on the New York project were completing a storey of brickwork every day.

It was the introduction of these methods which enabled Rosehaugh Stanhope to astonish Margaret Thatcher into keeping a promise made when she inaugurated the construction of the first phase of the Broadgate development (see Chapter 3). The then Prime Minister had promised to return to the celebration of the completion of the building if it was achieved within a year. So confident was she of that promise not having to be kept that she actually planned a trip to Canada. This had to be cancelled at short notice when it became apparent that her presence would indeed be necessary.

It should not be thought that the revolution in design and planning was confined to London offices, although that is possibly the most dramatic change, making obsolete a whole generation of buildings. The retail revolution of the 1980s was just as complete, both in the High Street and on the edge of town, involving the redesign of many of the familiar shop chains. The influence of Sir Terence Conran of Habitat, who took over the British Home Stores group and changed it into BhS, and of George Davis, who transformed Hepworths from a Yorkshire-based tailoring group into a design-driven group of retail and mail-order companies under the Next banner, is seen in the way that the fascias of British shops have been 'pastellized'. Even more striking is the plague of American town hall clocks to be seen on top of endless out- or edge-of-town Asdas, Tescos and Safeways. The growth of the shopping mall and groups of retail warehouses was predicted only by the prescient few at the beginning of the 1970s. Most observers believed that, Britain being an overcrowded island, such developments would not be possible, desirable or permitted.

The giant regional shopping centre, anchored by at least one large department store and food super- or hyper-market, although common-place in the United States, is a recent arrival on these shores. In the United Kingdom the large free-standing supermarket only dates from the mid-1970s. By 1976 there were only four supermarkets in Britain with a selling space of more than 50,000 square feet, a low threshold for the description hypermarket: Tesco in Irlam and Carrefour, a joint company formed with the French pioneer in the field, which had stores in Eastleigh, Caerphilly and Telford. Many new developments of city centre shopping had already taken place, such as the Victoria Centre in Nottingham, which Capital & Counties had built and sold most of to the ICI pension fund. The first true example of a regional shopping centre in Britain is the Brent Cross Centre in north London. Developed by Hammerson and Brent Walker with finance from Standard Life and built on the site of the old Brent dog-racing track, the centre opened on 2 March 1976. It looks unprepossessing from the outside, like a series of children's irregular building blocks placed end to end, but inside is a veritable cornucopia of the traditional High Street emporia: John Lewis, Boots, Fenwick, Marks & Spencer, Waitrose, C&A and W H Smith were all represented in the centre at its opening, and their stores took over 580,000 square feet of the 800,000 square feet air-conditioned space. Six months after opening, Brent Cross was attracting 55,370 shoppers on a typical Saturday, each spending an average of £43.60 (in 1979 money), nearly 90 per cent on non-food items. By comparison after six months the Caerphilly Carrefour attracted 16,800 shoppers to its 100,000 square feet almost wholly given over to food, and they spent an average of £18.40 each.

The rise of the retail warehouse, selling Do-It-Yourself goods, furniture, electrical goods and carpets was consumer-driven and mostly carried out by owner-occupier retailers. Not until the late 1980s was the institutional investor generally prepared to finance or own these properties, neither pure warehouse nor pure retail store. The growth of the national chains of retail warehouses also stimulated the development of much larger warehouses from which operators distributed stock to far-flung stores. In 1979 MFI bought a 31-acre site outside Northampton on which to develop its main warehouse. The million square feet initial building has been added to over time, and the investment was eventually sold to John Ritblat's British Land Company. Asda opened a similarly vast distribution centre on a disused airfield outside Lutterworth in Leicester.

The retailers made their case in both economic and environmental terms. John Sainsbury, now Lord Sainsbury, speaking to the Oxford Preservation Society in 1981, said: 'Large stores with car parks cannot be accommodated in ancient cities . . . indiscriminate development of large stores in green fields is not acceptable.' The growth of car ownership had made these edge of town developments accessible and had created the environment in which they could be built: the by-pass or motorway created a natural barrier to town expansion but the immediate environs of these roads were unsuitable for residential development; the retailers filled the gap. By 1989 two-thirds of households had access to a car for their personal use, up from just over 50 per cent at the end of the 1960s. New operators were being attracted to these revolutionized shopping practices: IKEA from Scandinavia and Toys 'R Us from the United States were well established and, as had happened across the Atlantic, many retail parks now have a McDonalds as an added attraction.

The retail design and architecture revolution was matched by dramatic changes in the style of new factory development. Many of the dark satanic mills of the nineteenth century have been demolished and replaced by modern, light work-places, something between a laboratory and an office. This has again been a consequence of both technological and planning changes. The technology change has been the shrinkage of the traditional heavy industry with which Britain led the Industrial Revolution in the nineteenth century. This is not the place to discuss whether this move away from low value-added industry to the less labour intensive industries of the late twentieth century was desirable or merely inevitable, but the effect on the workplace has probably been even more dramatic than the change in offices and shops.

The planning change came late in the period covered by this book, although the final alteration to regulations simply reflected a weakening of the relevance of the previous rules. Until 1987, the use of property in England and Wales had been ruled by the class into which the planning permission fell. In that year the Use Classes Order introduced the concept of B1 space. This permitted office, research and light industrial use to be carried out at one property with one planning consent. Hitherto, the planners had tried to separate the factories from the offices from the research establishments, in nice neatly coloured parts of their planning maps. As industries such as pharmaceuticals or computer software grew in importance, it became increasingly difficult and potentially highly damaging to distinguish between these uses. In fact, mixed-use property had been increasingly accepted by the planners before this; industrial units would have some office space tacked on to the front. The change in the Use Classes Order altered the balance, so that the percentage of offices in these later developments is much higher than on previous industrial areas. Three early and important examples were the Cambridge Science Park, Aztec West outside Bristol and Stockley Park near Heathrow. All predate the legal alteration to Use Classes, and are examples of how the changing needs of commerce forced the change.

The story of Stockley Park is told later in the book (Chapters 4 and 5), but the importance of both the Cambridge Science Park and Aztec West are worth more than a passing mention. Trinity College, Cambridge has for 35 years had as its Senior Bursar Dr John Bradfield. (Trinity has a tradition of long-serving Senior Bursars, there having been only three since 1900.) The Senior Bursar's job is to oversee the assets of the College so that its endowment income is maximized. Dr Bradfield was one of the first college bursars to understand the importance of equity investment for these funds, eschewing the higher immediate income available on fixed interest securities in the reasonable expectation that better long-term returns would be earned. Because Trinity has, like so many Oxbridge colleges, a large property endowment, the college has tried to manage that estate to the best advantage: new student buildings have been developed, (much like the similarly endowed St John's, Oxford), and other property improved.

Bradfield's predecessor, Tressilion Nicholas, who had taken over in 1929, followed a policy of buying farms during the Depression. One of these was a large estate outside the Suffolk port of Felixstowe; as Britain's trade with Europe began to supersede that with North America and the Commonwealth, so the amount of sea trade which went through east coast ports burgeoned at the expense of cities like Liverpool. European Ferries took the opportunity to expand Felixstowe, and as the port grew, it needed the land that Nicholas had bought for Trinity all those years previously. So the idea that long-held land investments could suddenly become prime development sites was not new.

Trinity, inspired by a university committee, imported from the United States the idea that a university town could support flourishing commercial research and development centres. Route 128 around Boston is flanked by 'high-tech' industries attracted by the Massachussets Institute of Technology. Very much as the experts did not believe that edge-of-town retailing could come to Britain, there was great scepticism that the science park concept would translate well to a British city. In 1970, Bradfield began the planning of the Cambridge Science Park on land which had belonged to the College for centuries. The first units were begun in April 1973, and the park was officially opened in 1975. By June 1990, 875,000 square feet of space was complete, with a further 270,000 square feet planned. Trinity has not developed all the buildings itself, often preferring to sell building leases to developers, but it keeps a strict control on the Park as a whole: the use of buildings is limited to scientific research, 'light industrial production dependent on regular consultation with the tenant's own research, development and design staff established in the Cambridge area', and 'ancillary activities appropriate to a Science Park'. The building density, at one square foot of space for every six square feet of land, (16 per cent site cover), compares favourably with the traditional 50 per cent cover of many industrial estates. Although there are few formal links between the University and the Park, the fact that so many academics are either principals in or consultants to the companies means that the development has long passed 'critical mass' in attracting similar companies. Even in the 1990 recession, few of the tenants had gone out of business. Tressilion Nicholas was able to see the fruits of his successor's stewardship; he died in 1990 aged 101. Now Trinity is in the early stages of developing a successor, the Eureka park at Ashford, Kent, an important road and rail link to the Channel Tunnel.

Aztec West was a purely commercial venture. As land and buildings became more expensive and skilled workers more difficult to find in the south-east of England, developers sought to attract industry to other centres. The Electricity industry pension fund, Electricity Supply Nominees (ESN), developed Aztec West on a site bounded by the junction of the M4 and M5 at Almondsbury, north-west of Bristol. The initial buildings were simply industrial units with a higher-than-normal level of office space, and the architecture of the site was certainly no breakthrough. As the development proceeded, however, more enterprising designs were incorporated. At the same time the development changed hands, being acquired by Arlington Securities, which in turn was taken over by British Aerospace. In 1986 John Outram designed some small light industrial units and in 1987/88 CZWG, (Campbell Zogolovitch Wilkinson and Gough), produced some Art-Deco buildings of unusual form. Piers Gough describes the work of his partnership as 'B-movie architecture'.

In contrast to the dynamic changes in commercial architecture, there are few signs of any real movement forward in the large building projects of the state sector. Although the *Sunday Times* awarded its Building of the Year 1991 accolade to a Hampshire primary school with a block of six council flats in Walthamstow as close challengers, the Hyatt Hotel, part of Birmingham's new Convention Centre complex, won the wooden spoon. The whole Convention Centre, part of Birmingham's well-intentioned attempt to re-establish itself as England's second city, is pure state monolithic in design, as if the 1980s had not happened at all. Whereas the inside of the buildings may be perfectly suited to their roles, particularly the new concert hall with its meticulously adjusted acoustic, from the outside we are back to the uncompromising blocks of buildings that the 1970s led us to learn to loathe.

The property boom of the 1980s saw a dramatic change in the architecture of business premises. It is far too soon to make final judgements about whether the new styles will age well and be identifiable in a hundred or more years' time as a worthy testimony to a decade. There are some who are already condemning the new buildings as meretricious and appropriate memorials to the commercialism of the 1980s. Those who work in and around them would, I believe, prefer to let future architectural historians decide, and merely be grateful that fewer buildings of the 1980s than of the two previous decades are unpleasant to work in and a positive irritation to the eye. Some of the buildings from Modernists, Post-Modernists and Neo-Classicists alike may indeed become treasured legacies to future generations.

3

A STRONG BREW

IN JULY 1978 an obscure tea company, Rosehaugh, was re-listed on the London Stock Exchange having bought 28.3 per cent of an even more obscure company named Sunbourne Properties for the princely sum of £850, and 20 per cent of the altogether more substantial Tannergate, which had earlier bought a mixed property portfolio from the Legal & General for £15.5m; the shares of Rosehaugh had been suspended in May at the equivalent of seven pence a share. These modest transactions launched the public company career of one of the most complex characters in the British property boom of the 1980s, Godfrey Bradman, a soft-spoken accountant with a most unlikely background for a property tycoon.

Bradman's paternal grandparents were Jewish immigrants to England in 1902 who had set up a shop in Brick Lane, now the centre of the Bangladeshi community. Godfrey was born in Willesden in 1936. When he was only four he was evacuated with his mother to Long Melford in Suffolk while his father served in the RAF. He describes his 'very rural' life in Suffolk, where his brother and sister were born, as being 'in somewhat reduced circumstances'. Leaving the local school at 15 with no 'O' levels, he went to work as office boy in nearby Sudbury for the local accountants Bensusan, Butt Eves. Apart from the traditional task of making the tea, he also had to stoke the boiler, fetching the coal from the cellar, and collect parcels from the bus which conveyed documents to and from the partnership's head office in Colchester. Bradman describes it today as 'a Dickensian existence; you could only write in the clients' books with dip-in pens with steel nibs.' Being a bright boy with ambition, he set about gaining the qualifications necessary before he could be articled to the accountancy profession. He took his GCE 'O' Levels by correspondence course with Wolsey Hall, perhaps their most successful client ever. There were disadvantages to trying to pass exams this way, particularly in such subjects as Chemistry where opportunities for practical experiments were non-existent. Bradman showed his typical attention to the fine print and realized that to pass Physics-with-

Chemistry required a mark of 47 per cent and half the marks for the exam were awarded for Physics. Since this was a subject with a more theoretical bent which he was good at, he concentrated on that part of the exam, treating any marks he picked up in Chemistry as a bonus.

His employers would not take him on as an articled clerk without the traditional premium of 500 guineas, which he and his family simply didn't have, so he found a partnership in London which would take him and at the age of 19 he moved to the capital. While still an articled clerk he took an interest in property but it was not until he qualified that it played an important part in his life. As a newly minted 24-year-old ACA he set up as a sole practitioner, taking the lease of one floor in an office in Baker Street for £400 a year. He immediately sub-let part of the space to a firm of actuaries for £720 a year, leaving him with an office, which he lined with yards of books bought at Foyles, and an income of £320 a year. Since he had only three accountancy clients at the time, one paying 10 guineas a year, one £40 a year and the third four pounds per month, this was not going to be sufficient to fulfil Bradman's ambitions. Making something out of nothing is the hallmark of the Bradman story and his next step was a classic example.

As a professional person, he was entitled to commission on any life assurance policies he sold; these commissions, as the life offices are still reluctant to admit, often eat up the first year or two of the monthly premium payments. Bradman took out a £20,000 life policy on his own life, without-profits, for an initial monthly premium of £18; the commission receivable was two per cent of the sum assured, or £400, payable immediately to him. He then took out another policy for £110,000, the first premium being paid for with the commission on the smaller policy, and he had enough income from that commission to pay the premiums on both policies for some time and with cash to spare. He had also realized that, after a few years, there was a surrender value on the policies, which could be as much as one year's premiums. In the meantime he had use of the life offices' money to keep him going while he built up his accountancy practice and property interests. 'Armed with that I had enough income for two years and was able to spend them reading and continuing my studies. I had few clients but I gave them an extremely good service and so the practice quickly built up.' As it grew Bradman took on partners, initially Bernard Faber, who later became involved in property himself with a company called London & City, and Bradman's younger brother.

The Bradman family had not allowed their modest background to hold them back: Bradman's brother had qualified as a biologist and taken a degree in parasitology but, while studying for his PhD, also qualified as an accountant. Part of the practice was repeating the cash-flow ploy of the life policies for clients, on whose lives they wrote tens of millions of business. Bradman understood that while there were plenty of efficient 'tickers', keepers of proper books of accounts, his clients were interested in practical applications of accounting expertise.

By 1963 property was already an important part of Bradman's business. He bought a lease at 4–6 Savile Row from lessees who thought that their lease prevented them from sub-letting at a rent lower than that which they themselves were paying. 'But they hadn't read their lease properly. They paid me £30,000 to take the lease off their hands and we were able to sublet it in ten days at the market rent, slightly less than they were paying.' With the profit from that deal Bradman then bought a 20-year profit rental on 18/19 Savile Row for 'a very small amount of money.' By now the size of the deals was beginning to escalate, since the next purchase was of a lease on 29/30 Leicester Square for £550,000 from the industrial company BICC. The superior landlord of this property was Max Joseph, the entrepreneur who built up what is now Grand Metropolitan, and who was John Ritblat's [of British Land] property sponsor. Joseph held a 986-year lease on the property at £13,000 a year payable to Legal & General, the freeholder. The two men put their interests together and sold them for £1.35m; 'quite a nice deal' says Bradman today, especially for one who had so recently been a mere articled clerk. By this time Bradman had moved offices to 83 Wigmore Street, over a restaurant called Platos.

Property was not the activity in which Bradman made his name and first fortune. His skills at understanding the detail of any transaction had built him a reputation as a master of tax planning, which evolved into the tax avoidance industry of the late 1960s and 1970s. The subject is covered in great detail in Nigel Tutt's book *The History of Tax Avoidance*, but the art is worth describing since it demonstrates briefly how Bradman's obsession for detail developed. The UK had become, under Harold Wilson's Labour government of 1964–70, a high tax area, particularly on 'unearned' income and short-term capital gains, where, in one year the rate of marginal tax reached 137 per cent of earnings. As Godfrey Bradman comments this was 'quite a strong motivation' to minimize an individual's or a company's exposure to such tax rates. Tax law at that time was governed by the principle that, if the law did not specifically rule out a scheme by which the tax could be avoided or the taxable event postponed indefinitely, then it was valid. Tax evasion, the deliberate hiding of income or gains from the Inland Revenue was then, as it is now, illegal. Governments were aware of the problem and had introduced specific legislation to head off the most obvious sources of avoidance such as bond washing and dividend stripping; these were processes by which investors turned income, which was heavily taxed, into capital, which until the early 1960s had not been taxed at all. Similar schemes now surfaced in the 1960s whereby such pop stars as Tom Jones and Engelbert Humperdinck sold the rights to their future income to a company in return for a lump sum or shares in the company, which would also pay them a modest salary. Management Agency and Music and Hemdale were two companies which flourished in the late 1960s from such schemes, which were perfectly legal at the time. Bradman's schemes were simple in concept and entirely artificial but 'hideously complicated' in execution according to Tutt. He describes meetings in Bradman's Wigmore Street office where the participants were sworn to secrecy, since the value to Bradman was in the fact that no-one else knew how to construct such schemes.

Tutt quotes a scheme as an example of how tax could be avoided involving the Rose brothers, well-known property investors, whose publicly quoted company owned the Woolworth head office in Marylebone Road. Just before the end of the tax year in 1969 the brothers and a third partner had sold shares in five companies to a Bradman company, Excalibur, for £471,998. They were not to receive that sum immediately however; instead they were to be paid £150 a year for 200 years and a final payment of £441,898 on 3 April 2169, together with interest charged at ten and a quarter per cent. On 8 April, in the new tax year, Excalibur leased the properties just purchased to another company, Geltan, for 999 years with an optional break at 49 years, Geltan paying £982,862, to be settled over the period of the leases. Geltan then sold its interest in the leases and Excalibur sold its interest in the remaining freeholds to another Bradman company called County. County then sold the remarried interest in the properties to a company, Central, controlled by the Roses and their partner, for £989,095. Meanwhile yet another Bradman company had bought the property owners' interest in the 200 years of payments from Excalibur for £471,848. The Roses had retained ownership of their properties but had received nearly £500,000 cash which the Revenue could not tax since it was in exchange for the deferred payments from Excalibur. The Roses had to invest the £472,000 straight back into Central as a loan to pay for the repurchase but a loan can be refinanced and its repayment does not give rise to tax. Confused? This is a very simplified version of the scheme which actually involved 25 separate transactions. The Inland Revenue tried to block the scheme, taking it to the House of Lords, but their Lordships ruled in the Roses' favour. Bradman had earned his £80,000 fee. In August 1971 the Inland Revenue announced that such schemes were to be stopped and legislation was introduced to give that intention the force of law in the 1972 Finance Act.

In 1974 Godfrey Bradman made his first appearance in the public eye. The coal miners had been on a go-slow since late in 1973 and the Heath government had imposed a three-day working week, with the use of electricity being forbidden at certain periods to preserve coal stocks. The government finally accepted the need to put the case to a special tribunal, but the miners' leader Joe Gormley would not postpone the all-out strike which the miners had voted for. Prime Minister Heath eventually called a General Election for 28 February, which he failed to win, allowing Harold Wilson to form a minority government. At the beginning of February, Bradman proposed to Joe Gormley that, in exchange for reconvening his National Executive and voting to postpone the strike until the tribunal's findings were known, a group of businessmen would pay the miners an extra sum during that period; the total cost would be

£2.4 million, 'modest money by today's standards. The slightest embarrassing thing was that the week before he had refused Edward Heath's request to reconvene the National Executive.'

The change of government in March 1974, after a week-end of comings and goings as Heath tried to save his government, which had actually won more popular votes than Labour, saw two notable changes in Bradman's life. On the one hand the even higher tax rates which Denis Healey the new Chancellor of the Exchequer brought in to make 'the pips squeak', increased the demand for good tax planning and avoidance; on the other hand the new administration was determined to act tough with the tax avoiders. One of the new Chancellor's first measures was to introduce interest penalties on late payments of tax. For most tax avoidance schemes this was a serious blow since they often relied on the complexity of the substance to keep the Revenue tied up for years before a final decision was made as to their validity. Meanwhile the taxpayer would have the use of his money. 'Ten years use of the money is almost as good as not having to pay it at all' said Bradman. By this time Bradman had a company which acted as holding company for his many interests, London Mercantile Corporation, and the tax avoidance schemes had moved onto a new footing. This time the idea was the 'reverse annuity'; a company, instead of paying a lump sum in exchange for a future flow of income, as is the case in annuities, would receive a lump sum and promise to make a series of cash payments in the future. The cash received would either be wholly or mostly exempt from tax, whereas the yearly payments would be deductible for tax by the payer, even if some would then be taxable in the hands of the recipient. However, increasingly tough legislation, coupled later with the progressive reduction of direct taxation by the Conservative Government elected in June 1979, meant that tax planning schemes were in less demand.

By 1977, Godfrey Bradman had had enough of tax planning as a career. 'To be honest I wanted to do something that was more productive.' His property interests were by now quite substantial, and they were structured in the typical Bradman fashion with plenty of partners who were prepared to put all the money up but to share the profits with Bradman's companies. In February 1977, Bradman bought the portfolio of 'probably 2,000 individual units' from Legal & General for £15.5 million through Tannergate, of which Bradman owned only 20 per cent. In the same year a company named Sunvale bought Maple House in Tottenham Court Road, now known as International House. Sunvale was itself a subsidiary of Sunbourne Properties, of which Bradman owned 28.3 per cent. Sunbourne took a lease on Riverside House, Wood Green, North London and sold the resulting investment with its continuing obligation to pay rent on the 85,000 square foot offices, to the Coal Board pension funds, 'for a profit of £5–6 million', (although since Coal Industry Nominees, the Coal Board funds, sold the same property in 1987 for only £6 million this seems an unlikely profit figure). The profit, whatever it was, was the equity invested that same afternoon in Maple House, a 175,000 square foot office and shop development which cost Sunvale £11.25 million, the balance financed by borrowings.

It was in 1978 that Godfrey Bradman finally emerged as a public company director. The vehicle chosen could not have been more obscure: in May 1978 the Stock Exchange announced the suspension of the listing of shares in Rosehaugh, a tiny tea company with assets of 12.8p a share and no profits, trading at seven pence a share, (equivalent to under two pence in the share's current form). In July the shares were re-listed on the announcement of two acquisitions from London Mercantile of shares in both Tannergate and Sunbourne. Rosehaugh now held 20 per cent of Tannergate, which, over the year since its purchase by Bradman, had sold enough properties to give it net assets of £1.5 million, with the remaining properties in the books at £8 million but valued at £13.7 million. Sunbourne meanwhile had sold its major asset, International House, to the British Steel pension fund for £15 million. The purchase of 28.3 per cent of Sunbourne by Rosehaugh valued the shareholding at £850, each one per cent being valued at £30. Over the next three years Rosehaugh bought out its partners at prices which demonstrate the rewards of successful property dealing in companies where most of the purchase is financed through borrowings. In September 1980, Rosehaugh bought out two of its three partners, Henry Davis and Blackwood Hodge, for a total of £305,235, valuing their 16.67 per cent holding at £18,310 per one per cent, paid for in Rosehaugh shares. When Bernard Sunley Investment Trust sold out its 50 per cent interest in May 1981, the price Rosehaugh paid was £1.4 million, equivalent to £28,000 per one per cent share in Sunbourne, an immodest return on their investment only four years earlier.

Godfrey Bradman is far removed from the traditional picture of a property developer. A small, quietly spoken man, he has none of the bonhomous persona of so many of his rivals and colleagues. It is typical for instance that he has never changed the name of his public company vehicle, despite the fact that for the first few years of its existence investors could not make up their mind whether the pronunciation was 'Rosehuff' or the correct 'Rosehaw'; there was a cost and no particular value involved in a name change and Godfrey Bradman is not a vain man. What everybody agrees about is that he is clever. One investment man who became close to Bradman returned from their first meeting to inform his colleagues 'here you have the greatest money-making machine ever.' Another property man who has worked with him over many years described him as being 'a first class tax accountant with a very, very determined, persevering, precise mind. He is never happier than when he is working his way through tax and other mechanistic deals.' True property men speak rather disparagingly of his property acumen, as not understanding the concept of how property values grow. Indeed he is said to have confessed at one stage that he never goes to see a property because he wouldn't know what to look for and he finds most of it appalling anyway. Nevertheless he built up one of the largest development companies in the UK and been party to some of the most striking developments. Unfortunately the locomotive became derailed at some stage and from being a man who could do no wrong he spent 1990 and 1991 striving to save his company.

The early deals done by Rosehaugh after it came under the control of Godfrey Bradman were similar to its initial investments: low risk. In October 1980 a subsidiary, Bolansbourne, bought for £9.875 million a portfolio of six properties from the Coal Board pension fund's new subsidiary British Investment Trust, immediately selling two of the assets for £7.2 million, leaving properties in Hammersmith, Victoria, Old Street and Berkhamsted with a net cost of only £2.7 million and a rent roll of more than £750,000 per annum. The sellers insisted on receiving cash for their assets, not knowing too much about Mr Bradman or Rosehaugh and not wanting to depend on the company's shares for realizing value; this initially proved to be a poor decision.

In December 1980 came the transaction which set Rosehaugh on the way to the major league. Another company with an 'off-the-shelf' name, Jamplane, announced the purchase of two buildings in Wilson Street on the northern fringes of the City, actually in the Borough of Hackney, from National Freight and British Rail for £3.925 million. Rosehaugh paid only £5,000 for 50 per cent of this company and lent it £400,000. The other 50 per cent of Jamplane, later renamed Rosehaugh Greycoat Estates, was bought by Geoffrey Wilson and Stuart Lipton's company, Greycoat. There was a third equity partner, Ronnie Jarvis, whose company Ravensale took a 19.4 per cent share of the project, leaving each partner in Jamplane with 40.3 per cent. Jarvis, who had once been the owner of Conway Stuart, the pen company, earned his shareholding by producing the cash for the initial purchase of the development site. Even if Ronnie Jarvis took most of the risk in this way, his rewards have been handsome, since 19.6 per cent of Rosehaugh Greycoat was worth £34 million by June 1990.

The achitecture and building methods used in Finsbury Avenue were deemed to be the area of expertise of the Greycoat partners, and are dealt with in following chapters, but Godfrey Bradman's acumen with finance was to drive a coach and horses through conventional methods of raising development capital for a speculative office building project. Because both Rosehaugh and Greycoat were relatively small companies and the development was in an area hitherto unproven for offices, Bradman was advised that his proposition would be unlettable and he would also find it impossible to raise the bank finance necessary to build it. The longer-term institutions too were reluctant to join as partners for various reasons. Bradman recalls that 'I don't think the institutions had any money at that stage.'

The idea for a way around this impasse came to him in a meeting with

Eagle Star's David Jessel, who liked the idea but had no funds with which to participate. Bradman suggested that Rosehaugh Greycoat would issue a nil paid debenture stock, secured on the development, with a generous interest rate. The trick was that this debenture could only be called down three years after the initial issue date, before which time no money would change hands. The holders of the debenture would be obliged to provide the funds when they were called upon to do so. If the holders were not quoted investment trusts or acceptable insurance companies or pension funds, a guarantee that they would provide the funds would be obtained from a reputable bank. In June 1982 'we procured a number of debenture holders to subscribe for the issue, but no call was ever made. For the holders, there were no negative cash-flow implications, since no money passed, it didn't appear as a property since it was a security, it didn't appear in their balance sheets since it was nil paid; the only place it could be picked up was as a "contingent liability" in the notes to the accounts.' The reason why the debenture holders never had to pay the call was that Bradman, armed with their bank-guaranteed obligations, was now able to raise finance from more conventional sources. An American bank lent the construction finance secured only on the obligations of the debenture holders, not on the property itself. It remained the debenture holders who were secured against the development itself and a right to 30 per cent of the eventual net post-tax value of Phase 1.

The property was let at a higher rent than had been anticipated in the original plan and in November 1985 Rosehaugh Greycoat was able to issue a conventional 30-year debenture, listed on the Stock Exchange, secured on the completed and let investment, pay off the bank loan and not draw down the original debenture. The total cost of the development was £34 million, but the listed debenture raised £40 million, releasing some of the profit from the building of Phase 1 for reinvestment in the rest of the project. The debenture holders, British Land, Globe Investment Trust, Dixons Photographic and J. Rothschild, 'kicked up a rumpus' according to Bradman, because they were never required to provide cash at two and a half per cent over the London Inter-Bank Offered Rate (LIBOR), which would have made them a profit over their own cost of money. The 30 per cent equity interest they earned from subscribing to the nil-paid debenture is now worth over £40 million, but it is only British Land which remains a shareholder, having bought out the other holders for £18.25 million in 1988 and 1991. This suggests that British Land has almost doubled its total investment (including its own original entitlement) since that date. The other two phases of Finsbury Avenue were later successfully completed and let. The first rent review of Phase 1 took place in September 1989 and saw a substantial increase over the intial £19.75 a square foot rent paid by the tenants in 1984.

As well as this critical property development, Godfrey Bradman became closely involved in the revival of one of the dinosaurs of the High Street, Woolworth. The UK stores of Woolworth had been part of a separate UK publicly quoted company for many years but the controlling shareholding was still held by the American parent. The UK Woolworth group was a byword for old-fashioned retailing, best known for its 'mix 'n' match' confectionery and its ability to offer anything from a can opener to child's clothing. Despite attempts to improve its image, ('The Wonder of Woolworth' was a prolonged marketing campaign), it was making a derisory level of profits for the capital it employed. Much of that capital was tied up in the many High Street stores which Woolworth, unlike most of its competitors, still owned. In 1981 Godfrey Bradman went to see the US Woolworth management with a proposition to buy their shares in the UK company. The US company was receptive to this idea since it too was under pressure to make its assets 'sweat'.

The deal fell through and a company name Paternoster bought the British Woolworth company in 1982. Bradman's reward for the original concept was an option on Paternoster shares and convertible stock which gave Rosehaugh a net pre-tax profit of £16 million by the time the options were fully exercised and the shares sold in 1985. Paternoster soon renamed itself Woolworth and then, after the take-overs of B&Q and Comet, its name was changed to Kingfisher. The success of the buy-in was in substantial measure a result of the breathing space afforded by utilization of the underlying property assets while a new and more specific retailing formula was developed.

The Finsbury Avenue development and the Woolworth transaction were the most financially important matters with which Rosehaugh became involved in its early years under Godfrey Bradman, and by 1981 the benefits had already become apparent to the company's shareholders. In today's price terms, adjusted for subsequent issues, the shares, which had reopened at 13p in July 1978, had risen to 48p by July 1981. Rosehaugh's advance was not restricted to the large projects. As well as making low-risk investments in portfolios of property, (as in the early Tannergate and Sunbourne examples), with Bolansbourne and Tolverne, the early development of new areas of activity may be discerned. In June 1981 Rosehaugh bought 90 per cent of housebuilder Pelham Homes for £458,000 from Ray Whatman, who joined the Rosehaugh team. At the same time another subsidiary, Copartnership, was being developed by Christopher Collins, an ex-executive of surveyors Montagu Evans, the senior partner of which, Jack Nardecchia, was and is on the board of Rosehaugh.

There were hiccups in this progress. One subsidiary failed to complete a contracted £2.28 million purchase of four acres of land for residential development from Camden Council in December 1981, a very rare circumstance for a subsidiary of a flourishing public company. In January 1982 Rosehaugh bid for the public investment company London Shop Property Trust, but failed in the attempt, and in March 1982 an 85 per cent owned subsidiary, Cardwool, was set up to buy two and a half acres of land at East Croydon railway station for £1.1 million. The projected development on the site has yet to commence. In October 1982 the stockbrokers Bone Fitzgerald were suspended from trading; one of the company's shareholders was Godfrey Bradman. He had been a large client of the firm under its previous name and owner, Victor Sandelson, particularly in Treasury Bills.

These disappointments were as nothing against the successes, and by the end of 1983 the germination of Rosehaugh's greatest project was advancing. 'Armed with the success of Finsbury Avenue I had every year, probably two or three times a year, put to British Rail that they should let me get at the adjoining site.' The adjoining site was Broad Street and Liverpool Street Stations. In November 1983 Rosehaugh Stanhope was set up by Bradman and Stuart Lipton of Stanhope, ex-Greycoat, to bid on the development. 'There was a competition and I suppose that the submission I made to BR, which I wrote and did in a way which I don't think any competition had before, was the forerunner of the competition that took place for Kings Cross. It took me a month to write an analysis of every conceivable thing that affected their site, including the fact that their planning consent was very near, within 28 days, of expiry. We were selected and we had to move very quickly actually to commence the first phase within that 28 day period from the date of selection. Until that competition people had made submissions of 5 or 10 pages, but to make a submission which when you looked at it was that' (making a hand gesture indicating about one foot) 'deep, with bound volumes, reports from experts on town planning and engineering, was new. I suspect that there was really no competition, although Norwich Union were rather miffed that we got it and they didn't.'

Why was Stuart Lipton selected as his partner rather than continuing the successful partnership with Lipton's erstwhile colleagues at Greycoat? 'Stuart had expressed some interest (in the project) and rather than be in competition I cleared it with Greycoat that they would not object if I invited Stuart to join Rosehaugh on that project.'

Although at the time of the competition in March 1984 Rosehaugh Stanhope had only a sketch of Arup Associates' plans for the site, the next 12 months were a frenzy of activity, carrying out research into what the potential tenants of the proposed buildings wanted from the new generation of office buildings. It was determined by Frank Duffy's firm DEGW that clients needed floors of 15,000 or 20,000 square feet, rectangular and with as few columns as possible. Cores and lifts should be on the perimeter rather than in the middle of floors. Such space scarcely existed. The research did turn up some rather strange preconceptions from some of the prospective tenants. One bank thought that, since one of their dealers used 12 VDUs, maybe everyone will want to use 12 VDUs, and since some are in colour, perhaps everyone will want colour. They didn't want it cooled by chilled water in case of leaks, so they must have chilled air. The ducting and pipes for chilled air are about 17 times the diameter of water. If you go on this exponential analysis of what you need you very quickly find that the tenants would have buildings designed which would hardly be affordable by anyone.

The letting of the initial phases of Broadgate, as the development became known, was made much easier by the fact that Finsbury Avenue had already proved a success. Broadgate was financed in almost as innovative a way as the neighbouring development. The first Phase was pre-let to Security Pacific, the Californian bank which had taken over the London brokers Hoare Govett, and Phase 2 to Shearson Lehman, the investment banking subsidiary of American Express. Phase 1 was financed through £4.25 million of capital and loans provided by Rosehaugh Stanhope and a £35 million 2½ year non-recourse loan provided by County Bank, the merchant banking subsidiary of NatWest Bank; Phase 2 by £5 million of capital and loans from the joint company and an £85 million loan from Amex Bank, another American Express subsidiary, whose associate company was to be the tenant.

Non-recourse loans were commonplace in the US but, prior to the 1980s, not known in the UK. The basic premise of a non-recourse loan is that, if something goes wrong and the borrower is unable to keep up the agreed flow of interest or capital payments, then the lender has no more security than that represented by the specific asset against which the money has been lent. In the case of Broadgate, therefore, the lenders have no recourse to the general assets of Rosehaugh Stanhope nor to those of the respective parents. Although this is true in law, and in the US it is by no means uncommon for an investor to walk away from an investment which is making losses without ruining his future in the business, (much as many home-owners in the UK have thrown their keys back at the building societies), it is far more questionable whether a British public company could abandon a property to the lender and hope to have future access to bank funds. Godfrey Bradman responds to the question of responsibility over non-recourse loans rather circumspectly: 'That's a big issue. It would be very difficult to walk away from a wholly-owned and managed non-recourse loan, but if it was in a company where you had only a 15 per cent interest then one has to consider what one's responsibilities are.'

Another feature of the Broadgate development and one which was crucial in persuading the British Rail Property Board to back Rosehaugh Stanhope rather than any of the other potential developers was the profit share deal agreed between the two parties. The payment to BR consisted of two parts, the initial purchase price and a subsequent deferred purchase price. On Phases 1 to 4 the initial purchase price was £87.8 million. The deferred element of the purchase price on these Phases depended on the cost of the development, the rents achieved and the time at which BR claimed its share. By 30 June 1990 BR had been paid £125 million as its share of Phases 1 to 3, with a further £40 million outstanding on Phases 4, 6, 7, 9/10 and 11 at that date. One other party has an interest in the Broadgate development, David Blackburn, who was director of

Rosehaugh until 1985 and previously an associate of Godfrey Bradman in his tax planning days. Blackburn resigned from the Rosehaugh board but maintained a consultancy with Rosehaugh Stanhope which gave him 5 per cent of the surpluses on all Broadgate's Phases except numbers 1 and 2. Outside observers have commented that the loss of the talented David Blackburn as a second voice at the top of Rosehaugh was a significant factor in the later problems that the company faced. Godfrey Bradman himself commented that Blackburn liked to 'work very intently on one single thing.' That single thing was Broadgate. By the end of June 1990, David Blackburn's company had received commissions of almost £12 million out of nearly £15 million which had been provided for in the accounts of Rosehaugh Stanhope.

By this stage Rosehaugh had begun to move away from the relatively focused approach to development, based on large, well financed projects, often in new locations. As well as Pelham Homes in house-building, Bradman had in 1984 set up a subsidiary to develop shopping centres. His partner was Ian Pearce and the subsidiary, in which Pearce had a share, was named Shearwater. Initially this subsidiary seemed to be following the successful pattern of Rosehaugh's office developments. A joint company was formed between Shearwater and Hepworth, the clothes retailer soon renamed Next, to redevelop Northampton's Peacock Way shopping centre, and in July a further joint company was formed with Associated British Ports (ABP) to create a new shop, office and housing project in Southampton to be known as Ocean Village. Smaller schemes included the new shopping centres in Kendal, Cumbria and Prescot, Merseyside, which received £3 million from public funds as a stimulus to development in such a run-down area. In the development of housing, Rosehaugh was the 50 per cent partner in a group which built 24 houses on the site of Witanhurst, one of the grand Highgate houses overlooking Hampstead Heath. Each of these houses was priced between £750,000 and £1.5 million in 1985, before the late 1980s housing boom took off; one of the partners in the scheme was the Finnish bank KOP. A company was also set up with John Duggan, the Irish property man, later to form Phoenix, which was in turn taken over by Tony Clegg's Mountleigh.

The joint venture between Bradman and Duggan did not succeed. Duggan's approach was to find a deal which would make money fast. Bradman liked a methodical approach and fully researched. Duggan makes a gesture with his hands to describe it, 'You have to have the book. At my first board meeting he turned down something that would make us an instant £500,000, and really it was over from that moment.' It did not help that Duggan was a keen shot and Bradman a vegetarian: 'The first lunch I had with him was a disaster' says Duggan. In Duggan's view Bradman 'didn't understand property feel. You can nickel and dime any deal, any piece of paper, but if you don't have a feel for it, it's no good.' After 14 months the two went their separate ways. The risk-averse, methodical Bradman and the dealer Duggan were a strange mixture and it is surprising that either felt such chemistry would work.

As Rosehaugh grew, it began to need more equity itself to support the rising tide of development and in April 1986 the company raised £58.9 million through a rights issue, gratefully taken up by the growing band of Bradman admirers. Shearwater was proving to be an active developer, winning the right to redevelop the centre of Eastleigh in Hampshire and forming a joint company with Blue Circle Industries, the cement manufacturer, to develop a retail and leisure park on the site of one of the worked-out limestone quarries left by BCI in the green belt of Kent at Swanscombe. A further diversification was the setting up of another subsidiary, Rosehaugh Heritage, based in Bath, to redevelop architecturally sensitive sites.

Meanwhile Broadgate was continuing to advance with a further letting agreed before Prime Minister Thatcher returned to top out the first two Phases on 11 July 1986. Union Bank of Switzerland decided to take the 380,000 square feet of offices in Phase 3, facing onto Liverpool Street on the site of the old Broad Street Station buildings, for its newly acquired brokerage subsidiary, Phillips and Drew, on a rent of £35 per square foot. The bank agreed to provide the bank finance for the building of this Phase themselves, as Amex had done before them. By the late summer of 1986 Rosehaugh Stanhope had taken an interest in land in Docklands on which they planned a 3.8 million square foot development of shops, offices and homes designed by Richard Rogers. Rosehaugh's own trading subsidiary Baxtergate bought South Quay Plaza 2 on the Isle of Dogs for £22 million. The attraction was not wholly the building itself; the purchase enabled Rosehaugh to shelter much of its profit in that year from tax.

In December 1986 Rosehaugh entered into another joint venture to develop an office at the junction of Crosswall and Crutched Friars in the City with Wimpey and Haslemere Estates. This building has since had a chequered history. The consortium built and let the development to Jardine Mathieson, the company which was the model for James Clavell's book on Hong Kong, *Taipan*. The property was then sold in 1989 to Land and Property Trust, run by Berish Berger, a family member of one of London's foremost residential landlords, for £60 million. Land and Property was put into administration in 1991, but by then it had already sold the building to a 'European consortium'. The curse of Crusader House was then visited on those investors too as they defaulted on payments to their bank, Banque Bruxelles, which in 1991 took possession of its tainted asset.

Bradman was not content to be responsible for the biggest single development in London; he had plans to be involved in them all. In 1986 he became involved in the competition to redevelop Spitalfields market across Bishopsgate from Broadgate and by the end of the year Rosehaugh Stanhope had announced plans to develop one million square feet along the line of the railway which carried trains from South London between

Blackfriars and Holborn Viaduct. By 1987 Rosehaugh Stanhope was also showing interest in the redevelopment of Paddington Basin, a little known enclave of London hidden between the Westway elevated section of the A40 and St Mary's Hospital and the hinterland of Kings Cross Station. The propensity to think big was instilled into the management of Rosehaugh's subsidiary companies. Ian Pearce, who ran the Shearwater retail development subsidiary, was quoted in 1986 as having been told by Bradman 'You can lose as much on a small development if it goes wrong as on a major project, but the upside is not nearly as exciting.'

Godfrey Bradman had, by early 1987, established himself as perhaps the pre-eminent property developer in the UK, certainly amongst the quoted companies since Stuart Lipton, his only realistic competitor for the title in public eyes, had not yet brought Stanhope to the Unlisted Securities Market. His reputation was enhanced by his extra-mural involvement in many activities not usually associated with the property developer. As long ago as 1982 Bradman had financed the initial publicity for the campaign for lead-free petrol, CLEAR. He convened an ad-hoc committee of scientists which decided that it needed a professional campaigner as its executive director: Des Wilson, veteran of single issue campaigns such as Shelter, the campaign for the homeless, and the Liberal Democrat's 1992 election campaign director, was appointed by Bradman, the start of a long association between the two men. Bradman's initial £100,000 financing brought its reward in the 1983 government commitment to phase lead out of petrol and in the 1988 Budget when Chancellor Nigel Lawson applied the strongest impetus to the campaign by introducing an attractive tax differential to the pricing of lead-free petrol, since which time lead-free has gained over 40 per cent of the petrol market. Wilson and Bradman have been associated with various other public campaigns since then including the Campaign for Freedom of Information at a time when civil servants were being prosecuted for leaking confidential information to the press. Bradman was also closely concerned with the campaign to force the pharmaceutical company Eli Lilly to pay compensation to people who had suffered serious side-effects from its anti-arthritis drug, Opren.

As Chairman of Friends of the Earth Trust Bradman has also contributed to the development of environmental issues in the building trade. In 1985 he commissioned a study Hazardous Building Materials, edited by two lecturers at the University of Salford and published in 1986; in its preface he wrote 'In my own business, I have sought to ensure that great care be taken in the selection of safe and suitable building materials, and that it is recognized that we owe to people buildings which are safe environmentally as well as structurally.' In 1988 Rosehaugh itself published a guide to Legionnaire's Disease and Bradman organized a conference at the School of Hygiene and Tropical Medicine, of which he was also on the Council, to discuss the bacteria. In the same year he sponsored a study of the use of CFCs in Buildings. The culminating publication in this area of interest was *Buildings and Health – The Rosehaugh Guide to the Design, Construction, Use and Management of Buildings* which was published by the Royal Institute of British Architects in 1990. This 520 page book contains all the information necessary to avoid threats to health in buildings, from CFCs to mice. Bradman has also concerned himself with many other health campaigns varying from Parents Against Tobacco to an Aids Policy Unit.

Although 1987 was a year of dramatic further progress for Rosehaugh, the stock market crash on 19 October sowed the seeds of the substantial problems the company eventually faced. Earlier that year the company had raised a further £82 million through the purchase for shares of General Funds Investment Trust, the portfolio of which was easily liquidated in the euphoric bull market which marked the first part of the year. Rosehaugh Greycoat's second and third phases of Finsbury Avenue were let, and Reuters contracted to buy a development in Docklands. Broadgate was letting well, with Japanese interest in Phase 4 (confusingly known as 6 Broadgate) and County NatWest took Phase 6. In December 1987 the Prince of Wales formally opened the Broadgate development, an occasion marked by a skating demonstration in the pouring rain by British Olympic gold medallists Torville and Dean on the ice-rink in Broadgate Circle. The Prince, the well known architecture critic, restricted himself to an anodyne comment about the redevelopment itself.

Perhaps the first sign of potential trouble for Rosehaugh was the rise in interest rates in August 1987, although this was quickly shrugged off by the markets. The effect of economic policy on the property market at this time is described in a later chapter, but the pace of lettings in the City, and in Broadgate, began to decelerate as a result of the crash, while building continued apace in all quarters of the capital. Rosehaugh's own share price was among those most severely affected by the market fall, and, although it recovered for a time, it never regained those levels. Bradman ignored the implicit warning contained in the market's gyrations and the company became involved in a veritable orgy of new projects. In February 1988 the American bank Bankers Trust actually bought Phase 5 of Broadgate outright for about £100 million which gave the Rosehaugh Stanhope company two years of large reported profits. Stockbrokers Laing and Cruickshank, which had recently been taken over by the French bank Credit Lyonnais, took the bulk of space in Phases 9/10. Rosehaugh Stanhope was selected by the LDDC as the developer of the huge Royal Albert Docks at the eastern end of Docklands and by British Rail, after a bruising contest with Speyhawk on which Rosehaugh Stanhope spent £6 million, as the developers of Kings Cross. The Kings Cross development created a lot of suspicion among local residents and politicians and drew the comment from Godfrey Bradman that 'If it were not for the (legitimate) desire for commercial secrecy on the part of British Rail and the other public owners of the site I would be happy, in principle, for the public to have access to the commercial calculations which will determine the density and balance of development on the site. Otherwise people become suspicious. They ask "What are these chaps creaming off?".'

At the same time Rosehaugh embarked on the largest housing development in the UK, the 5,000 homes and related buildings of Chafford Hundred, a glamorous name for a rather dull piece of flat Essex land in Grays, built in partnership with Blue Circle (again) and the publishing and banking conglomerate Pearson. Shearwater too was wasting no time: new projects included retail developments in Trowbridge, Camberley, Newcastle and Caernarvon. It had not yet proved difficult for Rosehaugh to raise finance for its projects; in July 1988 County NatWest raised a syndicated loan of £350 million to finance the building of the later stages of Broadgate, just beating the £300 million loan raised by NatWest for Phases 6 and 7 in January 1987. The bank executive responsible for that deal, the funds for which were 60 per cent provided by Japanese banks, was Paul Rivlin, later to join the Rosehaugh board.

Although everything continued to progress along its normal ambitious path during late 1988 and into 1989, the rise in interest rates and, certainly from early 1989 the slow-down of parts of the economy, particularly retail sales, house price rises and the financial services sector, were starting to affect the outlook for property. By September 1989 Bradman was threatening to withdraw from the Royal Docks scheme as he was frustrated by the lack of progress with the LDDC and there was an uncharacteristic dearth of new projects announced during the year. Bradman had in fact agreed to step back within Rosehaugh: 'We did take on a number of people to deal with the expansion of the Group as a whole. I agreed to the idea of having joint chief executives with me being executive Chairman. If there's any idea I really regret it's for that period of time I was not chief executive and in retrospect it was not helpful.'

The fundamental strength of Bradman's concept for Rosehaugh was the 'principle that I had enunciated originally about minimizing and laying off risk. At a certain stage a lot of people tended to forget how important that was.' The secret of Rosehaugh's success was that it 'developed with someone else's money on someone else's land' as Trevor Osborne of Speyhawk describes the formula. The money came from the banks, who embraced the 'non-recourse' concept with enthusiasm, especially the US banks who were familiar with it at home and the Japanese banks who were so anxious to increase their market share for most of the 1980s.

By June 1990, Rosehaugh Stanhope had property assets of almost £1.7 billion, supported by only the £1,012,000 original cash equity investment from its two shareholders; a company with over £1,200,000,000 of borrowing on such a low investment is probably unprecedented in recent history, and is only possible because the properties threw up a valuation of £450 million more than their cost, including the £29 million after-tax profit taken on selling Phase 5 to its occupier, Bankers Trust. The problem for the developer is that, even when the properties are built and let, there is still a deficit between rent and the interest payable on the loans. When much of the debt was taken on, in the mid-1980s, interest rates were in single figures for a time and it was possible to forecast that this cash shortfall might be quite small, but as rates rose to the 15 per cent level they reached in October 1989 and stayed at that level for exactly a year, then the cash-flow deficit became less manageable.

Other property developers insured themselves against such eventualities by buying a 'cap' on their interest rate costs, by which the banks, for a relatively modest payment, will not charge more than an agreed rate on the loan, a liability they themselves can lay off in the money markets. Rosehaugh chose not to do this with all its loans, and, as one developer says, 'Bradman got it wrong. He really thought interest rates were coming down to 6 per cent.' The accounts of Rosehaugh Stanhope show that the banks paid £5.9 million as a result of 'interest rate protection agreements', but this has to be set against total interest paid of £163 million. Although Rosehaugh and Stanhope seem to have invested only £½ million in their joint company, their involvement is much greater. They had lent the development company £187 million by June 1990 and they were owed a further £64 million on interest due to them but not paid over. The loans are unsecured and rank behind the bank loans which are secured on the properties being built.

Raising the further £45 million of capital that Rosehaugh effectively had to put into the joint company in the year between June 1989 and June 1990 was a serious burden. It was made worse because other areas of the business were not able to provide the resources. Although Pelham Homes had a very cheap land bank, house sales came to a grinding halt; many of the Shearwater developments proved impossible to progress with and it became known that Rosehaugh was an aggressive seller of assets. The final confirmation that all was not well was the announcement on 5 February 1990 of a rights issue to raise £125 million. The Rosehaugh share price was already very depressed, so that a rights issue at this price, well under half its peak level, was deemed a mark of weakness and the shares fell sharply towards the issue price. The issue was not underwritten by institutions in the normal way and there was no guarantee that the money would be subscribed by the existing shareholders, in which case the company would have received nothing, with incalculable consequences for Rosehaugh.

The following months contained little good news for the company. Rosehaugh was pulled out of the planned development of the Royal Docks, frustrated by the delays of dealing with the LDDC and leaving Stanhope still involved. Godfrey Bradman then confirmed what had been the talk of the industry in recent months, that the Ludgate and Kings Cross schemes would be the last to be carried out by Rosehaugh Stanhope; (Ludgate was the ambitious plan to build a string of offices down the line of the railway linking Holborn Viaduct and Blackfriars railway stations). There has been a lot of lurid speculation about the reasons for the break-up of the most productive property partnership between two separate companies of the decade, but the truth is probably more prosaic. 'It's true to say that both companies did not originally have the full range of personnel to undertake such big developments and it was a marriage of convenience to share in the resources and skills, but as both companies grew neither company, frankly, needed the other', explains Bradman. There is no doubt too that the personalities of Bradman and Lipton are diametrically opposed, the former being relatively introverted and the latter being more characteristic of a property developer with his extrovert personality. Another close observer notes that by the end of the partnership each was encroaching on the businesses of the respective parent companies, which was unwelcome.

It was Shearwater's activities which were probably the most adversely affected by the economic recession which had finally taken grip in 1990 after nine years of uninterrupted growth. The subsidiary was sacked as developer of a Sheffield canal-side scheme for failing to come up with funding in good time, and the same happened in Camberley; of its own volition it pulled out of the Blue Water scheme, which was sold to the partner BCI for only £5 million. By the time the half-year figures to 31 December 1989 were announced in April 1990, the company had decided to take a £12 million write-off on 'projects which may not be progressed.' In October Ian Pearce of Shearwater and Ian Rowberry of Copartnership left Rosehaugh and the operations of those subsidiaries were cut back. Rosehaugh was forced to sell its own head office in Marylebone Lane just north of Oxford Street to a Swedish company for £23.5 million, and Rosehaugh Heritage was sold to a subsidiary of Kingfisher, the Woolworth holding company, for £35 million, incurring a further write-down of £16.5 million against the value at which the company was carried in the books.

The news was not universally bad for the company in 1990. The Ludgate development was given a welcome boost by the announcement that Coopers and Lybrand Deloitte had agreed to take over 500,000 square feet of the 600,000 square feet development, and project financing was secured for its completion. Coopers had earlier taken Greycoat's Embankment Place development, and, although they were now not going to occupy it, would still be liable for paying the rent on that property too until it found another party to take over the lease. In the event it became known in 1991 that Coopers had never signed a lease for Ludgate, leaving Rosehaugh Stanhope without an anchor tenant for the development.

Lettings in Broadgate continued, albeit at a slower pace, but no buyer appeared for Phase 6 (4 Broadgate), for which the developers were seeking over £200 million. During 1990 Rosehaugh acquired three important new shareholders: JMB Realty, Olympia & York and Ravensale. JMB is a privately owned American property investor with a $20 billion US property portfolio, and had previously bought the British property trading phenomenon Randsworth; Olympia & York is the Reichmann's company, which owns a third of Stuart Lipton's Stanhope company and is developing Canary Wharf; Ravensale is the company in which Ronnie Jarvis, the original investor in Finsbury Avenue holds his property interests. The first rent review on 1 Finsbury Avenue also contained good news, with the rent rising from £19.75 a foot to £46 which will increase further the profit of Rosehaugh Greycoat. That company will soon be generating surplus cash at considerable rate, enabling it to pay back its bank loans. On 25 October 1991 it was announced that Rosehaugh had negotiated the sale of its interest in Rosehaugh Greycoat, the owners of the Finsbury Avenue properties, to British Land. In a complicated deal, both Rosehaugh and Ronnie Jarvis's Ravensale (now the owner of more than 10 per cent of Rosehaugh's shares), realized their interest in this successful development. Rosehaugh's share of the sale amounted to £44 million, because, on the same day, it also sold Rosehaugh Copartnership, its residential development company, to Ravensale, for the princely sum of two pounds. Jarvis's company took on that company's debts, and, as a result, Rosehaugh's proceeds from Rosehaugh Greycoat was a smaller proportion of the approximately £70 million total consideration paid by British Land than its 40 per cent shareholding (against Ravensale's 20 per cent) in the associate company would have suggested.

Bradman's future depended on several things. First of all he had to hope that interest rates would continue to fall back from the 1989–90 peak levels. The second potential saving grace might be the rent reviews on Broadgate. Phases 1 to 3 were let at rents of £35 a foot or below, but in today's depressed letting market, there was unlikely to be much, if any, immediate uplift. The third idea of hope was that the institutions would buy some of the group's assets, reducing debt, even at the expense of long-term benefit from its prime assets. The first breakthrough for the company was the sale in August 1991 of Bishopsgate Exchange, 155 Bishopsgate, Phase 7 of the development, not the widely marketed Phase 4 at 6 Broadgate. The buyer, for a reported £180 million, was the US Prudential Insurance's Global Real Estate Investment Programme. The European Bank for Reconstruction & Redevelopment (EBRD) finally chose 1 Exchange Square, 175 Bishopsgate, as its headquarters, leaving only 199 Bishopsgate as substantially unlet by the end of 1991. It is likely that the EBRD was able to negotiate a very attractive lease. None of these improved elements was enough to save Bradman.

Godfrey Bradman has, in the last ten years, been praised beyond his probable value and, more recently, unfairly criticized for a life-style which does not conform to the usual mould of the property developer. The property world is eager to hear the latest Bradman story, and it is certainly true that his lifestyle invites some quizzical looks. He is a vegetarian, a teetotaller and a rabid non-smoker. It is said that he will only turn off hotel lights using a handkerchief for fear of germs, and my visit to his office gave some more grist to the story mill. Bradman was suffering from a cold and he refused to shake my hand, for fear of giving me his germs, claiming that he himself had been infected in this way. His office lavatory is mute witness to this obsession with cleanliness: the flush is a foot-pedal and the basin taps work by a magic eye, meaning that no human hand will touch anything that any future user of the facilities, including presumably Godfrey Bradman, will touch. Property men relish too the occasion on which he came to speak to an industry lunch, accompanied by someone carrying a tantalus in which there were his own bottles of purified water. Others tell of his rejection of several coffee cups as being cracked or not clean enough.

On one occasion, in the building Rosehaugh occupied before moving into its headquarters in Marylebone Lane, several people had gathered for a meeting and were waiting for Bradman to join them. The room was quite small, and there was a powerful wall air-conditioner at work: the visitors were cold. With great presence of mind one took a piece of plain paper and wrote in large letters 'OUT OF ORDER', placing it on the air-conditioner before turning it off. When Bradman eventually joined the meeting, he walked anxiously around the room before spotting the sign. 'It's a practical joke isn't it?' he said. Baffled, the visitors enquired how he knew that. 'The notice does not have a date on it' came the reply. Everything was properly ordered in the Bradman empire.

The merger discussions between Rosehaugh and Stanhope which began in mid-1991 were widely interpreted as a sign of the weakness of Rosehaugh. As the negotiations wore on it became clear that all the negotiating clout was in the hands of Stanhope. Bradman fought for his company and for a dignified exit for himself as the man so closely identified with the fortunes of the company. It did not happen. On 6 December 1991 Rosehaugh announced that it had made a loss, in the year to 30 June 1991, of £226.6 million, after providing for the decline in value of its portfolio; its borrowing limits had been breached and the accounts qualified by its auditors. Net assets per share fell to 130p against 373p at the end of June 1990. The company had sold £148 million worth of property in the year to June 1991, with a further £93 million by the end of that calendar year being realized. Rosehaugh and Stanhope had been obliged to convert £50 million each of their loans to Rosehaugh Stanhope into equity and waived over £40 million each of interest accrued on those loans. Rosehaugh Stanhope was still, even after the repayment of the loan secured on 155 Bishopsgate, 'Bishopsgate Exchange', labouring under bank loans totalling over £1 billion, all related to market interest rates. A full year of the reduction in interest rates from 15 per cent to 10.5 per cent will itself save the joint company interest of £45 million, bringing the joint venture almost back into profit, provided that there are no further capital write-downs.

For Rosehaugh itself the problems proved more urgent. The declared losses and write-downs had given the banks the right to demand repayments of their loans, and all £300 million and more of net borrowing needed to be renegotiated. The group still showed gross assets of almost £600 million, and the parent company had guaranteed only £82 million of the borrowing, but it was increasingly clear that it was indeed impossible for Rosehaugh to walk away from subsidiaries with non-recourse loans. Even a further fall in interest rates would not create a profit in Rosehaugh itself, since it has little in the way of a completed and let investment portfolio; that is held almost exclusively in its associated companies, such as Rosehaugh Stanhope.

To mark the end of the era, Godfrey Bradman stepped down as chairman of the company, and it was understood that he had no long-term plans to remain on the board. At his final annual general meeting in the slack days between Christmas and the New Year 1991, Bradman came in for criticism from shareholders who in earlier years would have been praising his unerring judgement. He even had to announce that Rosehaugh would be moving from the Marylebone offices which he had so carefully organized to suit his whims; although the freehold on them had already been part of the asset realization programme, this was an admission that Rosehaugh was a small company again.

On 23 January 1992, it was announced that merger discussions between Rosehaugh and its partner Stanhope had been abandoned, and the Rosehaugh share price dipped to under 5p. Stuart Lipton's Stanhope had become unwilling to take responsibility for a company which had already admitted that 'the Directors have assumed that their negotiations with the Group's bankers will result in the provision of sufficient facilities after 31 January, 1992 to permit the Group to pursue its business plan.' As Arthur Andersen, Rosehaugh's auditors, put it 'Should the negotiations not result in such agreement, the going concern basis [on which the accounts had been prepared] may cease to be appropriate'; Rosehaugh's future still hangs by a thread.

Bradman has proved that he has vision, having believed in Finsbury Avenue, Broadgate and Ludgate when many wise souls were shaking their heads knowingly. His original *modus operandi* was truly low risk, high reward and it is a shame that the group lost sight of this in the later years. It is not enough for him to say that he blames the people he put in charge of the operating companies. At least part of the trouble was attributable to him telling them to think big, and another part is a result of his not protecting Rosehaugh from the risks of suffering higher interest rates (and for longer than almost any analyst was forecasting in 1988). Perhaps he did not have anyone who could tell him he was wrong and he began to believe his own publicity as the genius who could do no wrong. As one developer said to me of Bradman 'I do not believe in wizards'.

- INNOVATIVE FINANCING
- TENANTS (BANKS) PROVIDING DEVT FUNDS
- INTEREST ON LOANS NOT 64 CAPPED
- VERY HIGH GEARING
- LIQUIDITY PROBLEM IN MARKET WILL LEAD TO COLLAPS

4

CREATING SPACES

NOT MANY MEN can lay claim to have changed the environment of a city to any lasting degree. Some have achieved it through acts of vandalism, such as Nero setting fire to Rome or Hitler to the cities of Europe, but others have made a more positive contribution. Christopher Wren and Nicholas Hawksmoor changed the skyline of London after the Great Fire in the late seventeenth century; Baron Haussmann in nineteenth century Paris drove his boulevards through the slums of the Right Bank. More controversially, Colonel Richard Seifert could boast that his designs in the 1960s and 1970s changed the face of London more than those of any architect since Wren. Not many voices were raised to suggest it was for the better. Stuart Anthony Lipton, an unqualified property developer, might reasonably claim to have been involved in the creation of more high quality working environments than any of his contemporaries, as a director of Greycoat, Stockley and Stanhope.

Lipton was not in fact the name he was born to in November 1942; his father, Bertram Green, and mother were divorced and Stuart took his mother's maiden name. After a middle-class upbringing he entered the property industry in 1960, working for agents Yeates & Yeates. After a period with Chamberlain & Willows and another firm, in 1966, at the age of 24 and the year he was married, he founded his own firm, Anthony Lipton & Co. One of his most vivid memories of this period was marvelling at the sheer size of the sale the site of what is now the Mirror Group Newspapers building at the corner of Fetter Lane and Holborn; it changed hands for what seemed the astounding sum of £1 million.

At Anthony Lipton he was still learning his trade. Something his partner Mike Gilbert had learned while at agents Donaldson was the value of short leaseholds. This arcane subject had been a closed book to most investors; it involved the purchase of the tail-end of a lease before it reverted to the landlord. The investor receives a flow of income for a period, at the end of which he is left with nothing. It is the property equivalent of buying an annuity, but the property market was not looking at the value of these interests in a rigorous fashion. For instance valuers would take no notice of the fact that, since rents are paid quarterly in advance, the initial purchase price of such a lease is effectively reduced by the quarterly rent received immediately. The problem is simply one of calculating accurately the internal rate of return, but most agents relied on a set of valuation tables which gave a much lower value than the true one. Gilbert and Lipton quickly understood the concept, which was introduced to Gilbert by John Smith, descendant of Captain John Smith of Pocahontas fame and sometime Conservative MP for the Cities of London and Westminster. His Manifold Trust became the biggest investor in such leases, and John Smith was later a significant supporter of Lipton and Gilbert's property ventures.

The biggest client of the new firm was Amalgamented Investment & Property, the company headed by Gabriel Harrison. Among the executives Lipton's company dealt with were Geoffrey Wilson and Peter Olsberg. In 1971 these two left Amalgamated to join Lipton and Gilbert to form Corporate Estates, backed by the then-ubiquitous Jim Slater of Slater Walker, which held a quarter of the company. It was quickly backed into the tiny quoted company Sterling Land in a deal worth only £3 million, and before long, in June 1973, was subject to an agreed bid worth £28 million from the rapidly expanding Town & City Properties. The Sterling Land board was 'totally unaware' that Barry East, the head of Town & City, whose board colleagues at that time included David, now Lord, Young, and Elliot Bernerd, was simultaneously negotiating the purchase of the much larger Central & District Properties portfolio from fringe merchant bank Keyser Ullman. This excessive expansion at the top of the market was almost to cost Town & City its existence. The sale of his company, 'more by luck than judgement probably' according to Lipton, was mainly for shares. The management of Sterling Land was retained to give advice on its old portfolio and it still had shares in Town & City. In September the Sterling Land directors resolved to sell most of their shares and Joseph Sebag, Town & City's stockbroker, apologized for only being able to achieve a price of 75p per share. In the next 12 months they were to fall to 10p.

Although Stuart Lipton was able to extract himself from his first public company with aplomb, the property crash of the next three years did not leave him unscarred. Together with Peter Olsberg he then started a company named Westwood. Although Lipton today says that this company did not actually go into receivership, it was not a success and the memory of it is clearly not a happy one. Olsberg had been called back by Jessel Harrison to try to rescue the doomed Amalgamated Investment and Property which he had left only a few years before. Gabriel Harrison had died suddenly in December 1974, and in the event no-one could save the company; those who looked at a rescue suggest that the book-keeping and records of the company were in a chaotic state.

Lipton rebounded with a company set up in 1976 with his old colleague

Geoffrey Wilson and Ron Spinney, Greycoat Estates. The company was named after one of its initial projects, a refurbishment of 16,000 square feet of offices at Townsend House, Greycoat Place, Victoria, let to London Transport; another project was the refurbishment of Country Life House in Tavistock Street, the first Lutyens office building, commissioned by his long-time patron, Hudson. The four initial deals were financed by Standard Life Assurance with Greycoat making relatively little from the properties.

It was at this stage, in 1977/78, that Lipton sought to put into action some of the lessons he had learnt from close observation of the US development and construction industry over the previous decade. On his initial visits he was largely 'watching with amazement' at the quite different techniques employed in the US industry but now there came the opportunity to put the idea that they were indeed exportable to the UK to the test. The test-bed was a range of eighteenth and early nineteenth century warehouses on a 5-acre site to the north of the traditional limit of City buildings although administratively still part of it. Cutlers Gardens had been built by the East India Company as its Treasure-House, designed by Richard Jupp and his successor Henry Holland. Latterly the property had been owned as the upstream warehouse of the Port of London Authority (PLA), and as the sea cargo trade moved further and further down the Thames the more dilapidated the old buildings became. In 1973 the PLA exchanged contracts with Ramon Greene and Jack Walker's company, English & Continental, for the sale of the site. An Office Development Permit was obtained for the resiting of the Baltic Exchange, the centre of merchant ship chartering, which had threatened to leave Britain unless the permit was forthcoming. The 1974/75 property collapse prevented Greene and Walker from completing the deal and in 1978 Greycoat stepped in with its partner Standard Life Assurance, paying £5 million for the site. The developers inherited Richard Seifert and Partners as architects; they had been the architects retained by the Baltic Exchange, who no longer wished to move to the new location.

There was substantial irony in the combination of Seifert and Greycoat, since Lipton later became notorious for his criticism of the traditional 1960s 'rent slab' buildings, many of which had been designed by the Seifert partnership. The new partners had to gain planning permission within six months, after which time the ODP expired and, with a Labour government in power, there could be no certainty of another being issued. For all his later criticisms, Lipton found Seifert to be 'a master planner.' Four ground plans were seriously considered before planning consent for 790,000 square feet of offices was granted in November 1978 by the City Corporation. The development was the first which London had seen in recent years which, as Lipton expresses it,' 'created a place'. Paternoster Square and the Barbican were earlier attempts to create a coherent new city area, but they failed to gain acceptance with the general public. Cutlers Gardens established new courtyards and walkways, with arches inserted in the ground floors of the old buildings. New blocks were also built in the complex and these caused controversy. Conservationists were aghast at the demolition of the massive warehouse which backed onto Middlesex Street, (the famous Petticoat Lane), 'one of the grandest pieces of street scenery in London', but the construction began.

The new buildings were designed to blend with the cleaned Georgian brickwork. The granite needed to achieve this match was found on a mountain on the Rio Grande in Brazil. With an attention to detail which was to become a trade mark, some would say obsession, of his developments, Stuart Lipton flew to Brazil to see the rock for himself. The granite was transported to Italy for polishing and now sits easily in its environment, although polished granite soon became the cliché of 1980s development. As well as refurbishing two Georgian houses guarding the entrance to the development, Quinlan Terry, the classical revivalist, built two pillars to support the wrought-iron gates. The project won over most critics and is a popular office location, despite the fact that is not built to any revolutionary ground plan. The criticism of the standard 45-foot wide office had begun but the technological revolution was far enough in the future to allow serious debate between Greycoat and Peter Henwood of Standard Life as to whether the building should even have the extra cost of air-conditioning. That question was resolved in the affirmative by a survey of the possible tenants by the Economist Intelligence Unit.

The widest building, only 55 feet, was the controversial new one at the rear of the site replacing the original blank warehouse wall. The developers expected this to be the most difficult building to let and bear the lowest rent. It was the burgeoning American presence in the London financial markets which revealed a new demand: Lehman Brothers were among the initial tenants of the rear block and proceeded to build one of the first modern dealing rooms in the City of London. They were joined by other US investment banks. Letting the development was something of a problem. Creating a new place was fine in theory but Cutlers Gardens was well off the beaten track for the financial services industry. Most companies at that date would not think of moving operations out of a rough square bounded by Bishopsgate, Cannon Street, St Martins-le-Grand and London Wall. Cutlers Gardens was even more off-pitch in that it backed onto the distinctly scruffy Petticoat Lane.

The solution was to market the buildings at lower rents but promote the location. In 1981 when the development was well advanced the agents quoted £18.10 per square foot for the new space and £17.50 per square foot for the refurbished buildings, against the rents on prime City offices at the time of something approaching £25. A video featuring the TV personality James Burke asked: 'What do the Guildhall, Bank of England and Stock Exchange have in common? They are all within easy walking distance of Cutlers Gardens.' The proximity to Liverpool Street Station and the working environment eventually won over the sceptics. Another achievement of the developers and contractors, Sir Robert McAlpine, was the sheer speed with which the building work was done. The 27 months which the work took was found, in a study by the University of Reading, to be the fastest 'spend', (the running cost of the construction work), of any contemporary development. Greycoat's reward for the project was a six per cent interest plus a management fee for overseeing the development.

STANDARD LIFE

In June 1978, at about the time that the contract to develop Cutlers Gardens was signed, Greycoat became a publicly quoted company. This was achieved by the reverse takeover of a small company named Chaddesley Investments, which was effectively controlled by the South African Schlesinger family. The deal valued Greycoat at only £560,000, since the quoted company issued 3.42 million shares to the Greycoat shareholders and those shares were quoted at 16½p each at the time. Lipton and Wilson also subscribed for a further 1.4 million shares at the same price, ending up with 68 per cent of the newly merged company. Under the rules of the Stock Exchange the shares of Chaddesley were suspended while the transaction was ratified by both sets of shareholders and when the shares' quotation was restored in August they immediately rose to 44p. Geoffrey Wilson made clear what the Greycoat team had already determined as its credo: 'We have a commitment to high standards of design and construction which enables us to attract first-class tenants at good rents.'

Two other buildings developed over the four years 1978–82 justified this claim and established the reputations of both Greycoat and, separately, Stuart Lipton, as imaginative leaders of a new generation of developers. The first was an office block at Hammersmith commissioned by Sir William Halcrow & Partners, the consulting engineers, for their head office. Halcrows appointed Greycoat as their developers after a competition, and Lipton claims that the resulting building is the first of the new generation with a really efficient floor-plan and is 'the best building in Hammersmith'. Again, as Greycoat could not afford the building themselves, they funded the construction by a forward sale to Norwich Union, leaving the company with only a small interest in the ultimate investment.

NORWICH UNION

The second building was on an even more controversial site, on the corner of the Euston Road and Hampstead Road, backing onto Tolmers Square. This site had been fought over long and hard in the 1970s with Camden Council anxious to create council flats but developers Stock Conversion seeking permission for offices. By the time Greycoat came along in January 1979 with Sir Robert McAlpine, with whom it set up a 50–50 company, Greycoat London Estates Investment, both Council and developers were ready to compromise. The partners were granted permission for 200,000 square feet of offices and agreed to fund a new Tolmers Square residential development for the Council; the Council received £2.25 million on granting the developers a building lease of 99 years with an option to extend for a further 26 years, and would receive 50 per cent of the net profits on completion. The reflective glass building is not deemed by Lipton to be one of his successes, although he remains content with the interior; 'not great' is his verdict. It was initially let to Davy Corporation but is presently occupied by Prudential.

By now the old Chaddesley company had been renamed Greycoat Estates and profits were benefiting from Wilson and Lipton's involvement; pre-tax profits in the six months to September 1978 rose to £200,000 from £6,000 a year earlier even though the new management had been in place for only three of those months. The management was taking forward agreed developments and adding properties to the portfolio such as Imperial House and Regent Arcade, Regent Street, bought for shares from Rank Organisation.

The major new project of Stuart Lipton between 1979 and 1983 focused on another important site, the Coin Street development on the South Bank of the Thames between Blackfriars and Waterloo Bridges. This site became notorious as the scene of a show-down between commercial and community development. On the one hand was Greycoat, with its Richard Rogers plans for a 'new place' rather than a succession of office slabs; on the other were the political activists who believed that the only development possible for the area was of new low-cost housing and related infrastructure. After a protracted series of enquiries Greycoat finally decided to withdraw from the scheme in January 1983.

Coin Street was not the only important development in which Greycoat was involved during this period. Two which broke new ground in terms of design and building techniques were the offices above Victoria Station and the Finsbury Avenue development. In February 1981 the joint Greycoat/McAlpine company submitted a planning application for 220,000 square feet of offices to be built on a raft over the tracks of Victoria Station, the first of BR's stations to see such a development; at other stations buildings had risen over the concourse or on peripheral bits of land. The techniques for building floor-plates on rafts bearing the weight of large offices had been developed in the US by a contractor named Schal which had built the Sears Tower in Chicago, the world's tallest office building, and had worked for the legendary Harold Diesel. As Lipton says, they had the technology which 'allowed me to turn the dream into reality'. This building was also a ground-breaker in another sense. One floor of the building was 75 feet wide, far above the convention of 40–45 feet. Sam Levy of agents Jones Lang Wootton, the doyen of office lettings, was convinced that such a wide building would not let. It did prove difficult, but it was finally selected by Salomon Brothers, the US investment bank, as its new European headquarters, and plays a starring role in that memoir of the yuppie 1980s, *Liar's Poker* by Michael Lewis. The second development in this period became the precursor to a project which was to dominate Stuart Lipton's life for most of the next ten years: Finsbury Avenue, next to Liverpool Street Station.

The Finsbury Avenue development, as we have seen, was the brainchild of Godfrey Bradman of Rosehaugh. He had seen what Greycoat had been achieving in its other developments and invited it to join him in this new investment. The site was certainly a fringe one, like Cutlers Gardens. Next door to a bomb site used as a car park and without a frontage to the only street in the area which could be considered at all respectable, Eldon Street, the northern boundary, on Sun Street, was in that area of light industrial buildings which throng the streets of Hackney, and was not even in the City of London. Despite the innate suspicion with which the Hackney Council viewed speculative office development in their borough, outline planning permission was obtained on 6 October 1981 for 501,360 square feet of offices, to be built in three phases, and detailed planning permission for Phase 1 with its 295,000 square feet of offices came in late 1982.

The architect chosen for Finsbury Avenue was Arup Associates, who had at that time designed very few speculative office developments. Arups, like Sir Denys Lasdun and other prominent partnerships, had relied for a living in the 1960s and 1970s on the patronage of the public sector. The partnership had seen set up in 1963 by Ove Arup, the renowned consulting engineer, who died in 1988, and Philip Dowson, the architect, and had specialized in university buildings. The partner to whom Stuart Lipton turned to realize all the aspects of the demands for new-style offices built in new ways was Peter Foggo, with whom he was to work closely for much of the next seven years. By this time Lipton had developed what one observer has called his kitchen cabinet, a team of ad hoc advisors on whom he relies and with whom informal discussions on all aspects of design, building and legal matters are often held. Among this group are Frank Duffy, the architect head of DEGW, Gary Hart of lawyers Herbert Smith, and executives from the Economist Intelligence Unit and Schal.

The principles on which the developers worked were very much those which had been researched by Lipton and others in previous years. Eight floor-plates were looked at, including a tower, before the team settled on twin buildings linked by an enclosed atrium, a feature that was to prove ubiquitous in 1980s office design. 'It became the definitive building' says Lipton, with metal-tiled ceilings, movable air-conditioning and proper services. The exterior was a lattice of steel, less 'inside out' than the Arup Associates designed building at 80 Cannon Street or Richard Rogers's Lloyd's building. Architectural journalist Jonathan Glancey comments: 'A stern building, 1 Finsbury Avenue nevertheless displays a certain flamboyance with its dramatic courtyard roof and its sequence of steel struts and braces that further echo the architects' passion for the great engineer-designed structures of the high-Victorian era.' The design was also dictated by the technical needs, and ceiling heights reflected the new demands for cable ducts under the floors and air conditioning.

The building was contracted to Laings and budgeted to cost £70 per square foot over 21 months. In the event the first tenant was in the building only 15 months after construction began, and the cost was £60 per square foot. Again, because the building was 'off-pitch', rental values were expected to be low, and the project was deemed economic at £14.50 a square foot, against rents which were now approaching £25 in the best areas. The letting of the building, primarily to stockbrokers Rowe & Pitman, (part of Warburg Securities), at £19.75 was a great bonus. Incongruously, Rowe & Pitman, the blue-blooded firm said to be stockbrokers to the Queen, tried to recreate the atmosphere of the panelled partners' room on the top floor of the building where the lunch and meeting rooms were situated. Rosehaugh Greycoat presented the building to tenants as 'shell and core' with no internal fittings, and paid an allowance of £5 per square foot to the lessees for those costs rather than wasting its money and that of its clients by building fittings which the tenant would then rip out. Such an idea became as commonplace in Britain in the late 1980s as it had been in the US for many years. Stuart Lipton is still clearly pleased with his award-winning development: 'An innovative building, it's still one of the best buildings I ever built.'

By the time both Victoria and Finsbury Avenue were completed and let Stuart Lipton was no longer involved either in their future, or in the death throes of the attempt to develop Coin Street. In March 1983, he resigned as joint managing director of Greycoat, although he stayed on the board for a brief period as a non-executive director. 'I wanted to stop the world and wanted to get off' is the simple explanation for this dramatic move. Lipton and Wilson had worked together since 1969 and had been seen very much as a team, although Lipton was gaining more media attention. Lipton would not say there was a disagreement between the two men: 'I just wanted a change of scene and I was getting more and more involved in the detail and I wanted to have the opportunity of thinking what to do.' Wilson too maintains that this was a perfectly friendly parting: 'We have different working styles but we work together very well. I have a great admiration for Stuart, he is a most professional developer.' Lipton had no specific plans: 'when I left I had no idea; I just took a tiny office in Stanhope Gate.' He was not idle for long. His new company, named Stanhope after its location, was soon involved in two important new projects.

The first was an investment brought to him by agent Elliott Bernerd and banker Jacob, now Lord, Rothschild. The project was to take control of Trust Securities, a company with a large scale project at Stockley Park north of Heathrow Airport. Trust Securities had come to the stock market in October 1980. Its chief executive was Peter Jones, who had been a leading light in 1970s developer Compass Securities which had been taken over by Guardian Royal Exchange. Earlier that year Jones had been fined £500 and given a 12 month prison sentence suspended for two years after being convicted of plotting to defraud the Inland Revenue. This fact was not disclosed in the original prospectus, although the issuers claimed that every potential investor had been told orally.

In February 1981 Trust Securities' shares were suspended on the Stock Exchange pending details of a substantial acquisition. This proved to be the purchase of the Nearcity Group which controlled W. W. Drinkwater; that company in turn was the parent of a group of businesses in the waste and ballast business. The reason why it was attractive to Trust Securities was its vast holdings of land, some 900 acres in all, including 247 acres north of the M4 currently used as a rubbish tip. Trust was able to buy Nearcity for only £75,000 together with its matching assets and liabilities. By May Trust had sold off the major operating subsidiaries of Drinkwater for £2.4 million, leaving it with the 247 acres near the M4, known as Stockley Park, 63 acres at Denham and 22 acres at Hayes for an all-in net cost of £975,000. In October 1981 Peter Jones took over as chairman of Trust Securities and in December it was announced that the Universities Superannuation Scheme (USS) had agreed in principle to provide £50 million for the first phase of a development of 500,000 square feet of industrial and office space at Stockley Park.

By 1983, when Bernerd and Rothschild came to Stuart Lipton, Trust Securities was finding the going difficult. The problems of building a high-tech industrial park on a rubbish dump were formidable, and Trust's other development projects had not made enough to finance the scheme. The consortium formed by Bernerd, Rothschild and Lipton was able to persuade the major holders of Trust Securities to grant them options on Trust shares, or sell them shares in exchange for shares in a new company, to be named Stockley, valued at 15p, well below that then prevailing on the market of 45p; the whole company was worth only £4.7 million. This recognized the fact that Trust could not sustain its plans on its own; Peter Jones kept some shares in the new company but did not remain as an executive of the reformed company. The role of managing director was taken by Michael Broke, who had been working for Jacob Rothschild, but the major shareholders were the new non-executive directors, Bernerd and Lipton and the various Rothschild interests.

The Stockley development was originally conceived as a 'high-tech' estate; this was a light industrial or research facility with ancillary offices, with two storeys of offices at the front and a single storey at the back. The new owners decided instead to create an American-style office park, although they maintained flexibility by making the ground floors higher than other floors and a floor-loading limit of 600 lbs per square foot, 'so that anybody who wants to use high-tech space can do so.' The blue-prints were the many business parks established in the US, particularly by Stanford University in California which had managed to attract precisely the type of tenants that Stockley was targeting. The change in Use Classes Orders, the technical definition of what businesses may be carried on with what planning consents, did not come about until 1987, but the new description of the space which Stockley was building is B1, office space interchangeable with industrial space, an idea which proliferated as the 1980s progressed.

73

Stuart Lipton looks upon Stockley as his 'most interesting' development. Because the site was a recently used rubbish dump, known as 'stinky Stockley', there was an enormous amount to do before construction started. Trust had originally planned to build directly on top of the old dump but engineers Ove Arup suggested a more satisfactory long-term solution, albeit at higher initial cost. The dump was at the south end of the site, while the eastern side was virgin Green Belt scrub land. Arup discovered a gravel deposit under the clay and planned the wholesale removal of the rubbish to a temporary position to the west, filling the resulting hole with the gravel from the east, covering it with clay, and removing the rubbish again to the now-empty gravel pit before covering that in turn; after contouring, a golf course will be built on top of the rubbish.

Despite all the scepticism, which included doubt that office-type rents would be achieved in this quasi-industrial location, (although only a stone's throw from the M4, M25 and Heathrow), the first phase of the project was well on the way to completion by the time the Prince of Wales officially opened the development in June 1986. The Prince, already known for his interest in architecture, was relatively complimentary about the project in his speech, calling it 'an international showpiece in an international location'. The roads and three buildings totalling 350,000 square feet of the USS-funded portion had been completed in a year, and lettings to companies such as Fujitsu had been agreed at around £13.50 a square foot, a premium level for an out-of-town office park. Lipton had another interest in Stockley as well as a direct shareholding: his company, Stanhope, had been appointed project manager of Stockley Park in early 1984, its fee rising to 2.4 per cent of the cost of the development.

The other development which rapidly filled the gap in Stuart Lipton's diary was the massive Broadgate project. British Rail had existing plans for developing the site of Broad Street Station and the surplus land around Liverpool Street Station in conjunction with Taylor Woodrow and Wimpey, but by 1983 had decided that progress had not been rapid enough. They put together a tender list of potential developers and suggested to Lipton and Godfrey Bradman, with both of whom BR had worked previously, that they should make a joint approach. The combination was seen as having clear synergy between a brilliant financier, Bradman, and a development manager of some panache in Lipton. There were 11 consortia in the original list of tenderers, reduced to a shorter list of eight. 'In the end it was between us and Norwich Union' says Lipton: 'Norwich were going to pay £75 million in cash for the front portion of the site; our deal was for £90 million in phases and a profit share.'

The Broadgate project led to the formation on 11 November 1983 of Rosehaugh Stanhope Developments (RSD) owned 50/50 by the two companies. In the first 14 months only £550,000 of equity capital was invested by the two shareholders and until 1991 the total equity subscribed was only £1,012,000, against a total development cost of almost £2 billion. The initial phase of the development of Broadgate followed quite closely the pattern of Finsbury Avenue, with the exception that, in the case of Broadgate, the canvas was four times the size. The intention was again to 'create a place', but the size of the project enabled a rather more grandiose plan to be developed by RSD and its professional advisors. Arup Associates, in the person of Peter Foggo, were again appointed as architects but their designs were more American in inspiration than the Victorian engineer's building of 1 Finsbury Avenue. The steel-framed buildings were faced with a skin of coloured polished granite and the first four Phases made an arena in the centre of which was an ice-rink, used in the summer as a concert stage, after the example of the Rockefeller Center in New York.

Duffy's firm DEGW was employed over the next year to determine the needs of the likely tenants. Alexei Marmot of DEGW reported that 'financial service companies are increasingly dissatisfied with the buildings available to them in the City. They are very clear about what their premises should be like: prestigious, well-built, with large floor areas designed for maximum flexibility to accomodate frequent organizational and technological changes, especially in telecommunications.' Some clients would also like to occupy buildings finished only to 'shell and core'. The buildings were designed for speed: design was completed before work started, unlike the fashion for 'design and build' in which details are designed while the building is constructed. Most assembly is carried out off-site and parts simply bolted together. If all this seems familiar, it is very much the method noted by Mr Bossom who was an architect in the heyday of skyscraper building in America in the first 30 years of this century.

The 'fast-track' techniques were used to great effect: Prime Minister Margaret Thatcher and I were both guests, though not of quite the same importance, at a lunch in August 1985 to mark the ground-breaking of the first and second Phases, where she made a symbolic pass with a bulldozer, and promised to return in a year to mark the development's completion. This timetable was considered unsustainable by those used to British working methods, but it was beaten. On 11 July 1986, having had to cancel a trip to Canada to fulfil her promise, Mrs Thatcher returned to the Broadgate site, thanking 'Mr. Bradman and Mr Stanhope (sic)' for their efforts: 'We have everything here I admire – good design and superlative teamwork.' Foundation work took eight weeks, steel erection 14 weeks and 20 weeks were used for cladding the structure, a total of 42 weeks.

Stockley plc meanwhile had not been idle. In June 1984 it bought a row of unmodernized properties, 29–36 Sackville Street, W1, from the charitable Sir Richard Sutton Settled Estates for £12 million, paid in shares. This group of properties became a parcel bought and sold regularly in the late 1980s until the music stopped. Stockley gained planning permission for each house to be converted separately into offices and then, in 1986, sold them to Tony Clegg's Mountleigh Group; this company in turn sold to Peter Taylor's now bankrupt Sheraton Securities for £13 million. In late 1990 it was announced that 36 Sackville Street had been bought by Genepierre IV, a French investor, from Mercury Asset Management. No. 36 thus had six owners between 1984 and 1990. Stuart Lipton regrets the Stockley sale, saying that he was 'chicken' to sell the development before doing the building work.

In March 1985 Unilever brought in a consortium consisting of Stockley, British Land and the Barclays Bank Pension fund to redevelop its property between Blackfriars and Fleet Street, to be known as Dorset Rise. A more important change was the purchase by Stockley of the European Ferries property portfolio in April 1985; this company was the Townsend Thoresen ferry operator, its fleet's ships often carrying explicitly in the names on their sterns the 'Free Enterprise' philosophy of the controlling Wickenden family, which had diversified into property. The company now took Stockley shares as its payment for its portfolio, becoming owners of 44 per cent of the enlarged Stockley, albeit being restricted to voting on only 29.9 per cent. The new shareholder also undertook not to sell these shares or make a bid for two years, giving Stockley a further two years beyond that in which they would have pre-emption rights over their holding. By this time the Stockley share price had risen to 70p and the market value of the company to £140 million. Later on in the month Stockley bought a 26.5 per cent stake in Stock Conversion Investment Trust, a veteran of the 1960s and 1970s development, which had given up trying to redevelop the Tolmers Square site that Greycoat had eventually turned into 250 Euston Road. There were long discussions between the two companies as to the possibility of some merger or deal, but they failed to come to a satisfactory conclusion. Stockley's holding in Stock Conversion was sold to P&O in April 1986 when that company made a full bid; the sale raised £100 million for Stockley.

In June P&O and Stockley announced that they were jointly to redevelop Beaufort House on the eastern edge of the City, backing, like Cutlers Gardens, on to Petticoat Lane. This monolithic 550,000 square feet building was another example of Lipton trying to 'create a space' since the architects made a piazza in front of the entrance and built a huge arch over the front doors, larger than Marble Arch. By now Stockley had become the sixth largest property company by market value.

By April 1985 Lipton's company, Stanhope, still privately owned, brought in three large institutional investors, the merchant banks Kleinwort Benson and Robert Fleming, and the investment trust Globe, as shareholders. These investors paid only £1 per share for their holdings, which amounted to 32 per cent of the company. This act of generosity on Stuart Lipton's part was not unqualified. The new shareholders had to provide loans totalling £10 million at a sub-market rate of interest and on which actual cash payments were postponed until Stanhope was moderately profitable. Perhaps for this reason Fleming's investment was on its own behalf, rather than for its investment clients, unlike Kleinwort's. The £10 million was a useful addition to Stanhope's resources at a time when its net assets were still only £100,000, despite the fact that Broadgate was now under way.

In November 1985 Stockley, with its partners British Land and the Barclays and Unilever Pension Funds, (the Paternoster Consortium), won the closed tender to buy the bulk of the Paternoster Square development by St Paul's Cathedral. The vendors were the Church Commissioners, Laing Properties, Wimpey and Trafalgar House, who had been partners in the original development in the early 1960s. Stockley and its partners paid £80.25 million for the six offices and the shopping precinct. Part of the purchase price was immediately recouped by selling, for £14 million, to Charterhouse, the merchant bank, the office block it occupied itself. Stuart Lipton's private company was, as with Stockley Park, appointed as project manager. The debate over the plans for redevelopment of Paternoster Square is described elsewhere. The whole episode left Stuart Lipton rather bewildered. He went to great lengths to meet what he had understood the public to want with schemes such as these: an initial overall plan, not detailed design of buildings. 'It was a real taste of, if you give the public what they ask for, they don't understand it.' Stockley was a little coy about its initial plans, with Michael Broke even claiming that a complete redevelopment was only 'a possibility.'

Rosehaugh Stanhope's ambitious plans were not confined to Broadgate. With the architect Richard Rogers Lipton began to negotiate with the London Docklands Development Corporation for permission to redevelop the old Royal Docks, the eastern extremity of the area, to provide 1.5 million square feet of retail space. The joint company also made proposals for the Spitalfields fruit market site across Bishopsgate from Broadgate. These were designed by the classical revivalist Leon Krier and have been described by Jonathan Glancey as 'perhaps the most remarkable plan suggested by a commercial developer in the 1980s'. Krier's drawings suggested a recreation of the traditional narrow City street plan with crescents and squares. The buildings were an eclectic group of palazzos, basilicas and a campanile, introducing an Italianate touch to the granite-clad City. The plan lost out to one put forward by London & Edinburgh and, in early 1991, the produce market finally moved. The winning consortium has yet to start work on its development, although it now has planning permission for a scheme including a new building designed by Sir Norman Foster.

Discussions were held between Lipton and the board of Stockley as to whether Stanhope and Stockley should merge. With both sides knowing each other perhaps too well, it became a difficult negotiation, but in May 1987 Tony Clegg of Mountleigh told the Stockley board that he would like to buy the company. The bid put an implicit value of £150 million on the Paternoster Consortium's holding by St Paul's and an explicit price of

£365 million on Stockley as a whole. The board of Stockley accepted the bid, but this was not the end of Lipton's involvement. For the present at least Stanhope maintained its management contracts on Stockley Park and Paternoster as well as a supervisory role in the Beaufort House development.

Stuart Lipton soon returned to a role in a public company. 1987 was witnessing the most frenetic stock market boom for 20 years and property companies were the particular darlings of investors as rents rose rapidly around the country. On 8 October 1987 the subscription lists were opened and closed for investors wishing to buy shares in Stanhope on the Unlisted Securities Market. At the minimum issue price of 180p, each share the institutions had subscribed to only 30 months earlier had multiplied in value by 1,224. In fact the tender price struck was 250p so that Kleinwort's and Globe's investments of £17,000 each were now worth more than £28 million and Fleming's £13,000 had become over £22 million. This profit was more than adequate reward for the investors putting up £10 million of low-interest debt between them. Flemings, having pocketed the profit from this period of investment for themselves, now transferred all the holdings into the names of their investment clients. Stanhope had gone from being a high-risk speculation to an institutional investment in two and a half years. The issue also made Stuart Lipton even richer: his initial cash investment in Stanhope of £100,000, held by his wife and himself, was now worth over £130 million.

The issue prospectus of Stanhope gives a good flavour of the absorption of Stuart Lipton in the architectural and artistic elements of property as well as the purely financial facets. 'Stanhope's objective is to produce developments which combine aesthetic appeal and architectural merit with efficiency in construction and use, and which command premium rents in locations with outstanding growth prospects.' The latter has not yet been established in Broadgate, but few would dispute the superior qualities of a typical Stanhope development compared with its predecessors of previous decades. 'The Directors believe that the Group's insistence on good architecture contributes to its commercial success by satisfying the growing awareness of tenants that a distinctive building is an important aspect of their corporate identity. The requirements of major commercial tenants are no longer confined to location, size and cost, but also encompass configurations and flexibility of space to meet the changing needs of their businesses, together with suitable amenities and ambience.'

The prospectus also gave a detailed account of the Rosehaugh Stanhope finances. The tangible assets of Rosehaugh Stanhope Developments, (RSD), had risen in the year from 30 June 1986 to 30 June 1987 from £83 million to £388 million. The first two Phases, already completed and let, had cost £174 million but were now valued at £258 million, and Phases 3 and 4, costing £129 million to that date, were nearing completion; these figures did not deduct the payments due to British Rail of £120 million.

British Rail, as landlord of Phases 3 and 4, had imposed a rent of 'one red rose if demanded without review', a new twist on the traditional peppercorn rent. Debenham Tewson & Chinnock, the property valuers, opined that Phases 1–4 and 6–7 would have a capital value of £1 billion gross when complete. The first four Phases of Broadgate, like Finsbury Avenue, had been designed by a team at Arup Associates under Peter Foggo. They turned down the commission to design the other Phases, not wishing to distort a balanced partnership to meet the extraordinary demands the further Phases would make on their staff; RSD appointed the US architects Skidmore, Owings & Merrill instead. The facade of Broadgate seen from Bishopgate is by this partnership.

Other ventures were being undertaken by the Rosehaugh Stanhope joint company. In Docklands they had agreed to sell a quarter of a site at Blackwell's Yard to Reuters where a building designed by Richard Rogers and costing in all £35 million was to be built by the end of 1988; the electronic news group took options on the rest of the land. Adjacent to this site, in a joint venture with Berkley House, RSD had bought the 17-acre site of the old Brunswick Wharf power station. Another twinkle in the RSD eye was a plan to develop above the line of the railway which ran from Holborn Viaduct station to Blackfriars. British Rail planned to connect the north London termini to the Southern Region by driving a tunnel from Kings Cross to Blackfriars, rendering Holborn Viaduct station unnecessary and removing the railway bridge at the bottom of Ludgate Hill. Stanhope by itself had bought a leasehold interest in 1 London Wall, a 1973 building beside Route 11, which they planned to link to the Museum of London across the dual carriageway. The company had also been negotiating with the South Bank Board to improve the environment of the arts complex between the Shell Centre and the LWT building, which had turned into a free skateboarding park and haunt of the homeless. Terry Farrell, the Post-Modernist architect, was working with Stanhope to develop plans.

The Bradman-Lipton team had one other scheme on which they were working which could eclipse even Broadgate in terms of 'creating a space'. The hinterland of the main north London termini for the north and east of Britain, Kings Cross and St Pancras, was a derelict mess of railway lines, roads, the Regent's Canal, gas-holders and goods yards. British Rail and the recently privatized National Freight were the major landowners in the area and the government was anxious for all these wasted acres to be put to a better and more remunerative use. By the beginning of 1988 RSD had been confirmed as one of the two developers in the running for the comprehensive redevelopment of the whole area, the other being Speyhawk. In June 1988 British Rail announced that the London Regeneration Consortium, of which Stanhope owns one third together with Rosehaugh and National Freight, was the winner of the competition to build on the 100-acre site. The outline design for the project had been provided by Norman Foster's partnership, and this was revised on

October 1988 after local criticism. As well as bridging the road between the two termini, the plan creates an oval park using the canal as a focal point, with the housing and offices round it. The original intention was for Kings Cross to be the freight terminal for the Channel Tunnel route. The development will probably have to wait until the next property boom since speculative development on this scale in a recession is very difficult to finance.

Having tied in his company so intimately with Godfrey Bradman's Rosehaugh, Lipton now sought to create new ventures separate from that successful partnership. One important new project was developed with the Japanese construction company, Kajima, in March 1988. Kajima had already acquired 101 Piccadilly for the Japanese Embassy but now sought a British partner. Lipton had visited Kajima in Tokyo and his reputation was sufficient to convince the Japanese company that this was the right coventurer. The first project was the purchase and redevelopment of Hanway House in Red Lion Square, Holborn, which was sold on in 1989 to Cable & Wireless as the headquarters of their Mercury telephone network. (Stanhope's Chairman, Lord Sharp, had been, until 1989, Chairman of Cable & Wireless). Other projects undertaken with Kajima include 1 London Wall and the office blocks which face Euston Road in front of Euston Station.

The critical change in 1988 for the long-term health of Stanhope was the sale of one-third of the company in May to the Reichmanns' Olympia & York company (O&Y). This coup was a result of an earlier introduction from Stanley Honeyman, an old friend of Lipton's. Honeyman had been a director of English Property Corporation which the Reichmanns had bought in a bid battle in 1979 (described in Chapter Ten). He suggested that Lipton call on the Reichmanns who had just taken over the Canary Wharf project from the US bankers who originated it. 'I thought I was going for half an hour' recalls Stuart Lipton 'but stayed two and a half hours. I was interested in what they were doing because they were continuing the theme of building expertise. You can talk to Paul Reichmann about the cores, the toilet details, the floor plan.' In 1988 Michael Dennis of Olympia & York approached Lipton, expressing admiration for what Stanhope was doing and asking to do 'some kind of venture' with Lipton. Buying one-third of Stanhope cost £137 million, at a share price, 250p, which, though the same as the initial tender price, was well above that prevailing in the market at the time. The attraction from Stanhope's point of view was that this was a large equity injection at a time when the property boom was already faltering in the wake of the 1987 stock market crash and at the end of the trend to lower interest rates. Paul Reichmann was quoted at the time as saying that the investment was 'a way of helping Stanhope expand and was a major gesture of confidence in Stuart Lipton and his team and, through them, in their joint ventures with Godfrey Bradman and his colleagues at Rosehaugh.' It did seem slightly odd that the developers of Broadgate should now both have O&Y as large shareholders since the Canadians were developing Canary Wharf which is competing with them for many of the same tenants. Lipton did not find this a constraint: 'Canary Wharf is a different product and London is a series of villages.'

A rapid use of at least part of Stanhope's new-found financial muscle was the repurchase in July of Stockley Park from Mountleigh by a consortium led by the Stanhope-Kajima joint company, for £200 million. Other members of the consortium of which Stanhope-Kajima holds 58 per cent are Chelsfield, the private company of Elliott Bernerd, which originally bought 16 per cent but has sold half to Shimizu, another Japanese construction company; the Prudential owns the other 25 per cent. This surprising reversal on the part of Mountleigh enabled Lipton to take back total control of the development of which his company had been project manager throughout. In September Stanhope announced two more important developments which would distance itself further from the perception that the company was merely a play on the RSD portfolio. ITN commissioned Stanhope to manage the development of its new headquarters designed by Foster Associates at 200 Grays Inn Road; Lipton had known ITN since buying its old Wells Street headquarters for it while he was still an agent. Stanhope bought the new site and leased the building back to ITN, with the intention of letting some of the surplus office space to provide an income for ITN with which to pay the rent. The development took only 21 months from start to broadcasting. Unfortunately for ITN much of the surplus space was still vacant at the end of 1991.

Another new joint venture partner was Trafalgar House, the entrepreneurial vehicle of Nigel Broakes and Victor Matthews in the 1968–1972 property boom, which had bought Cunard and Express Newspapers and moved away from direct property investment. This project is on London Regional Transport's Chiswick depot site near the M4 and the North Circular Road. Planning permission was finally granted in early 1991 for an office park development on the 32-acre site. Stanhope also built an office in Staines which has been let as British American Tobacco's worldwide headquarters, showing a yield of 10 per cent on cost.

Because Stanhope has operated mostly as a developer and in joint ventures, its profitability has not yet been high. Since the cost of money has almost always been well above the rental return immediately available on development, the goal of the company has been an increase in net asset value. The net assets at the time of the issue in 1987 were £135 million or 123p per share, well under half the price that investors were willing to pay for the shares. Over the three succeeding years, net assets rose to £458 million or 275.6p per share at the end of June 1990. Profits have been derisory, arising mainly from interest payments on loans made to related companies and on the capital subscribed by O&Y. Only in 1988/89 did real profits accrue from Broadgate, resulting from the sale of Phase 5 to Bankers Trust. If Stanhope manages to hold onto its portfolio, as rents rise over time the profitability of the company will be transformed. This assumes that the company does not then seek more ambitious projects – a rash assumption.

Lipton and Bradman agreed that the Holborn and Kings Cross projects are the last on which they would work together. At the start the partnership was one of complementary skills: Bradman the financier and Lipton the developer. As both Rosehaugh and Stanhope grew each began to assimilate the skills of the other so, as Lipton puts it 'the rationale was less'. Although both men have a reputation for being blunt there is no suggestion that the partnership ended in a blazing row, even if there is little warmth between them now. Observers suggest that, as they grew to have some expertise in each other's original areas of strength there came a point at which each felt the other was treading on his toes. Lipton simply feels that, in joint ventures, two is probably the right number; being in a company together is a different sort of partnership. Bradman and Lipton had been involved together in Finsbury Avenue, the 12 Phases of Broadgate, (each like a separate project), the Reuters development, Kings Cross and Holborn. In joint ventures separated by many years, such as those Lipton has done with Jeffrey, now Lord, Sterling and Bruce McPhail of P&O, 'you don't get involved into personality' as Lipton puts it.

Stanhope was one of the few clear winners of the property boom of the 1980s. Although it announced a £77.4 million pre-tax loss in the year to June 1991, Lipton was able to say 'we remain confident that, when the current difficulties are over, Stanhope will emerge stronger, more competitive and better equipped to take advantage of the opportunities which lie ahead.' During the year Rosehaugh Stanhope became roughly cash-flow neutral, after the sale of Broadgate Exchange and the conversion of £100 million of its shareholders' loans into equity. Nevertheless, the company had to write down the value of its projects in Broadgate, Ludgate, Stockley Park, Docklands and elsewhere by £43.4 million. The net asset value of the shares fell back to 192 pence from 276 pence, and the shares fell to a distress level 37p. Making predictions in a book is notoriously dangerous, but my betting would be on Stanhope being, like British Land and Town & City in the previous property crash, a survivor. It has interests in some of the best developments and its finances are not in a truly distressed state. The company's shares remain difficult to value since there is only asset value to fall back on and many of the projects in which it is involved are in related companies. Its weakness is an inability to control directly most of its assets in these companies. While Stanhope and its partners were strong and operating in a growing economy all was well, but in periods of recession and high interest rates, doubts arise about short-term viability which may not be justified. As the company's ambitions moved from development to survival, Stanhope's managing director since 1988, Nigel Wilson, left to become a managing director of GPA, the Irish aircraft leasing group. He will join a board which has on it, as non-executives both Nigel Lawson and Sir John Harvey-Jones, both commanders of thousands of column inches during the 1980s.

Stuart Lipton is a man who arouses strong opinions in most of those to whom I have spoken. One property man describes him as 'not a very sophisticated investor, a man who is very tough in business and hasn't made too many friends. He is very self-centred and doesn't give a damn.' Yet Lipton, who describes himself disingenuously as 'a bit player' of the 1980s property market, says that what keeps him in the business long after he feels any need to make more money is his relationship with his partners. 'I have tended to work for long periods with groups such as McAlpines and Bovis,' and there have certainly been long associations with Richard Rogers, Norman Foster, Arup, (particularly Peter Foggo), and Frank Duffy of DEGW. 'What drives me is the people and people relationships. People have been very kind to me.' This comment makes Lipton sound like an implausible Blanche DuBois, but the apparent contradiction is difficult to reconcile. While it is true that he has terminated relationships with two long-standing partners, Wilson and Bradman, he has also kept around him a loyal team of highly talented people. It may be that he is so tied up in his own affairs that he does not sense the unintentional slights which others feel. One competitor thinks he has become too big for his boots and dislikes the way he treats his staff, 'shouting at them in front of other people.'

It is certainly true that he has a reputation for being able to lose his temper. During one negotiation with John Ritblat of British Land, Lipton was due at British Land's office, at which he was confidently expected to tear a strip off the assembled company. John Ritblat, who knew his man, was prepared. On arrival, Lipton was greeted by a receptionist sporting a large button reading 'WE LOVE YOU LIPTON'; on being shown into the meeting room, he found that John Ritblat and his whole team were also wearing the buttons. Stuart Lipton may have a temper, but he has a sense of humour; he was totally disarmed and dissolved into laughter.

While Lipton and Elliott Bernerd were engaged, as directors of Stockley, in the discussions with Stock Conversion, a meeting was held one evening between the two sides at Morgan Grenfell. The negotiations were as close to success as they ever were, and at one point the Stockley team of Lipton and Bernerd left the Stock Conversion representatives to have discussions by themselves. The two partners in Stockley found themselves in the Morgan Grenfell partners' room, where the traditional high desks still stood. Before long Bernerd and Lipton were crouched under the desks, (not easy for a large man like Lipton), trying to throw paper darts into each other's waste paper baskets; which is how the Stock Conversion team found them when they emerged from their meeting.

Lipton has taken on many 'civic' duties, which he calls his 'pro bono stuff' and which he is anxious should not be forgotten. He was assistant building superintendent of the Hampton Site, (the National Gallery extension), is on the DTI's Property Advisory Group, the governing bodies of the Royal Academy, Whitechapel Art Gallery, Imperial College, National Theatre, Glyndebourne and the National Fine Arts Commission. He likes to think of himself as a patron of the arts, filling his developments with sculptures and commissioning 150 paintings of the building of Broadgate by Robert Mason, one of which, 'Phase II (Rainy Day)', hangs in his office, alongside an architectural drawing by Norman Foster and an engraving of the Great Exhibition of 1851. But Lipton does not have to worry about what others think of him now. His reputation will depend on how his developments last. If in 20 years Broadgate is still seen as a desirable place to work rather than an ageing rent-block then he should be satisfied. The problem is that it is the name of the architect, rather than his own, which may be associated with developments for which he, as much as anyone in the decade, was responsible.

- DEVTS PRE SOLD /LET
- TRADITIONAL FUNDING

5

FROM RAG-TRADE TO RICHES

TWO OF THE new stars in the property firmament in the 1980s had their roots in the nineteenth century textile industry. Peel Holdings was the company on which the fortunes of the family of Prime Minister Robert Peel had been built; its story is told in Chapter Nine. The other textile company which transformed itself in the 1980s, at one stage becoming the fourth largest company in the quoted property sector, was Mountleigh, a company whose career was inextricably linked with its driving force, Tony Clegg.

Mountleigh was the direct descendant of a business named The North Warwickshire Worsted and Woollen, Spinning and Weaving Company, incorporated in Coventry in 1863, giving the company the statutory registration number 587; only 21 of the first 600 companies registered in England retained their listing by 1988. The second Lord Leigh (1824–1905) was the company's first chairman, which had been founded to relieve unemployment among Coventry's ribbon weavers. Six years after its foundation the name of the business was changed to Leigh Mills in the chairman's honour. Initially the cloth was spun in the north by other companies and woven in the Leigh Mills works in the Midlands, but in 1896 a new works was leased in Stanningley, Pudsey in Yorkshire. The business suffered the usual booms and busts associated with the textile industry: its centenary in 1963 was marked by one of the low points of activity and the original Coventry mill was closed. It was a merger in 1966 with Mountain Mills, a rival worsted manufacturer, which brought in Tony Clegg; the joint company was renamed Mountleigh, with Clegg's partner Ernest Hall as its chairman.

Tony Clegg is a short, stout man with a winning persona. Although he now lives in Yorkshire he was born in Littleborough on the other side of the Pennines in Lancashire. After National Service in the Army he worked as a merchant converter in Manchester, linking up with Ernest Hall when the latter bought Mountain Mills from the Francis Sumner Group in 1961. Clegg was then working for the Broughton Bridge Mill

Company, another part of the group, and Hall asked him to be production and administration director for Mountain Mills. Clegg moved to Stanningley in 1966 with the acquisition of Leigh Mills.

The worsted business continued to be an erratic performer; at its low point after a fire in 1971 losses mounted to £132,000 and the share price fell to 3p. Hall and Clegg set about diversifying the company into property. This happened, like most happy developments, through an act of pure serendipity: 'property chose me, I didn't choose property' says Clegg. Over the years Leigh Mills had assembled a substantial estate; in 1966 the company owned 137 acres of land of which only 250,000 square feet were occupied by mills and buildings. Other property had been sold by the previous management years before. One day Tony Clegg took a telephone call from agents Conrad Ritblat. They had found a buyer, an engineer, for the old mill adjacent to the Stanningley headquarters of Mountleigh. Although Mountleigh no longer owned the property, when they had sold it the previous managers of Leigh Mills had placed a restrictive covenant on the mill that it could only be used for textile manufacture. 'This was pretty surprising' laughs Clegg, 'I would have imagined that they might have put a restrictive covenant on that it couldn't be used for textiles; I can't think what their thinking was.' The agent asked for the covenant to be removed. 'I thought about it a bit and then phoned back and said I didn't think I really wanted to do that, but how much would they sell it for. I bought it for £24,000.' The old mills were demolished, at no net cost since the stone was sold, and a 12,000-square foot building constructed and let as a warehouse at £1 per square foot. This left seven acres on the site vacant for future development.

Before this Clegg had dealt in property only as textile man: 'I'd bought and sold a few mills but I'd probably done that pretty badly; I didn't know what I was doing'. From 1976 he decided to devote one day a week to property matters; on Tuesdays he would go round properties with a surveyor, Simon Duckworth. In the year which ended on 30 April 1979, Mountleigh's total turnover, including the worsted business, was £5.24m and the company declared a pre-tax profit of £347,000; of this £254,000 was contributed by the property development division. A year later the property division was able to help turn a loss of £86,000 on textiles into an overall profit before tax of £740,000. Only eight years later, Mountleigh had transformed itself into a company with a turnover of £529.5 million and pre-tax profits of £70.7 million. Mountleigh was a possible bidder for Sir Terence Conran's High Street Storehouse chain of Habitat, Mothercare and British Home Stores, and the company was mentioned in the same breath as the giant and venerable Land Securities. Yet within a year of the announcement of the record profits, Tony Clegg had sold control of his company to two Americans and the company had been dramatically reduced in size. How could have this happened so rapidly to a company and a man with no background in the property industry?

Tony Clegg's style in managing Mountleigh was not like that of the merchant developers such as Stanhope, Rosehaugh or London & Edinburgh. Mountleigh's growth was almost all built on the facility for buying something which outside critics often thought overpriced and then selling it on, often before the original purchase had been completed. Clegg was unapologetic about this style of management. In an interview in May 1987 he complained 'People ask me how I can buy for £50 million and sell almost immediately for £60 million, but nobody asks Tesco how it can buy a case of baked beans at 10p a tin and sell them at 12p.' It would be impossible to count Mountleigh as a developer because the biggest deals and greatest profits the company generated came almost exclusively from trading rather than adding physical value to a site. Although many of the company's early deals were developments, particularly in its local Yorkshire market and Aberdeen, and Clegg constantly protested that he was interested in carrying forward developments such as Stockley Park or Paternoster Square, the headlines the company made were almost all about rapid dealing on of portfolios or companies which it had acquired.

Even in its early days of developing property in 1979/80, the trading mentality was apparent from the wide fluctuations in the turnover of the group coming from that activity. Among the first important deals was the development and letting of a 105,000 square feet warehouse at Benyon Park, Leeds to Hepworths, soon to become itself the temporary darling of the stock market under its transformed name and style of Next; this development had been financed by Hampshire County Council Pension Fund. The company also let an industrial development at Dyce Airport, Aberdeen. During the 1980/81 financial year further lettings had been agreed, of warehouse space on the Euroway Estate, Bradford as well as an office development in Golden Square, Aberdeen to the Royal Bank of Scotland; this latter was then sold to the Ready Mixed Concrete Pension Fund. These deals gave a property valuation surplus of £2 million, and the total value of property held had risen to over £6 million. In May 1981, the loss-making worsted interests were sold for around £400,000 and property became the only activity of the company; property assets had risen by the May 1982 year-end to a value of nearly £8.25 million.

It was a dramatic and slightly off-beat investment in November 1982 which transformed the finances and perception of the company in one deal. (It is symptomatic perhaps of the flurry of activity carried out by the Mountleigh Group in the 1980s that the company's own mini-history wrongly gives the date of this deal as 1981.) Mountleigh agreed to purchase from Possfund, the Post Office pension fund, (then incorporating British Telecom), for £5.25 million, three housing estates of a total of 800 houses, at Saxmundham, Lakenheath and Eriswell in Suffolk, let to the US Air Force. The purchase was financed by a rights issue of one million new shares, increasing the size of the company's equity share capital by a quarter, which raised a net £825,000, and a floating rate loan of

£4.5 million, on which interest of 2 per cent over the wholesale short-term money market rate was to be charged. Since at that time the interest rate would have been around 13 per cent and the net income to Mountleigh was estimated at £734,000 per annum, there was a profit after interest for Mountleigh of around £150,000 a year. The investment was immediately revalued by surveyors at £8.25 million.

There had been a potential risk in the USAF houses deal since it was possible that the USAF might not renew the leases on the estates which expired in 1982 and 1983. 'Over a period of time one would have made an awful lot of money out of those 800 houses had the Americans vacated them, but I couldn't stand the fact that there would be no income over the period, and my covenant was not good enough for somebody to lend me money without them being income producing.' The estate had been on the market for some time and buyers had balked at that possibility. Clegg had an ingenious solution: he bought, for £35,000, an option to insure against the possibility that the USAF would not renew its lease. The income he thus guaranteed enabled him to raise the necessary bank finance. The valuers had estimated these were worth 'considerably in excess' of their £8 ¼ million valuation should they be available for individual sale. Far from walking away from their estates however, the USAF renewed their existing lease for a further ten years and, in January 1985, commissioned Mountleigh to build and lease to them three further estates of 650 houses. The renewal of the existing leases increased the gross rents payable to Mountleigh to over £2 million from £1.2 million, and the company also received a maintenance charge; in exchange, Mountleigh was to spend about £1.5 million upgrading the estates. The contract for the new estates involved rental payments to the company of about £4 million, payable in Swiss francs, and the development was financed by a Swiss franc loan of £30 million with an interest rate of only 4.5 per cent per annum. In true 1980s fashion, this whole second phase of the USAF relationship was kept off the balance sheet of Mountleigh, since the lending was entirely secured on the houses and the banks had no recourse to the other assets of Mountleigh should things go wrong.

The relationship between Mountleigh and the USAF soured a little in later years when the USAF sued the company for non-performance of the 'build for lease' agreement of the second contract. 'We had such horrendous problems getting planning permission. I had an extremely good relationship with the Americans but they were very cross that we were finding it so difficult. So were we, since the rent was fixed and, as time went by, the contract was getting less and less interesting to us. On every occasion I had gone to Ramstein [USAF headquarters in Germany]. On the one occasion I didn't go one of my staff said we really wanted to pull out of the contract.' The USAF never pursued the writ, wanting only to have the houses built; eventually the two sides agreed not to try to build houses on the disputed site at Alconbury, but that more houses would be built on the Bentwaters estate.

The company's profits for the year to April 1983 had jumped to £811,000 from £554,000, helped by the absence of further losses on the worsted trade. Investment property assets had risen sharply to almost £23 million from the previous year's £8.2 million, helped by including the USAF estates at the valuer's figure of £8.25 million rather than its purchase price of £5.25 million; total debt had climbed to £12 million. In July Ernest Hall, Tony Clegg's partner for more than 15 years, resigned as chairman, taking a £75,000 ex-gratia payment, leaving Clegg in sole charge as chairman and managing director of the company. 'We'd worked tremendously closely and well for a long number of years' says Clegg about his ex-partner. 'It was unfortunate, but, by agreement, I looked after the property side and he looked after the textile business. The property side was pretty well all deal-driven and not at any time an income stream, and although the textile side was struggling like mad, I thought we ought to get rid of it. Ernest thought that this was the reason he was there.'

The second major deal establishing Mountleigh as a serious property investment company was the purchase, in January 1984, of Occidental Oil's European head office in Aberdeen from Jock Mackenzie's London & Northern Group. For a consideration of £6.4 million, the company bought a 122,000 square foot modern office block built on a ten-acre site by the Aberdeen outer ring road, let to the oil company for 25 years from November 1981 with five year, upward only, reviews.

There was an obvious advantage to Mountleigh in the purchase in that the surveyors valued the Aberdeen property immediately on purchase at £7.83 million, against its purchase cost of £6.4 million, which probably surprised the vendors. Since all that extra £1.43 million of value increased the shareholders' assets, Mountleigh was able to report a higher net asset value per share, which rose from 281.9p to 289.5p, even after taking into account the new shares issued as part of the purchase. Because the shares were trading at around 215p, the value of the company to potential investors was further enhanced. By the end of its financial year in April 1984, Mountleigh's investment property assets had risen to £39 million from the previous year's level of £23 million, with the Aberdeen office accounting for the bulk of new purchases; £7.7 million of the increase represented the transfer of property already owned from the 'dealing stock' of the company to the investment category. Smaller deals had included the redevelopment of a building in Glasgow, subsequently sold for £2.47 million to the BTR pension fund, the purchase of 44 houses in Maida Vale, London for £1.5 million and their subsequent refurbishment into 132 flats, a quarter of which were sold for £1 million within a year, and the inception of housebuilding in Scotland.

In the 1984–85 financial year several important acquisitions were made, and the figure of Paul Bloomfield becomes part of the Mountleigh story. Bloomfield was never mentioned in the publications which document Mountleigh's increasingly ambitious deals, but from 1985 he was a crucial element in the company's growth. Born in 1946, Bloomfield had been involved with a subsidiary of E. J. Austin, a company which had been one of the great scams of the bull market of the late 1960s, early 1970s. Bloomfield's business, which had nothing to do with the scandal-ridden part of that group, was a building sub-contractor named Metropolitan Hardcore. Austin's downfall came over the claim that it had found a modern equivalent of the philosopher's stone: the ability to turn dross, or at least very low quality ore, into economically viable gold. At one stage a group of London investment analysts was flown over to the US to see the prototype plant in the desert. Low grade ore was fed into this shed at one end and gold emerged at the other. Despite the inherent unlikeliness of such a claim, many were hoodwinked. The company collapsed and was heavily criticized in a Department of Trade report.

Although Bloomfield was not involved in this particular disaster, he was to hit trouble himself with his own business. A motorway contract went wrong and that subsidiary dragged all Metropolitan down with it. His next venture was property investment, which had just commenced when the 1974–75 crash hit home; he was able to buy properties such as the Phillimore Court apartment block in Kensington when others were desperate for liquidity. In 1975 he was taken to court by a disgruntled solicitor over an unpaid account, and the Inland Revenue became interested in this apparently substantial property dealer who seemed to be paying little tax. The Revenue assessed Bloomfield for several years of unpaid taxes, and while he was abroad a bankruptcy order against him was served for the relatively small sum of £34,000. The Inland Revenue spent more than ten years investigating Bloomfield's tax affairs, rifling through his books, about which he admitted to having been irresponsible. An undischarged bankrupt finds it difficult to be involved in business. He cannot be a company director or even run a bank account; he can however give advice for fees, which is the life that Bloomfield lived for the next ten years. It was in such a role that Clegg and Bloomfield came across each other over the purchase and onward sale of a garage in Halkin Street on the Grosvenor Estate in Mayfair. Mountleigh managed to obtain vacant possession on the site and sold it to a buyer who turned it into what is now the Halkin Hotel.

Before further important deals could be concluded, the finances of Mountleigh needed to be put on a firmer long-term footing. In January 1985 the company issued £7 million of a 9¾ per cent convertible loan stock, raising £6.8 million to reduce bank borrowings, which had risen to £7.6 million out of a total borrowing level of over £30 million. Conversion of the loan into equity shares would eventually lead to the issue of a further 2.17 million shares to add to the 7 million already in issue and then trading at 290p per share. Because the major existing shareholders in Mountleigh, notably Clegg and his Jersey-based family trusts, were unable to subscribe to this issue, Mountleigh's brokers Phillips and Drew introduced new institutional investors, notably the Target life assurance and unit trust group and Phillips and Drew's own investment management

Canary Wharf (*photograph by Edward Bridger*).

LEFT Godfrey Bradman of Rosehaugh. BELOW Rosehaugh Stanhope's Broadgate development (*photograph by Peter Davenport*).

ᵖ LEFT Stuart Lipton of Greycoat and Stanhope. TOP RIGHT Tony Clegg of Mountleigh. BELOW Stockley
·k.

ABOVE 17–22 Sloane Street. These shops were owned by six landlords in five years. BELOW These Sackvill
Street properties also had six owners between 1984 and 1990 (*photographs by Edward Bridger*).

TOP LEFT Elliot Bernerd of Chelsfield. TOP RIGHT Geoffrey Wilson of Greycoat. BELOW Cutlers Gardens, Devonshire Square, the Greycoat/Standard Life development showing Quinlan Terry's entrance gate.

ABOVE Terry Farrell's Embankment Place development for Greycoat (*photograph by Alan Williams*). BELOW Route 11 – London Wall. The slab blocks to the left and right are now being replaced, for instance, by Terry Farrell's Alban Gate astride the road (*photograph by Edward Bridger*).

ᴏᴠᴇ The Richardson twin's Merry Hill Centre in Dudley (*photograph by Edward Bridger*). ʙᴇʟᴏᴡ Sir John
ll's Metro Centre in Gateshead (*photograph by Edward Bridger*).

The Paternoster Consortium's proposed development of St Paul's.

subsidiary. A medium term loan of £10 million was also arranged.

The Annual Report issued in August 1985 showed the 1984/85 financial year to have been one of relatively little action for Mountleigh. Shareholders' funds had only grown by £3 million to £25 million, scarcely the pace expected of a dynamic company, even if the share price had now risen to 465p, well above the asset value of 359p. Fortunately Tony Clegg was able to report two substantial new transactions. The first was the acquisition in May 1985 of 42–70 Kensington High Street in west London for £6.5 million from the Imperial Tobacco pension fund. This was a row of shops, one of which had previously been a Woolworth store, plus 32,000 square feet of office space and 45 flats. Mountleigh's declared intention was to refurbish and let the retail and office space, which was expected to bring the property's value up to £14 million. In the event numbers 42–60 were sold for £8.2 million in early 1986 and Mountleigh let the major part of the rest of the development to Tower Records at £210,000 per annum. The second deal announced was the purchase in June of industrial land at Dagenham, east of London, variously reported by the company itself as 164 and 178 acres, for £3.15 million, on which there was a rental income of £250,000 per annum. In typical Mountleigh style, Clegg was able to reveal that 60 acres of this land had already been sold for more than the purchase cost of the total site and leaving the rental income almost intact. Both these property deals had been introduced by Paul Bloomfield. Bloomfield had identified the fact that Mountleigh was active and rapid in its decisions. His style and Clegg's fitted well: 'He has a very big vision of what you can do with property but he's not a detail man at all', says Clegg. 'That's why we worked well together. I was always a detail man and he can always see a very big picture.' One observer likened their relationship during this period to that of a father (Clegg) and his son.

The summer of 1985 marked the start of the most active period of dealing for Mountleigh, which pushed Tony Clegg and his company into the limelight as one of the most active property traders in the country. Clegg was by now known to be interested in deals so that all sorts of ideas were brought to his attention. His hyper-activity became legendary; he worked 16 hours a day but still insisted that he should be at home in Yorkshire with his family for Sunday lunch. He recalls that one year he reached the month of June having had at least one night a month in which he had failed to go to bed entirely.

Clegg was notorious for having meetings at night, and through the night; expensive lawyers and accountants would be lined up outside his office in the small hours waiting for his previous meetings to end. Business contacts tell of breakfast meetings with Clegg during which he would conduct three or four other meetings over his portable phone. Most of the proposals brought to him ended in the waste bin, but many deals were done. In September 1985 the company announced the purchase of 17–22 Sloane Street from Eagle Star Insurance for £6.75 million, partly financed by the issue of another one million shares, placed at 440p each. This property, a concrete monstrosity on the west side of Sloane Street, was held on a long lease from the Cadogan Estate, expiring in 2091. It occupies the roadside under the Chelsea Holiday Inn, as well as high fashion shops let to such names as Joseph Tricot and Kenzo. Even more gratifying was the fact that Peachey Property, an old-established investment company with large holdings around Carnaby Street, the famous 'Swinging London' fashion centre of the 1960s, was a tenant of the office portion of the investment. Peachey had been built up by Eric Miller, who had benefited from the famous lavender note-paper resignation honours list of Harold Wilson in 1976. In 1977, Sir Eric was the subject of scandal about personal expenditure made by him using the company's money. In April that year the board of Peachey announced 'that they have asked Sir Eric Miller to resign as director, but that he has refused to do so,' a very rare occurrence. Sir Eric was eventually voted off the board and on 22 September he shot himself, leaving Peachey in a sorry state. By 1985 it had been substantially rebuilt, but for a parvenu company to be their landlord gave a special pleasure to Mountleigh. The history of 17–22 Sloane Street in the 1980s is typical of the trading mentality of the 1980s property boom. In the space of five years the property was owned by six different companies: Eagle Star, Mountleigh, Randsworth, Next Properties, City Sites and Power Corporation. In all that time the property did not change physically; only the rents rose, and with it the value these various companies were prepared to pay for it.

In November Tony Clegg linked up with Brian Wolfson, then Chairman of Anglo-Nordic Holdings plc, to buy effective control of Wembley Stadium. A consortium which as well as Wolfson and Clegg included Throgmorton Investment Trust, London and Continental Advertising, C. H. Bailey and Meridien Holdings bought London Leisure and Art Complex (LLAC) from the Gomba Group for £10 million. Gomba, run by Abdul Shamji, was one of the companies which brought the Johnson Matthey Group to its knees, and the group's assets were all up for sale. LLAC owned 66 per cent of Arena Holdings and that company owned 51 per cent of Wembley Stadium itself, with the other 49 per cent of the Stadium company owned by the conglomerate, BET. A further 34 per cent of Arena was owned by another consortium, of Stockley plc, Harry Goodman of Intersun and Jarvis Astaire, the promoter of Viewsport. Stockley, as we shall see, became the eventual Achilles heel for Mountleigh, but at this stage they were no more than a potential partner for Clegg, whose 10 per cent investment in Wembley Stadium would cost £4 million.

The final, and largest, deal done by Mountleigh in the hectic closing months of 1985 was the acquisition of the privately held property company R. Hitchins for £28.4 million, again brought to Clegg by Paul Bloomfield. The selling Hitchins family were paid in 10% loan notes maturing in December 1988, guaranteed by the Royal Bank of Scotland, but Mountleigh decided that its balance sheet would become too highly geared after such a purchase and the year's second call on existing shareholders, in the form of a rights issue of 2.9 million shares at 475p, was made, bringing the number of shares in issue to 11 million from the 7 million extant as recently as April. Hitchins owned only one building which was fully developed and let, a Fine Fare supermarket in Luton, which accounted for about £5 million of the total purchase price. The rest of the portfolio consisted either of properties under construction but not let, four sites with planning permission around Luton and 60 acres of land on the Cote d'Azure in southern France with permission to build half a million square feet of a mixed residential and commercial development. Despite this rather speculative portfolio (which one property analyst admitted to me he didn't really understand), and the fact that the income received was only £480,000 per annum at the time of purchase, the valuers, Jones Lang Wootton and Hepper Watson certified the properties to be worth £49.25 million, well above the purchase price of the company, even taking into account the £4 million outstanding purchase commitment for land which Hitchins had undertaken.

By the end of 1985, Mountleigh had established itself as a rising star of the property world, but still capitalized at only £65 million, it could not be considered in the same league as the first division companies such as Land Securities or MEPC. Its great strength was in trading properties, but the company had now made a rod for its own back in leading the investment community to expect a rising trend of profits made from this source. There was little in the way of long-term investment apart from the USAF estates; trading profit in the 1985/86 year reached almost £10 million against the £5 million of net rental income. Investment property assets had risen in that year from £45 million to £79 million, but only £13 million of that increase came from investment properties acquired in the year; the rest came from transfers from the trading stock and a revaluation. Investment income is repeated, but every sale of a trading asset has to be replaced by profits on new assets. The Hitchins deal took into the trading account properties which were in the books of Mountleigh at £27.5 million but had been valued at the time of the deal at £39.5 million, so that Mountleigh could earn a pre-tax profit of over £12 million if it was able to sell those properties at the valuation estimates. Mountleigh was unable both to generate these trading profits and keep for itself investment properties of any significance as a result of the income shortfall between the cost of money and the rents earned. To achieve the sort of profit growth to which its shareholders were becoming accustomed, the company could simply not finance both investment and trading.

As a result in 1986 and 1987 Tony Clegg was forced to find larger and more spectacular trading coups to keep the show on the road. The first of these deals was the £58 million purchase from Samuel Properties of a portfolio of 180 properties, mostly in the south-east. Mountleigh paid for this purchase with a further issue of 1.05 million shares, this time issued at

805p a share, and a loan from the HongKong Bank of £50 million, secured on the properties purchased and with recourse to Mountleigh itself for only £10 million, so that if the company raised less than £40 million for the portfolio, that risk was borne by the bank, not Mountleigh. A fall in values of about 30 per cent may have seemed a distinctly unlikely turn of events in 1986, but four years later it may have been something a lending bank was faced with. Mountleigh stated that 'a substantial proportion of these properties will be disposed of within the foreseeable future providing significant profit contributions'; about £8.7 million of the portfolio was intended to be retained as an investment. By September it was reported that the company had indeed contracted to sell two-thirds of the portfolio for £60 million.

In addition to the properties bought there was included an option on the two sites by the south end of Vauxhall Bridge; these plots were on either side of the road. The northerly one became known as the Green Giant site after the physical attributes of an office block proposed and rejected for the area, and the southern plot is known as the Effra site. These empty sites had been the subject of several schemes over the years. David Goldstone of the Regalian Group eventually bought the northern plot and has developed an office block designed by Terry Farrell in the style of a D. W. Griffiths film set. The property was sold for £130 million by Goldstone to the government's Property Services Agency in early 1989 as a home for MI6, just as the property market showed signs of imminent distress.

In August 1986, Mountleigh published its annual report and accounts for the year which had ended in the previous April. These showed pre-tax profits up to £9.25 million from the £2.5 million earned during 1984/85; of the total for 1985/86 £3.5 million came from the sales of the Hitchins portfolio in the four and a half months since its acquisition, part of the £12.5 million profit implicitly stacked up in the trading account at the time of the take-over. Net assets per ordinary share in Mountleigh had risen from 344.15p to 548.83p. Tony Clegg had also seen a substantial increase in the beneficial interest held by him in the company during the year, increasing his holding from 477,308 to 1,492,683 shares; only part of this increase was attributable to the year's rights issue, which would have cost him over £1.25 million to take up. Since he did not have the personal resources to fund these purchases, Tony Clegg was putting someone else's money, the bank's, where his mouth was. The balance of the increase was the reversion to his own hands of the shares hitherto held by the HongKong and Shanghai Bank Trustee (Jersey) which was the nominee for Clegg family trusts.

The new deal which definitively took Mountleigh and Tony Clegg into the first division was the successful bid for the quoted United Real Property Trust. On 7 August 1986 it was announced that Mountleigh had agreed terms with United Real whereby their board would recommend Mountleigh's offer to buy for £117 million, quite a step for a company capitalized at £110 million. United Real was a company built up in the post-war boom by Maurice Wohl, which first went public in 1961, although only 26 per cent of the shares ever reached the hands of the general public. Wohl's intention had simply been to remove his company from the tax regime which, at that time, condemned it to paying 91.25 per cent tax on its income. United Real had built up a portfolio of 13 typical 1960s curtain-wall office blocks in London, one property in Birmingham and one in Sydney, Australia. At the time of the bid only one was being actively developed, in Victoria Street, SW1. Maurice Wohl had built United Real in a period during which investors were still very sceptical about property, and preferred to back those developers who had negotiated long leases with reputable tenants, even if the leases had no reviews for many years. At that time it was possible to raise long-term debt whose interest rate was below the income yield on the property investment. Many of the properties in the United Real portfolio were rented at well below the current market rents, but no review was in the offing. A shrewd investor could see that paying the tenants a capital sum to surrender their existing leases and either agreeing new leases at a market rent with regular reviews, or redeveloping, would turn these properties into marketable securities, well above the value attributable to them in United Real's books. State House in Holborn was typical, having been let to the government for 25 years at a rent of £1 per square foot without a review. When Clegg asked the United Real Chief Executive why this was, he was told it was only because the government wouldn't take a 35 year lease.

United Real had not been actively managed for many years because its effective owner, Maurice Wohl, had no reason to maximize his short-term income. Wohl had in fact become a tax exile and an absentee landlord, leaving England for Geneva in the mid-1970s at the time a Labour government had increased the marginal tax rate on investment income to 98 per cent. None of the directors other than the Chief Executive was a full-time employee at the time of the Mountleigh bid and there were only four administrative employees. United Real had not commissioned a valuation of its properties for over three years, (and no valuation was commissioned during the bid), but many analysts and companies had cast envious eyes over the portfolio for several years and some had made the journey to Geneva to try to persuade Mr Wohl to sell his company to them; all had failed hitherto. Maurice Wohl's advisors were J. Rothschild, in the person of Jacob, now Lord, Rothschild, Stanley Berwin of solicitors S. J. Berwin, and Morgan Grenfell Laurie, the surveyors headed by Elliott Bernerd. They had met Tony Clegg during Mountleigh's growth phase of the past two years and they gave him a fair wind with Maurice Wohl. As Clegg himself was quoted as saying, during the period between the announcement of talks and agreement of terms, 'The determining factor will not be price; the decision will be whether he wants to sell. He has had approaches before and has never got round to selling his stake.'

What would determine the outcome would be the emergence of a buyer dedicated to meeting Maurice Wohl's particular needs. One person who was close to this and many other transactions maintains that it was in this particular skill that Clegg excelled. 'He was very good at listening to people he wanted to do business with and finding out what it was they really wanted to do the deal', unlike many property entrepreneurs. 'A lot of people assume that what they [the sellers] want is the highest possible price', but there is often a personal factor to finding the key to unlocking a deal. Clegg puts his success in clinching the deal down to the fact that 'I was the first person who didn't argue with him. The whole market would have given pretty long odds that I wouldn't do the deal with him, and it was a very, very difficult negotiation. I had to go to Geneva to meet Maurice Wohl and set aside two hours, including getting to and from the airport. After that meeting it came back to me that he had wondered how this guy could think he was going to buy his company in an hour, so I pretty hastily reconvened a meeting to last the whole day.'

The form of the bid was cleverly packaged. Maurice Wohl wanted cash for his stake, and he wanted foreign currency, fearful that sterling would fall again, particularly if the bid was delayed at all and a General Election intervened with a Labour government taking over. On the other hand, the market was already beginning to suffer from indigestion with the weight of new Mountleigh shares that had been issued over the past two years and the bid could not be financed entirely from new borrowings. Clegg's solution was to issue 83 million £1 convertible preference shares, which count as equity in a company's balance sheet rather than debt, but might introduce a new group of investors attracted by the 5.25 per cent net dividend payable on the preference shares, equivalent to pre-tax dividend yield of more than 7 per cent at the basic rate income tax rate of the day; the balance of the purchase was financed through a £35 million one-year loan from The Royal Bank of Scotland, parent of Mountleigh's merchant bank, Charterhouse Bank, who themselves loaned another £5 million on the same terms.

The greatest coup over the acquisition of United Real may have been that in early 1987 the property portfolio, on the advice of the company's lawyers Berwin Leighton, was transferred to a Dutch subsidiary, renamed Mountleigh International, and could be realized free of capital gains tax. This was managed despite a similar case when the Daily Mail and General Trust, which controlled Associated Newspapers and other quoted shares, tried to do the same thing only to find themselves prevented from proceeding by the Inland Revenue. Clegg recalls that 'we identified from the very beginning that the big downside on the whole transaction would be the capital gains position. The whole deal was structured on the basis that it would be offshore at the point we bought it.'

Before the end of this important year for the company, Mountleigh refinanced some of its short-term debt through the arrangement of a syndicated loan from 27 banks of £110 million organized by Union Bank of Switzerland, the parent of brokers Phillips and Drew. There were also further large purchases: the Hoover building on Western Avenue was bought by Mountleigh's subsidiary Fanebrook for £10 million. This famous art deco facade fronted 440,000 square feet of factory on a 8.6 acre site, and was again brought to Clegg by Paul Bloomfield; there were to prove to be great planning difficulties with this building. Two other notable purchases were firstly the acquisition from the Electricity industry pension fund for a total of £22.5 million, partly financed by the issue of almost six million shares at 255p, (equivalent to 1530p in the old form), of the old *Times* offices, New Printing House Square in Grays Inn Road; secondly from a Docklands developer, the nearly completed and part pre-let Hertsmere House on the Isle of Dogs for £12 million.

There were two other transactions in the first few months of 1987 which were to be precursors of important future developments in the history of this extraordinary company. Another off-balance sheet company named Eagerpath had bought a wide range of assets, including Adnan Khashoggi's marina development in Antibes. Eagerpath was not apparently majority owned by Mountleigh and, therefore, the total assets and liabilities of the company were not included as if they were Mountleigh's. Only the net equity invested in it by Mountleigh was presented as an asset. In fact the other shareholders of Eagerpath were all close associates of Mountleigh. 'We took advantage of the model code as it stood then; you could not have done Eagerpath today' confesses Clegg. The company sold, for £9 million, a portfolio of properties in Eagerpath to Phoenix Property and Finance, headed by Irishman John Duggan, and entered into a joint venture with Phoenix to develop 24 acres of residential land at Hounslow Heath, West London. This land had no planning consent when the two men bought it for £7 million. Within two weeks of purchase the partners were given the planning permission they sought and within two months the estate was sold to Crest Homes for £14 million. John Duggan's first deal with Tony Clegg was to prove important to both men. Duggan had established his credentials to Clegg as a man with an eye to a good deal.

The portfolio sold to Duggan was part of a group of investments bought by Mountleigh the previous December from Stockley plc, the developers of Stockley Park, just north of Heathrow Airport, a company central to the story of both Stuart Lipton and Elliott Bernerd. This portfolio, bought for £25.25 million and sold for about £30 million, was turned round in rapid order, even for Mountleigh.

The snapshot of Mountleigh afforded by the year-end of 30 April 1987 shows how much was ventured and how much achieved in the previous 12 months. Reported pre-tax profits rose from £9.23 million to £33.57 million; £139 million of properties had been sold, £142 million bought, in addition to the purchase of United Real for a further £121 million. Of the profit, £3.76 million arose from United Real and a further £3.8 million from related companies which only paid cash dividends of £20,000 to the parent company. The great bulk of profit again came from trading, where £125 million of sales gave rise to a surplus of £32.86 million (up from £9.66 million the previous year), whereas the net rental income from investments only rose to £9.47 million from £5.1 million. The major achievement noted in the annual report was the sale of £120 million of the United Real portfolio, realizing an after-tax surplus of £26.77 million over the 'fair value' attributed to them at the time of the take over. The big buyer from this portfolio was the Norwich Union; they paid £20 million for a development in Victoria Street SW1, bought the minority interest in their own development over Moorgate station and the long lease of Clements House in Gresham Street in the City. This latter 130,000 square foot office building was one of the classic examples of a dated building with old-fashioned leases which would benefit from active management, and was valued at about £40 million. One of the most attractive features of these sales was that, thanks to the change in domicile of Mountleigh International, they had attracted tax of only £828,000. Norwich Union had engaged in a substantial spending spree on City of London office blocks in 1986/87, buying 120–125 High Holborn for £55 million and the architectural pattern-setting Fountain House in Fenchurch Street for £27.5 million as well as funding the development of properties in Liverpool Street, Holborn Viaduct and, as we shall see, Beaufort House on the eastern edge of the City.* The other substantial sale from the United Real portfolio achieved before the year-end was of 10/14 Stratton Street W1 to Elliott Bernerd's Chelsfield group. One further sale in the new financial year confirmed the success of the United Real purchase, when State House in Holborn was sold to interests of Robert Maxwell for £40 million, bringing the total realized to date to £160 million against the £120 million paid for the whole company.

The annual report also showed several other interesting snippets of information. Not only was Eagerpath a 'related company' but Clegg had indulged in some tax avoidance by buying two merchant ships, later added to, with borrowings of £6.8 million 25 per cent guaranteed by the parent company. The investment in Wembley was now accounted for in the same way. Tony Clegg's personal investment in Mountleigh and his rewards from the company had also risen during the year. Clegg's shareholding in the company had increased again, mostly through the exercise of stock options and conversion of his holding of convertible loan stock, but he had also purchased two million of the convertible preference issued on the take-over of United Real. Although his salary from Mountleigh had now risen to £169,000 per annum, there was no possibility that this could have been financed other than through further personal borrowing. With the shares standing at 288p (equivalent to

* In April 1992 it was reported that Norwich Union was intending to sell much of this portfolio at the depressed prices then prevailing: its late 1980s purchases had turned out very badly.

1728p in the pre-capitalization form) on 30 April 1987, Tony Clegg was worth over £30 million before netting off the loans he had taken out, and his company's ordinary shares were capitalized at more than £265 million.

Even before these 1986/87 results had been announced, the hyperactive Clegg had announced the deal which was not only to create the fourth largest UK property group but also expose a running sore which was to prove ultimately fatal to his plans. On 6 May 1987, the boards of Mountleigh and Stockley announced that agreement had been reached over an offer by the former for the latter. The early story of Stockley is told elsewhere in this book, but at this stage the greatest risk period had passed; the development at Stockley Park had begun to attract substantial tenants at rents which fully justified the initial concept, although most of the benefit was then accruing to the Universities Superannuation Scheme (USS), the pension fund for university staff, which had been the financier of the development. The board of Stockley was partly composed of the men who had undertaken the reverse take-over of the then Trust Securities, notably Stuart Lipton and Elliott Bernerd, as well as repre-sentatives of J. Rothschild, and two directors of European Ferries, whose portfolio Stockley had bought for shares in the year ending in November 1985. Although non-executive, these gentlemen all had other direct interests in the well-being of Stockley. Stuart Lipton's own company, Stanhope, had a management contract with Stockley to supervise the Stockley Park development. Elliott Bernerd's firm, which had now been taken over by Morgan Grenfell to form Morgan Grenfell Laurie, was retained as agent for parts of the Stockley portfolio and European Ferries had an effective shareholding of about one third of the fully diluted share capital of the company as a result of the earlier swop of properties for shares. Another Stockley non-executive director was Roger Seelig, a corporate finance director of Morgan Grenfell who was later to become embroiled in the Guinness affair. One of the factors which clinched victory for Clegg in this bid was the fact that he agreed to buy European Ferries' investment in Stockley, which was hedged about with restrictions as to voting and transfer, largely for cash at a lower overall price than available in the general offer. Although the Stockley board could in theory have blocked this purchase, they clearly thought the overall price was satisfactory for all shareholders, and agreed to the transfer.

The bid for Stockley would cost Mountleigh £365 million bringing in assets of £261 million, against the then market capitalization of the company's outstanding ordinary shares of £250 million and its gross assets of £367 million. Most of the acquisition was to be paid for by yet another enormous issue of 105 million new shares, to shareholders of Stockley who had no investment in Tony Clegg's record. These shareholders, particularly the USS, would prove to be constant suppliers of stock to the market over the next few years, making Mountleigh's ability to create new trading profits by taking over portfolios and companies for shares more and more difficult. Not only was this market problem created by the bid but there was no doubt that the transaction proved to be the wrong one at the wrong price at the wrong time for Mountleigh. Ron Peet, the chairman of Stockley made a pertinent point in his letter to his own shareholders recommending the offer: 'Your Board considers that the Offers made by Mountleigh reflect not only the current value of the company's assets but also substantially reflect the further value that could be expected to accrue from the current development programme.' With such property experts as Lipton and Bernerd on the board this statement could not be laughed off. After all the addition of Stockley's assets to the group, at the value carried in Stockley's own books, net of the £118 million of borrowing Mountleigh would need to finance the cash element of the bid, would add only £62 million to equity assets, diluting the net asset value for ordinary shareholders quoted at 30 April 1987 from 157p per share to about 100p.

The whole strategy of buying property for shares depended on the purchase of assets which could be put into the Mountleigh books at their purchase price, but had been bought with shares standing at a substantial premium to the overall asset value per share; this of itself would always increase the asset value per share for Mountleigh's shareholders. To achieve this result, the assets of Stockley were written up in Mountleigh's books by £211 million to 'fair value', which added 110p per share to the apparent asset value of Mountleigh. You may recall that a similar device was used in the case of United Real, and Clegg had demonstrated that his perception of 'fair value' in that case was superior to most analysts. As one observer put it, at the time Clegg was like the largest market maker on the Stock Exchange, being offered a vast array of deals and prices being put on properties, so that his market intelligence was probably superior to any other property market operator of the time. There was no reason to suppose that his judgement was going to be proved wrong in this case.

One other indicator as to Mountleigh's intention towards the Stockley portfolio was its reclassification of its property assets in Mountleigh's accounts from investments to trading stock, which meant that any surplus over 'fair value' would be reflected in Mountleigh's profit rather than its balance sheet.

The logic for Mountleigh buying Stockley has never been entirely clear. The Stockley Park development was well analysed and only a very rapid rise in rents on the estate would justify taking a more optimistic view of the assets. The other major assets of Stockley were a 50 per cent interest in the Beaufort House development, the other 50 per cent being owned by P&O; 50 per cent of the Paternoster Square site to the north of St Paul's Cathedral, where plans to replace the wind-swept 1960s development were in hand, and two investments, both fully let, off Fleet Street and by Victoria Station. It is true that Stockley had £30 million of near cash in its hands at the time of the take-over, having sold to P&O for £100 million its investment in Stock Conversion, another star of the 1960s property boom. Clegg is honest about at least part of the motivation: 'The deals had to get bigger hadn't they? It's impossible to change one's spots. We realized a profit out of the transaction.'

Trading in other property continued even in the wake of the Stockley deal. In June 1987 Mountleigh sold a portfolio of six properties to the quoted Control Securities, headed by Nazmu Virani, for £8.7 million, payable part in cash and part in shares making up eight per cent of Control's equity, which Mountleigh undertook to hold as an investment; the company also sold the 1960s office block Enford House in Marylebone Road to Sheraton Securities for £10.5 million in cash. In August it was announced that Mountleigh had sold 11 properties for £83 million cash to Randsworth Trust, one of the rapidly proliferating Mountleigh clones; included in the package was the Sloane Street property which Mountleigh had acquired for cash and shares worth £6.75 million as long ago as September 1985, a full two years earlier. The *Times* building in Grays Inn Road, which had originally been intended to be a substantial addition to Mountleigh's still small long-term investment properties was said to be subject to a 'stunning' offer for the property, generating the odd statement that 'current strategy planning may result in a rethink of this (original) decision'.

Tony Clegg seems at last to have fallen prey to the delusions of many of the initially successful subjects of this book: the idea that he had a formula for success which would enable him to make money in areas which were new to him. In September 1987 it became known that Mountleigh had bought several million pounds worth of shares in Storehouse, the quoted holding company of Terence Conran's retail empire of Habitat, Mothercare and British Home Stores (now modish restyled as BhS). 'I had the view, although of course it wasn't made particularly obvious at the time, that we could sell off everything except BhS, and then work BhS, continuing to run it. It's amazing how times change. There's no doubt that, at that time, the sum of the parts was considerably greater than the whole. People say now with hindsight "aren't you glad you failed?" The answer is that it was a bit closer call than I actually thought it was at the time, but we were in serious discussions with other retailers to sell off all the bits.' Fortunately for Mountleigh Clegg eventually thought better of making a bid for this group which would find the going even rougher in the years ahead. This had not prevented Benlox, a small company in the stable connected with Peter Earl of the mini-merchant bank Tranwood Earl and backed by Ashraf Marwan, from making a bid. Benlox and Tranwood Earl were to re-emerge in the story of Paul Bloomfield at a later date. For Mountleigh, the urge to move into retailing was not dormant for long.

In September Mountleigh launched another of its rapid strikes, buying the Pension Fund Property Unit Trust (PFPUT) for £271 million. During the early 1980s as described in an earlier chapter, pension funds' enthusiasm for property had diminished as the returns on that asset had paled into insignificance against that achieved on equity shares, both in the UK and overseas, and even fixed interest securities had bettered the growth of property in the early 1980s. PFPUT had been an early example of a unit trust restricted to non-tax paying investors buying property with the agglomerated smaller sums invested by funds who did not feel that they were big or knowledgeable enough to buy property on their own account. One of the problems with these unitized vehicles was that, to be able to meet occasional redemptions from unit holders, a substantial holding of cash was necessary, even when the property market was very strong, and when the market was weak and redemptions accelerated, the only properties which the funds could sell were their highest quality ones.

The PFPUT acquisition was made through the 'related company', Eagerpath. Included in the PFPUT portfolio were 24,000 acres of agricultural land, which, it was widely expected, Clegg would immediately put up for sale. This was despite the fact that Tony Clegg was an enthusiastic breeder of pedigree longhorn cattle. In fact the reported seller turned enthusiastic buyer of agricultural land, and as early as November had bought a £15 million farm portfolio from Distillers pension fund; he had reportedly negotiated the sale for £35 million of the only farm that analysts had thought he would retain. This was astride the A12 in Essex with outstanding planning permission for various commercial developments. Mountleigh was the buyer of more than half the let agricultural land sold during 1987, stemming a fall in values which had been gathering pace since the early euphoria over entry into the EEC had driven land prices to unsustainable levels at the end of the 1970s. Mountleigh continued to be an important buyer and seller of farms in 1988.

One notable development of the period was the introduction of Mountleigh as majority partner with Trust House Forte in the redevelopment of the Criterion site on the south of Piccadilly Circus, one of the rare cases in which Mountleigh persevered as a developer. It is a feature of Mountleigh's history that the number of developments in which it was involved at one stage or another outnumbered those which it saw through by at least a 10 to 1 ratio.

The Stockley bid also marked a change in the rhetoric of Tony Clegg. Hitherto he had glorified in the description of property trader, but he now seemed to yearn for the respectability that development and investment might bring to his activities. In announcing the company's results to 30 April 1987, Clegg was quoted as saying that the market would now see Mountleigh taking on more development and investment work, using the Stockley team as the development arm. The Paternoster Square redevelopment was supposed to be one such example, and for a time it certainly seemed likely that Mountleigh would press forward with this highly sensitive development. Stockley and its partners in the scheme, British Land and the pension funds of Barclays Bank and Unilever, had appointed Arup Associates as master planners for the project.

The take-over of PFPUT also aroused suspicion that one of the attractions to Mountleigh was the fact that PFPUT's largest single investment was City Gate House, a solid but distinctly old-fashioned office block in Finsbury Square. Its attraction to Mountleigh lay in the suspicion that there might be a mutually advantageous swap available between Standard Life and the company of that property and Juxon House, the major element of the buildings to the north of St Paul's which the Paternoster Group did not own, which was owned by the Scottish company. Juxon House, which protruded into the line of sight up Ludgate Hill towards the Cathedral, had itself changed hands regularly over the past ten years. In March 1979 the Prudential had bought, from the Church Comissioners, this 100,000 square foot office block, let to Barclays Bank, for £16 million; the Pru had in turn sold the property on to Standard Life. Standard Life angrily denied it had any intention of selling Juxon House or exchanging it for City Gate House which was next to two other buildings it owned on the corner of Finsbury Pavement and Finsbury Square. The property investment manager of Standard Life Peter Henwood said 'We have no interest in City Gate House. We looked at it three years ago before PFPUT refurbished it, but decided we weren't interested. I think if you tried to redevelop it you'd find that it would be listed and you wouldn't be able to pull it down.' As to the sale of Juxon House, Henwood claimed that the building was 'the front door' to the Paternoster redevelopment, while the consortium owned 'the back yard'. This was a little harsh but, undeniably, any rebuilding would be piecemeal without Juxon House. 'It is not for sale. It never will be', concluded Henwood. Those who have been involved in investment know that 'never' is a word that should be used sparingly if ever.

The interest in retailing as a business rather than as landlord resurfaced on 9 October with the announcement that Mountleigh had agreed to purchase, through its Mountleigh International subsidiary, the total equity of Galerias Preciados, the Spanish department store chain, for £153.4 million. While not on the same scale as the Stockley purchase, this transaction was to have equally damaging long-term effects on the company, and it is clear that the deal has not been a real commercial success. Galerias Preciados is Spain's second largest department store group, operating 29 stores of 2.9 million square feet in total at the time of the bid. The Spanish group had been in the ownership of the Rumasa family when they had their assets expropriated by the Spanish government in 1983. The buyers of the chain in 1984 were the Venezuelan Cisneros Brothers, the controllers of Organizacion Diego Cisneros, who were brought to Clegg by the ubiquitous Paul Bloomfield. After the October stock market crash the terms for the purchase were refined so that Mountleigh paid £72.5 million in cash plus £80.9 million deferred, interest free, until 3 May 1989. The purchase by Mountleigh from the Cisneros interests was peculiar in the sense that Cisneros immediately applied part of the initial down-payment of the sale to buying Mountleigh shares.

The unusual part was that by the time the Cisneros subsidiary was paying 300p per share for their 16.7 million shares the stock market crash of 19 October had occurred, Mountleigh shares had suffered more than most, and were currently trading at 140p, well below its summer all-time high of 322p. A similar agreement for the seller to reinvest a substantial part of the proceeds in Mountleigh shares at this now ludicrous price was made with the vendors of the much smaller Dutch company, Coroco, whose primary assets were two office blocks in Rotterdam. Mountleigh International, whose Chief Executive was Michael Cook, bought Coroco from a company controlled by the same Michael Cook for an initial £7.5 million plus 20 per cent of any increase over eight per cent per annum in the net asset value of Coroco over five years. The relative performance of Mountleigh against the stock market as a whole had indeed peaked at the time of the announcement of the bid for Stockley. The discrepancy between the nominal prices paid for Galerias Preciados and Coroco and the effective prices reduced the overall cost to Mountleigh shareholders by about £25 million, but the market collapse had much more serious long-term consequences than this short-term benefit. For the first time in nearly four years, the Mountleigh share price had fallen below the published asset value. No longer was it going to be possible to issue new shares at a premium and so increase the underlying asset value per share. The Galerias and Coroco deals were the last that Mountleigh were able to finance on this basis, although this did not prevent the issue of more paper.

The Galerias purchase revived fears about Mountleigh's strategy. On the numbers, the company was buying a group of stores with a net asset value of £304.1 million, way above the effective £125 million that Mountleigh had paid. Unfortunately the stores were chronic loss-makers and had made a pre-tax loss of £45.5 million in the year to 31 August 1987. The Cisneros group had put in new management and spent £25 million on refurbishing the stores. For Mountleigh the biggest change would be that from employing only 77 people in April, the workforce would now expand to 9,500. Clegg's intention was to return the retailing business to profitability with the eventual goal of flotation of the revived company on the Spanish market, meanwhile avoiding the penalty to current profits by taking the investment in Galerias as an 'unlisted investment' in its balance sheet. The capital structure of Galerias was reorganized 'so as to allow Mountleigh International to have control . . . and to receive the dividends and surplus assets arising on liquidation, but so that (it) is not a subsidiary of Mountleigh for the purposes of the Companies Act 1985'. This initially enabled the company to reflect the value of the investment in Galerias in Mountleigh's balance sheet without taking the trading losses into its profit and loss account. At the same time a substantial new shareholder and creditor, Cisneros, had appeared on the scene and was going to play a crucial role in the future of Mountleigh.

Tony Clegg took an active interest in the management of Galerias. At one meeting in London, while discussing an important deal, he was being shown racks of 'frocks', which he would either select or discard. He was helping select the dress ranges that Galerias would carry.

The purchase of Galerias and the stock market crash did not stimulate any obvious changes to the management of Mountleigh. At Stockley Park more prestigious lettings were agreed and the sale of elements of the PFPUT portfolio continued.

Mountleigh also announced its intention to seek planning permission for a new town west of Wetherby in Yorkshire and the option to purchase for a nominal sum a majority holding in the Norwegian developer Bygge Eiendorms, which had failed to raise new finance after the stock market crash; a conditional deal was concluded in March with Mountleigh paying £1 for 49 per cent of the parent company and £22.63 million for its British assets. More important, now that the share price had fallen below the quoted net asset value, Mountleigh began the process by which it could start buying in its own shares. Such purchases would increase the net asset value of remaining shares in an exact mirror-image of the earlier process of increasing asset value per share by issuing shares for a price above the quoted asset value.

Mountleigh's interim profit figures for the six months to October 1987 showed pre-tax profits up to £35 million, including a £14.2 million gain on sales of parts of the PFPUT portfolio, but there was a £7.7 million post-tax provision against the fall in value of the company's holding in Storehouse.

At this point, over the Christmas and New Year holiday there was the first hint of mortality for Tony Clegg, but in a literal rather than a merely business sense. He was rushed into hospital suffering from a gangrenous appendix, and, despite the public view that it was merely a standard case of appendicitis, Clegg was very ill for a week or so. 'Appendicitis can happen to anybody, but when I do anything, I do it in spades.' This may have been a substantial stimulus to the surprising move of the next month, the bid by Mountleigh for Phoenix. For an estimated £58.6 million, Mountleigh bought the smaller company for a combination of shares and cash, but the stated net assets of Phoenix, even including the assets of the recently purchased Rohan Group, were only £36.5 million. The logic for the bid was explained in the offer document: 'Over the course of the last 18 months, Phoenix and Mountleigh have been involved in a number of projects together; this has led to the belief of both Boards that the development skills of the Phoenix Group team and development opportunities already being held or being offered to the Mountleigh Group should be combined'. John Duggan, the Chief Executive of Phoenix, and Bruce Bossom, the property director of Phoenix and an ex-partner of Jones Lang Wootton, were to join the main board of Mountleigh and Duggan was to become Chief Executive of Stockley, 'the principal UK development arm of the Mountleigh Group'.

John Duggan's involvement with Phoenix had come about through an invitation by Professor Sir Roland Smith, the ubiquitous company director, who was non-executive chairman of the company, which was no more than a cash shell. Duggan makes no bones about how Phoenix was able to be another of the successful property companies: 'It was a bull market'. Rather than succumbing to the substantial pressure simply to add highly priced property assets to the company's portfolio, Duggan took over the quoted Irish company, Rohan. It was an introduction from Professor Smith that brought Clegg and Duggan together for their early deals. Duggan says that Clegg 'always had time for people like me who brought him deals, that was his life blood. You had to be prepared to take the time to see him, so you had to fit in with his schedules. I used to wait for him until three in the morning and tell him what I was going to do. He was a tremendous partner, once he had said yes to you he was there 100 per cent. When Black Monday came we all suffered and Tony got the notion that he needed me to come on board.'

Whether Clegg really needed Duggan or not, he was certainly prepared to pay a very full price for the smaller company. By the time Clegg had suffered his illness, Duggan had become quite a close friend, and while Clegg was recovering at his home over Christmas 1987 Duggan spent some time 'talking, just talking. He decided to do it [make the bid] and we had to work out how to do it. One of his greatest failings is that you can only be in so many places. I took advantage of the fact that he was not at the table all the time in the negotiations.' As a result Phoenix was sold for a 'fantastic' price.

Duggan and his colleague Bruce Bossom moved into offices in Hill Street, Mayfair, away from Mountleigh's main office in Berkeley Square. The two men looked through the Mountleigh portfolio and marked out the properties for which they wanted to take responsibility. Among the investments they took were Stockley Park and the Criterion site in Piccadilly Circus, assets which they believed suited their skills.

The offer document gave little new information about the trading of either company but it did give up-to-date information about the directors' shareholdings. At 30 April 1987, the annual report of Mountleigh showed Tony Clegg's beneficial holdings at 10,070,874 ordinary shares and 2,000,000 5.25% preference shares. The offer document showed Clegg as having bought another 65,000 shares on 20 October, in the immediate aftermath of the crash, yet it also showed his beneficial holding as only 9,891,264 ordinary shares (180,000 fewer) but 3,000,000 5.25% preference shares (1 million more); there is no explanation anywhere for this dramatic discrepancy.

In March the sale of Beaufort House to Norwich Union for about £200 million was confirmed, a transaction which Tony Clegg claimed to be the largest single property deal in UK history. The sale of this ex-Stockley property would produce a profit of around £20 million; the price was however no higher than the deal which Norwich Union had offered in 1987, a time when there were no tenants. The Prudential, which had formerly held a freehold over part of the site, then sold its interest to Mountleigh for £25 million. Another sympton of the more cautious view that Clegg was being forced to take over property values was the sale of New Printing House Square, 214–238 Grays Inn Road. In August 1987, Clegg announced that this property, which had been bought originally to add to the investment portfolio, was subject to a 'stunning' offer, and would now be traded on. The sale in March 1988 was for £28 million, a very acceptable return over the £22.5 million cost in April 1987, but not really justifying the hyperbole. The buyer was Elliott Bernerd's private company Chelsfield, whither Stockley's ex-managing director, Michael Broke, had moved. Another sale was of a package of 21 properties to Control Securities for £88 million, the third deal between the two companies within a year. Included in the portfolio were the original estates of houses let to the USAF which had put Tony Clegg under way six years earlier, and Hertsmere House, Mountleigh's purchase in Docklands. Control paid £68 million in cash and the balance in shares which took Mountleigh's holding to 17.5 per cent. Mountleigh was buying as well as selling in this period. One new development opportunity was the former Firestone headquarters on the Great West Road, bought from Royal Life for £20 million; a second was the partnership with the Leeds City Development Corporation, promising to invest £200 million in the City over five years (P&O signed a similar agreement). The new partners in Phoenix tied up the redevelopment of Camberley town centre, paying £31.6 million for a new 150-year lease, with the intention of spending £10 million roofing over the 1960s Arndale shopping centre.

The end of the year to 30 April 1988 gave no apparent signs of the imminent collapse in Tony Clegg's dreams for his company. The declared profit showed a pre-tax total 'on ordinary activities' of £70.7 million, up from £33.6 million in the previous year. £25 million of this total came either from the realization of the PFPUT portfolio or the acquired companies, particularly Stockley. The most startling figure of all was the trading turnover of the group, which sold almost £510 million of property in the year as well as a further £119 million from its investment portfolio. More worrying was the fact that, against the book cost of the property, (carried at cost or realizable value, whichever is the lower), Mountleigh managed a margin of just 12 per cent in the year, against a 36 per cent margin over cost achieved on a much lower level of activity in the previous year. The write-off against the decline in value of the Storehouse shares had risen to £13 million, which together with the loss realized on abandoning housebuilding in Scotland, gave rise to a total extraordinary loss of almost £18 million. Almost as extraordinary was the total of proceeds from the share issues that Mountleigh had made in the year, £337 million. The balance sheet issued in July showed the company still with a stock of £569 million of property held for trading purposes against £229 million held as investments. Stockbroker analysts were actually disappointed with the figures, which they had expected to show even higher profits, and the share price fell nine per cent to 156p in their wake. The mystery of Tony Clegg's shareholding was not clarified by the annual report: as at 30 April 1988 it showed his beneficial holdings to be 9,657,712 ordinary shares and 3,000,000 5.25% preference shares. This would suggest that Clegg had sold over 230,000 ordinary shares in Mountleigh since the announcement of the Phoenix bid, despite having bought shares at a higher level. The 1988 annual report also showed that Clegg's shareholding a year previously, on 1 May 1987, was of 9,826,764 ordinary shares and 3,000,000 5.25% preference shares, whereas the 1987 report had showed him holding 10,070,874 ordinary and 2,000,000 preference shares, again with no intervening document explaining the discrepancy; such inconsistencies may be explained by the switching of beneficial interests between various accounts, and no sinister implications are suggested.

Before the date of publication of this annual report another series of changes had occurred to make it of only modest use in determining the outlook for the company. The first step was the sale of Stockley Park back to the entrepreneurs who had originally sold it to him only a year previously. There had been trouble over the development of Stockley. Lipton's company had continued as the project manager of the project, and, according to one observer, he was still treating it as if he was the owner. There were huge rows between Stockley and Lipton; at one stage the owners asked Lipton to go to the US to market the project, but he is said to have responded that he didn't have the time. If Lipton was biding his time so that Clegg would become frustrated and sell the project back to him cheaply, he succeeded. By October 1988 Mountleigh was due to repay a £100 million short-term loan, and Stockley Park was the obvious candidate for sale.

The buyer was a consortium made up of Stanhope, Stuart Lipton's newly public company, Chelsfield, Elliott Bernerd's private company, Prudential Assurance and Kajima Construction, the Japanese building contractor. The price paid by the consortium was £160 million, and the profit over the 'fair value' assumed by Stockley the previous year was measured 'in the millions rather than the tens of millions' according to Clegg himself, which suggested that the investment did not match the returns available from putting the money in the bank for the same period. More worrying for analysts was the fact that Stockley Park had been seen as the prime development in Mountleigh's portfolio and the prime reason why their shareholders had been asked to pay such a hefty transfer fee for the services of Phoenix's Duggan and Bossom. Mountleigh had also sold Stockley House in Victoria to Bernerd's Chelsfield, which in turn sold it on to City Site Estates for £30 million only months later. Together with the sale to Chelsfield of the *Times* office in Grays Inn Road and Bernerd's sale of a 634-home housing estate in Hounslow to Mountleigh for about £13 million, Bernerd and Clegg had spent much of the last 12 months in negotiation with each other.

The second startling change made in the Mountleigh portfolio was the buying out of the other 50 per cent in the Paternoster Square Consortium,

British Land and Unilever Pension Fund, each with 20 per cent and Barclays Bank Pension fund with ten per cent, for £73 million. John Duggan justified the further purchase of this development site: 'It has got to be easier to take (the development) forward when there is just one owner, rather than a committee.' Stuart Lipton's Stanhope was to be retained as project managers of the still embryonic scheme. 'We have no complaints with Stuart Lipton. The only difference will be that whereas he has been acting as if he owned it we will now have a more significant input.' At least Mountleigh was throwing itself wholeheartedly into the preliminary planning stages of the Paternoster redevelopment. The story of the architectural argument is told elsewhere but Clegg was clearly keen to meet many of the criticisms from the Prince of Wales and other anti-Modernists, providing of course that such strictures did not make the project uneconomic; he was reported as saying that 'We acknowledge the very special responsibility which we have for protecting the immediate environment of St Paul's and we are confident that modern architecture can, and will, complement this unique part of our national heritage.'

The avowed intention of Mountleigh to change from merely trading to development and the creation of a portfolio of investment assets was the justification of the bid for Phoenix, but, apart from Paternoster, these new-style projects had hitherto been hard to identify. A series of announcements now suggested that such a change was indeed under way. Mountleigh was to co-ordinate the development of 800 acres of Barking Reach, on the Thames east of Docklands; in Docklands it was to develop a 'China City' with Tianjin Municipal Government on 12 acres around Poplar Dock; in Leeds it gained planning approval for a 500,000 square foot office block and it bought 20 acres of land in Harrogate from ICI for a business park development; in Slough it sought permission for an office block on the Granada Cinema site; in Aberdeen it persisted with plans for an out-of-town retail development; in Ashford, Kent it announced a joint venture to develop a 158 acre business park with Eurotunnel and 1,200 homes (with Rosehaugh's Pelham homes). Unfortunately, despite the protestations, few of these developments ever progressed to completion, and even fewer in Mountleigh's hands.

In August 1988, for the second time in the year, Tony Clegg was in hospital. The operation was to remove a tumour from his brain, and outside observers were preparing themselves for the worst; in the event the tumour turned out to be benign and Clegg had actually been much iller with his appendix earlier in the year. Clegg himself treated the whole episode very casually. John Duggan had just gone on holiday to his French house when he took a call from Clegg. 'He said "By the way, I'm going in for a minor operation". When I asked him what it was and whether it was serious, he said it could be but he would be out in two weeks. He asked me to look after the company.' There are many who still cannot accept the idea that the operation was as minor as Clegg maintains, pointing out that he had substantial radiation treatment after the surgery, and were amazed that he ever returned to business at all. Clegg explains the treatment: 'They leave an element of the tumour behind rather than damage too much inside one's head, and they kill it off with deep X-Rays. Every week-day for five weeks I had to go to the Royal Marsden. It was quite difficult because, although they had an appointments system, they never kept to them. I couldn't sit in a basement waiting for this machine, I was much too busy. I would phone up and find out how long they were running behind, then park the car outside. I'd wait for them to get nearer the point and send the chauffeur to find out when it was my turn. The poor people who were queuing in the seats thought I was queue-jumping, so the staff had to sneak me in the back way.'

The operation meant that Clegg was unable to be at Mountleigh's annual general meeting, which was chaired by Sir Ian McGregor, who had joined the board in April 1987. Sir Ian came under some probing about the investment in Galerias Preciados, which had been planned as a management turnaround and resale; the recapitalization of Galerias Preciados had involved the sale to Mountleigh of over £140 million of the stores which were then leased back. The interest saving for the stores group was substantial and McGregor could claim that the operation was now making a trading profit. This claim of good progress was not the first or last to be made on the subject of the Spanish stores, but the eventual flotation or sale is still waited.

On 13 October 1988 the end of the reign of Tony Clegg as king-emperor of Mountleigh seemed to be signalled by the appointment of John Duggan as Chief Executive of the group, leaving Clegg as Executive Chairman. Clegg sold his stake in Mountleigh to a consortium, represented by a company named Algver Investments of which he himself was a member, 'as a supporting gesture that I wasn't getting out completely'. The other members of the consortium were Duggan, Clegg's old friend Brian Wolfson of Wembley Stadium, and Geoffrey Simmonds, ex-chairman of Phoenix, who both then joined the Mountleigh board. The amount involved was £54.6 million, valuing Mountleigh's shares at 180p, well above the ruling price on the stock market. Duggan gave notice of his intention of taking charge: 'I don't envisage any sweeping changes. Only time will tell the difference in style between Tony Clegg and myself. One of my first tasks will be to make sure that, at a time when interest rates are high, our level of gearing is one we can feel comfortable about. Otherwise it's business as usual.' But it wasn't.

Duggan with his colleagues Bruce Bossom and finance expert Ioin Cotter looked for the first time at the totality of Mountleigh's position and were shocked enough to say to each other 'let's get out of here.' They decided to embark on an aggressive programme of sales. On Tuesday, 17 October 1988, Duggan announced the sale of Paternoster Square and other assets to Organization Diego Cisneros, who had sold Galerias to Clegg only a year before. On the face of it the £317.5 million transaction was a very good price to receive for Paternoster, together with Dorset Rise, another Stockley joint development with British Land and Barclays pension fund, and three other substantial London office blocks. Paternoster was in Mountleigh's books at £288 million, but the inclusion of the other properties suggests that it was sold for substantially less than this. The sale was at least partly the result of the Cisneros group's fears for the outstanding £80 million payment due to it from Mountleigh the following May. Duggan's approach was to tell them 'you ain't going to get paid, so why don't we give you something?' It does seem rather odd however to splash out over £300 million in order to make sure that the company you have sold an asset to can pay you. It is made a little less odd when it is revealed that the deal involved the debt boot being put firmly on the other foot. Cisneros did not pay for its new assets in cash on the nail. The £80 million Mountleigh debt to them was extinguished, but the bulk of the purchase price, £160.3 million, was not to be paid until October 1989. Thus for a payment of £70 million, Cisneros became owners not only of Paternoster but of four other fully let and marketable properties, (Babcock House in Euston Road, Hoskyns House in Shaftesbury Avenue, Dorset Rise and 36 Hill Street, W1), from which it might realistically expect to recoup its initial cash payment; indeed by May 1989 Cisneros had reportedly sold £70 million of these other properties and had Paternoster in exchange for its position as creditor of Mountleigh.

There is another strange contradiction in the history of this deal. Although Hoskyns House was reported to have been sold to Cisneros in the transaction, in February 1989 Land & Property Trust was reported to have bought the building for £23 million, from Mountleigh. The eventual payment of the balance due to Mountleigh from Cisneros for the purchase of Paternoster was as uncertain as had been Mountleigh's ability to pay Cisneros for its purchase of Galerias. The balance of £150 million was due at the end of September 1989, and an American investment bank was charged with the task of finding a buyer for the development. At the very last moment, a consortium of Greycoat and Park Tower Realty, an American private investment company, bought the development and the Cisneros group was able to pay its debt to Mountleigh.

The initial payment to Mountleigh of £70 million of loan notes was made in Amsterdam and Ioin Cotter disappeared in notorious Amsterdam for most of the afternoon, much to the prurient amusement of his colleagues. In fact his occupation that afternoon was entirely innocent. Cotter had arranged to deposit the loan notes in the safes of several different hotels for the night, nervous that such sums of bearer paper should be all in one place.

Duggan also negotiated another sale in this period, of the Eagerpath 'related company', to a Swiss-based company, SASEA. This company was run by Italian financier Florio Fiorini, ex-chief of the Italian state oil company ENI, and was associated with Giancarlo Parretti, the media entrepreneur who had earlier rescued the Cannon Film group of the Israeli businessmen Golan and Globus, the so-called go-go boys. SASEA paid Mountleigh £37.8 million in cash and took over £120 million of debt.

Not included in the sale were City Gate House, previously sold to CIN, the Coal Board Pension Fund, for a rumoured £80 million, nor, as it transpired later, an office in Gracechurch Street, EC3; the remaining assets of the old PFPUT portfolio, including some farms, were sold. SASEA was advised by Paul Bloomfield and Tranwood Earl, the mini-merchant bank of Peter Earl. SASEA had other fish to fry with Mountleigh: Fiorini and Parretti had joint interests in Spanish commercial property.

While this deal was being put together by Duggan, he was surprised to read in his week-end newspaper that the company of which he was managing director was in talks which could lead to a bid being made for Wembley Stadium, now a publicly quoted company after it had been reversed into the dog-track company, GRA. These talks had been carried on principally by Tony Clegg and his old friend Brian Wolfson. The price mentioned in the press, £180 million, surprised all the analysts of the situation, since the published net assets of the smaller company were only just over £100 million at the time. Duggan couldn't see value in such a deal and could only make it work financially at £75 million. 'I could see a tide running where I couldn't have stopped it. You look around a board table and say "who's going to be with me?" and I could see the Wembley deal going through. It was obscene, but I knew that, if I killed it, I couldn't survive at Mountleigh. Macgregor, [Mountleigh's Chairman] was a formidable opponent.' The talks were aborted, partly because their early revelation had been unwelcome, but Mountleigh promptly ordered its brokers, Phillips & Drew, to buy 18.5 million of its own shares (five per cent of the total outstanding) in the stock market at a price of 167.5p.

Then on 13 November came public news of two stunning developments. The SASEA investors announced that they had formed a new company which was bidding for Mountleigh International, the holding company of Galerias Preciados, and to give an edge to their negotiations, they had taken an option to buy the 7.6 per cent held in Mountleigh by Cisneros, and, amazingly, had bought at 200p each the shares in Mountleigh, another 5.4 per cent, held by the consortium to which Tony Clegg had sold his shares, and of which he himself was a member. The second announcement was just as dramatic: John Duggan was fired. The roles of Clegg and Duggan had not been established satisfactorily to either man, as Clegg was later to confess: 'I suppose both he and I read the cards wrong. I assumed that I was going to be an executive chairman and he assumed that I was going to be a non-executive chairman. It was a misunderstanding between us that needed clearing up.' Duggan agrees: 'Truthfully there's no place for a John Duggan in Mountleigh; Tony is a one man band in so many ways.' Clegg agrees at least to some extent. 'I can't say whether he [Duggan] was surprised [about the Wembley deal] or not. It would be very dificult, if one replayed the whole thing again to understand absolutely what did go wrong. It was bound to be difficult from his point of view, and mine, because I somewhat passed my baby to him, and so maybe I was over-sensitive. I certainly wouldn't apportion blame.'

By the end of November the Swiss-Italian Galerias Consortium had built up its stake in Mountleigh to 21.5 per cent through further purchases, at 200p, from some of the loose large shareholders introduced to the Company's share register in the take-over of Stockley. In this way the remaining credibility of Mountleigh was eroded. The bid for Stockley, not itself an obvious success, brought in large uncommitted shareholders and the Paternoster development. The bid for Galerias brought in the Cisneros interests, both as shareholders and as creditors; the deal over Paternoster was done by both sides from weakness and allowed SASEA to find a large shareholding which it could bring into play for its own reasons.

In January Mountleigh's interim profits and Chairman's statement were published. This is a very odd document since it refers to the events of the previous November only tangentially as 'some highly publicised disappointments'. The half-year profits, which included two months of Galerias Preciados as a subsidiary and were therefore not directly comparable, showed a fall to £24.8 million from £35.4 million on trading turnover up from £96 million to £450 million but rental income up only to £15.5 million from £7.8 million. Since most of that rental income would come through as profit, this suggested that the company made only £10 million on its massive programme of sales (including Stockley Park and Paternoster), barely any margin over cost. Another £6.7 million after-tax had to be written off the investment in two per cent of Storehouse. There was also a warning that the tax change might be much higher than that published in the statement since the sales of property had taken place well above the tax base price, even if the profit over Mountleigh's book cost was relatively modest. After Duggan's departure, not accompanied by his ex-colleague from Phoenix Bruce Bossom, business continued in a similar fashion to before but at a less hectic pace. Clegg added to Mountleigh's shareholding in Control Securities by spending another £20 million to buy a stake held by British Land; this 22.7 per cent was seen as a long-term investment. A Swedish investment group bought the unlet West Cross Centre on the A4 for £40 million, and Mountleigh abandoned a long-held development site in Gloucester.

The SASEA saga finally ended in March 1989 when, having failed to agree a sale of Galerias Preciados to the Italian entrepreneurs, Clegg personally bought back the SASEA 14 per cent stake in Mountleigh, SASEA having not exercised its option to buy the Cisneros's seven per cent holding. Clegg claimed that SASEA had indeed made a bid for Galerias but had not given enough further information for the deal to go through. There were some concerns whether the SASEA group was acceptable to the Spanish authorities and whether they had sufficient resources to complete the deal. This was a reasonable question since the Gracechurch Street property, which had originally been in the Eagerpath package sold to SASEA was now sold to another buyer, Culverpalm, for £40 million, and speculation suggested that this was the reason for the change in the contractual arrangement with SASEA for that portfolio, reducing its overall cost to the Swiss-based company. Parretti was to face similar questions when he bid for the MGM studios in California; (in April 1991 he was removed from control of his media empire by his major bank backer, Credit Lyonnais). How could Clegg afford to buy 14 per cent of Mountleigh when he had only owned just under five per cent when he sold in the previous autumn? Clegg was now a very highly geared investor. 'It was just a stake that was around. As I had ended up back as Chairman owning hardly a single share and this stake was loose, I thought it should be bought.' Clegg later added to his position by taking an option on the stake still held by Cisneros.

Paul Bloomfield was again involved on the other side of a deal when his new vehicle company, Benlox, offered £18 million for the Hoover Factory on Western Avenue which he had introduced to Clegg three years earlier at a price of £10 million, but on which the desired retail development with Tesco had failed to receive approval. The deal was never completed. Mountleigh then sold the Beaver housing estate, previously bought from Elliott Bernerd, to a housing association for £16 million, the price paid to Bernerd's company for it. This property had caused Mountleigh embarrassment when it tried to impose an increase in the ground rent on the estate; the adverse publicity which accrued from this apparently rapacious action persuaded Mountleigh to cut and run. Markheath, associated with Australian 'entrepreneur' John Spalvins of Adelaide Steamship, and headed by Paul Bobroff, who later became better known as chairman of Tottenham Hotspur football club, bought another office park site on the Great West Road from Mountleigh.

The final act in Clegg's involvement in Mountleigh was not long delayed. On 8 November 1989 it was announced that he had sold his 22.6 per cent interest in the company for £70.4 million to two Americans, Nelson Peltz and Peter May. Peltz and May had been one of the most successful teams which exploited the junk bond boom of the late 1980s in the US. They had made hundreds of millions of dollars through buying the major companies in the can business, taking the company private and selling it on to the French company, Pechiney. Peltz came to the UK to use Mountleigh as his vehicle for a similar success in the European market. He believed that Europeans were relatively unsophisticated investors and that the opportunities were now greater than in the well picked-over bones of American industry. He misjudged his market.

There is no doubt that Clegg was suffering tremendous pressure from the size of the bank debt he had taken on in order to buy his substantial holding in Mountleigh. His frustration at the inability of the shares to move to what he considered to be a reasonable reflection of the value of the company led him to seek a price for his holding which would enable him to close the position at a modest profit and remove the risks of such a highly geared investment.

Among those aware of Clegg's position was John Duggan. Duggan, who knew more than most about the promise and pitfalls of Mountleigh, told Clegg that he could not justify paying more than 175p a share, even though Clegg was asking 200p. Duggan worked on a bid for his holding, and sought a partner. The man he found was Werner Rey, the Swiss financier who had completely undermined the reputation of Swiss businessmen as being conservative, slow and cautious. Rey was as much a trader as many of the British property men; he believed that, having agreed with Duggan to make the offer, it was as good as done. He was not pleased to find himself outbid by the Americans. Rey and Duggan instead put their joint funds into a small company, Conrad, which, after a bid for Marler Estates and Rohan (bought again by Duggan, this time from Mountleigh), changed its name to Cabra Estates. Its major interests are in the football grounds of Fulham and Chelsea, on which planning permission exists for redevelopment. Werner Rey, meanwhile, has suffered the fate of many of the 1980s super-novas: his Omni group has had to seek protection from its creditors.

Why did Tony Clegg suddenly decide to sell, so soon after taking back the reins? 'My wife put a lot of . . . pressure is the wrong word. Both my wife and a number of my friends told me to get out simply because of my health. My eyesight was affected by the brain operation. There's a lot of nonsense talked about me working 18 hours a day; well, most of it is true. When you phone up the family lawyer to make sure that he phones the hospital just in case you can't talk to your wife. . . . The opportunity came along to sell my stake. It was fair and reasonable to assume that if the right offer came along I would probably look at it seriously.' Clegg does not deny that the level of borrowing he was carrying was a heavy burden, and he needed a reasonable price for his shares to be able to exit with a comfortable margin.

The final departure of Tony Clegg from Mountleigh was not a bang, more a whimper. His concrete achievements are difficult to identify. Very few of his projects were developed by him, the profits he made for Mountleigh in the good years were transitory and proved impossible to sustain. Yet Clegg was undoubtedly a phenomenon of the 1980s. As one of those who worked closely with him has remarked 'They thought it was a real business, but it was only a business in the context of the times they were in.' Clegg began to believe he could do anything, from taking over Galerias and bidding for Storehouse to buying ships, and he thought that it would never stop. Yet he has generated nothing but personal affection, even from those whom he crossed. The partnership between Clegg and the (then) undischarged bankrupt Paul Bloomfield is one of the more extraordinary of the decade. The deal finder Bloomfield with the deal maker Clegg were the property market for a period of the late 1980s.

Clegg is now working again in a company, United Dutch Holdings, backed by Danish businessman Jan Bonde Nielson. This latter man once owned 25 per cent of the Wembley company, and has faced charges of bribery in his native land, of which he was cleared, although he still faces appeal proceedings in Denmark, to which he has so far refused to appear. Much as Bloomfield was the *eminence grise* in the property dealings of Mountleigh, so has Nielson been a shadowy financial part of Clegg's life. It will be interesting to see whether Clegg defies precedent and becomes a significant factor in the property market as it recovers in the 1990s.

Mountleigh has continued to struggle under its new owners. The Peltz-May combination also found it more difficult to turn Mountleigh into a money-maker than their previous ventures together. In May 1991, half their shares in Mountleigh were sold to the Gordon P. Getty Family Trust for 100p each, half the price paid to Clegg 22 months previously. The idea was to enable Mountleigh to raise funds for the continued investment needed in Galerias. Only two months later Mountleigh announced a huge loss and that it was raising funds through a rights issue priced at only 25p a share, with the Getty Trusts and two other foreign investors underwriting part of the issue. The Stock Exchange also investigated the circumstances in which Peltz and May had sold shares in the 'close season' for director dealings: the two were censured. The rights issue was left almost entirely in the hands of the underwriters, who, in addition to Peltz and May and the Getty Trust included a Bahamian partnership of the US Pritzker family, builders of the Hyatt hotel chain, and Accumulator, a Danish property company. In May 1992, Mountleigh went into receivership, unable to raise funds to repay its Swiss loans. Its attempts to do so were finally frustrated by its inability to sell the Merry Hill Shopping Centre (see Chapter Nine).

Does Tony Clegg have any regrets about Mountleigh and his meteoric career? 'There have got to be things one regrets. But much, much more there is a feeling of enjoyment than regrets one might have had. Part of the problem of the business we were in was that we were really commodity traders. Commodity traders cannot walk around like Stuart Lipton and say "I built this and I did that." We didn't change the face of the UK. That was one of the difficulties of Mountleigh, and the reason I was interested in Storehouse and Galerias. I actually wanted to change the way forward for the company and I would have turned it into a retailer with strong property overtones. I saw it as a way of making the shift, because if one extrapolated Mountleigh's future, one had to take over Land Securities or the Pru and flog all that. And then what? I suppose the only thing one might have done with hindsight, and then one doesn't know how long the window of opportunity is, we might have taken it slower and create a larger investment portfolio behind the trading; to try to steady the thing a little bit and get to a point where one had a decent income.'

In April 1987, at the height of his success, Tony Clegg had spoken the words which best describe both the reasons for his rise and for his ultimate fall, in an interview with Jane Roberts in the *Chartered Surveyor Weekly*: 'I think the Land Securities of this world are good for the industry, they underpin the market. It may seem a bit boring when inflation is low, but I believe those companies will perform well in the long term. I admire them, but I don't deny I don't want to be one of them. I don't have that mentality.'

6

THE SURVIVORS

THERE WERE FEW, if any, companies which came through the 1974–76 period in anything like as healthy a state as they went into it; almost everyone had been caught up in the euphoric phase of that boom and everyone paid the price. There were even fewer managers of property companies who survived that period still in charge of their diminished empires, and only a handful went on to be significant participants in the 1980s property boom. Two who did survive and go on to greater achievements were John Ritblat of British Land and Jeffrey Sterling who, with his close colleague Bruce McPhail, progressed from the rescue of Town & City Properties to managing the fortunes of the venerable Peninsular & Orient (P&O), the shipping line which transported the Empire.

John Ritblat was born in 1935, the son of a dental surgeon from North London. Although like Godfrey Bradman he was evacuated during the war, to Warminster in Wiltshire in Ritblat's case, his upbringing was fairly typical of a middle-class boy: prep school at The Hall in Hampstead, where he is now on the governing body, followed by Dulwich College. His maternal grandmother had given him a little capital which was invested in shares. Young John could see the benefits accruing from these shares which seemed to provide him with a rising flow of pocket money, and when he was about to leave school he thought he would be a stockbroker, and having been to the offices of his own broker 'thought it was a marvellous business.' It happened that his uncle was Dudley Samuel, the eponymous head of property agents Dudley Samuel, Harrison of Bruton Street in the West End of London, where it still has offices today. Dudley Samuel was the doyen of his profession, if a little eccentric, and most of the successful property agents of the 1950s and 60s, such as Edward Erdman, Marcus Lever and Joe Gold, had passed through his office at some time to learn their trade at the feet of the maestro. Just before making his decision John Ritblat had lunch with his uncle who took him for a walk down Bond Street. In 1951 Bond Street still looked like an old hag with missing teeth, the bomb sites having not been filled in the post-war austerity period of building licences and other restrictions. 'We're not going to leave it like this' said his uncle surveying the sorry mess. 'If you become a stockbroker you'll know nothing about anything. I'm absolutely sure that if I send you along to Edward Erdman and he sees you have a twinkle in your eye, he'd be delighted to take you.'

In fact Erdman initially rejected the young man, saying in his memoirs that 'I thought he would be far too ambitious to settle down patiently to the disciplines and rigours of a professional career'; eventually he was persuaded to change his mind. John Ritblat became articled to Edward Erdman in 1952, and, in his own words 'I could see I was going to be quite good at it. I was a fully-fledged negotiator by the time I was 21.' While he was attending the College of Estate Management in the evenings to gain his surveying and auctioneer's qualification he met another young student, Neville Conrad, who was articled to his uncle's firm. In 1959, at the tender age of 23, he and Conrad set up their own agency, Conrad Ritblat. Their clientele was drawn from the people he had met at Erdman's. This was the big boom of the 1950s, with the names of Cotton, Clore, Fenston, Wolfson and Max Joseph prominent. 'All the developments were rubbish' says Ritblat today, 'in the 50s we were still putting up 30s buildings, while in the 60s we were putting up Paternoster and the things that are so ghastly.'

Ritblat had become very friendly with Max Joseph, the financier who used to run a business empire from an office with no staff. Joseph used Ritblat to run most of his property interests and in 1969 called on him to repair the fortunes of one of his companies, Union Property, which had fallen to a share price of six old pence, having been as high as twenty-one shillings. Ritblat warned Joseph that solving the company's problems was not a ten minutes a week job, so Joseph told him that he didn't care what was done, 'you've got to sort this out.' Joseph suggested that he buy the Conrad Ritblat practice or some part of the property assets that Ritblat and Conrad had by this time built up for themselves. Ritblat agreed to buy a large stake in Union, partly for cash, partly in exchange for his property assets and the agency practice, the two younger men ending up with about half the company. Conrad soon went on his own to build up Regional Properties, but Ritblat set about restoring the fortunes of Union. One of the early deals was the purchase and onward sale of the Classic Cinema chain, an asset deal, thereafter bidding in 1970 for British Land, a relatively small company with a worthy history. It had been set up in 1856 by three Liberal MPs as a way of enabling men of modest means to gain the property qualification necessary to be on the electoral roll.

With the name of the group changed to British Land, Ritblat then did the deal which has maintained his fortunes over the past 20 years. The simultaneous bids for two quoted property companies, Haleybridge and Regis, brought into the group Plantation House, a large Edwardian style office block occupying most of a freehold island site between Fenchurch

Street and Eastcheap in the City. Although many other property assets were added to the portfolio at the same time, it was the continued ownership of this flagship building which enabled Ritblat to survive the later economic blizzard.

It was a deal in the US which distracted British Land from the growing problems in the UK. In 1972/73 New York was in extremis. The city's finances were collapsing under the strain of a social security system which was attracting the underprivileged from all points of the US and from outside its borders. Businesses were leaving the city and the State of New York as the local taxes levied to meet this burden rose inexorably. One of the largest owners of offices in New York was the Uris Corporation, control of which had recently been inherited by Harold Uris from the estate of his brother Percy, the creator of the portfolio. Harold proved a rather ineffectual custodian of the inheritance and the company was known to be available for sale. John Ritblat looked with anticipation at the potential which Uris represented. Its portfolio was larger than the largest UK company, totalling some 20 million square feet of offices and hotels. The borrowing which it had was all non-recourse, so that if Uris failed it could not bring down British Land. The problem was that there was a growing number of empty New York offices, but Ritblat took the view that he could afford to sit out the bad times and wait for the market to improve. He took the idea to the National Westminster Bank and Schroders, the merchant bank; Gordon Richardson, later Governor of the Bank of England, and James Wolfenson of Schroders were old friends of Ritblat's. He persuaded the two banks to subscribe to 25 per cent of British Land and 25 per cent of the Uris Corporation and to guarantee to raise the balance of the purchase price, the main debt being a $600 million 20-year amortizing note carrying a six per cent interest rate. Ritblat rationalized the deal: 'All we've got to do is to manage it adequately, sit there for 20 years and after 18 years we will own the buildings free and clear, free of debt. They're marvellous buildings, just square boxes ideal for modernization to keep them up to scratch.'

After a year's negotiation in July 1973 the conditional contract to purchase was signed, the finance package was signed and everything was ready for engrossment. Ritblat returned to the UK on Friday only to find by the Monday that two sons-in-law of the Uris family had managed to complete a deal for control of the company at a dollar a share more for Harold Uris. 'We couldn't believe it' says Ritblat. The new owners had raised the finance through the car-park company National Kinney with help from Steve Ross of Warner Brothers: 'They believed that, after a year looking, we had unearthed some incredible goodies and value. We hadn't, we had simply created an incredibly complex financing package.' By the end of that year, after the Yom Kippur War, interest rates rose sharply in New York and National Kinney found themselves in trouble; Warner Brothers had to find a further $200 million immediately and the Uris portfolio had to be liquidated. At the end of 1977 the rump of the business was bought for $320 million by a little-known Canadian company, Olympia & York, run by the Reichmann family, 'with marvellous timing' says Ritblat, 'they made billions'. It was a critical element in the development of the global property empire now owned by the Reichmanns, whose development in Docklands has been described in Chapter Two. O&Y's involvement in British property is discussed further in Chapter Ten.

Ritblat still expresses real regrets over the failure of the Uris deal. 'We'd have made, we calculated, two billion dollars. It was the most exciting year and the best thing I ever conceived, but it was a disaster because it unhinged the finances of British Land. Everything had been predicated on the rights issue and we had left everything unfinanced.' By taking their collective eye off the position at home British Land's management had put themselves at the mercy of their banker, NatWest. Fortunately, since the bank had been party to the Uris expedition, it sympathized with British Land's plight when the UK property market collapsed in 1973/74. In March 1974 British Land gave the first hint of serious trouble. While reporting pre-tax profits of over one million pounds for the six months to 30 September 1973, it also forecast a loss for the second half of the year. This loss turned out to be over one and a half million pounds, as annual interest charges rose to £12 million from under six million pounds a year earlier. By September 1974 British Land shares had fallen to twelve new pence each and the whole company's equity was worth only five million pounds. 30 September 1974 was a critical day for the company as on that date it was due to complete the purchase of an office in Aldersgate Street on the western fringes of the City for four and a quarter million pounds, and there were real doubts whether the company was in a position to fulfil its obligations.

At British Land's Annual General Meeting that month, John Ritblat faced questions from anxious shareholders. He assured them that purchase and the payment of £1.3 million of interest due on 30 September would be 'made on the due date', but he accepted that discussions were necessary with the banks and that some investments would have to be sold. Ritblat is proud to claim now that British Land received 'no help from anybody. We rolled up a bit of interest but we paid every cent and didn't sell any property until after 1977.' The Ritblat memory seems a little faulty about property sales, since in April 1976 the company announced it had lost three million pounds in the six months to September 1975 and had sold properties worth £10.5 million in the year to March 1976 and negotiations had been completed for sales of a further £20 million. These later sales included two parts of the Croydon Centre, to Legal & General and Nestlé.

At the worst the company was down to the last eight million pounds in banking facilities. In August 1974 British Land had a facility to draw ten million pounds from the finance house Mercantile Credit, but their position was equally difficult and they could not pay the money over.

Ritblat threatened to issue a writ, which the Bank of England would not have welcomed in that environment. Instead John Quinton of Barclays, the lead banker to Mercantile Credit, gave Ritblat a new facility.

The process of selling some assets and waiting for the rents on the remaining portfolio to rise sufficiently to cover the interest costs was a slow one. It was made worse by the economic crisis of 1976 which drove the Minimum Lending Rate up to an unprecedented 15 per cent. The gradual reduction of short-term debt culminated in September 1977 when about £25 million of maturing debt needed refinancing. £10 million of this had been a loan from the Crown Agents, one of the odder participants in the 1970s property boom and one into which there was a government enquiry; the other £15 million was in the form of a nine and a half per cent unsecured loan stock. On 10 September British Land announced that it was to issue £21 million of a 15 per cent debenture stock and £7.7 million of a 12 per cent convertible loan stock. The interest cost on these new instruments was much higher than that on the debt they replaced, and set back further the time that British Land was going to be able to declare a profit, but it moved a substantial proportion of the company's £200 million debt burden further into the future.

The only reason British Land was able to secure such finance was because the company had, in Plantation House, a truly prime asset. That one property was valued for the purpose of establishing the security on the debenture at £51 million. The 515,000 square feet of offices were then producing rents of £2.7 million, well below the interest cost of the debenture alone, but rental values had recovered sufficiently to make it certain that rent increases were to be forthcoming. Modern air-conditioned offices in the City were now commanding rents of up to £16 per square foot, up from only £12.50 at the low.

John Ritblat then engaged in a succession of deals which represented a creative solution to his company's problem. Using British Land's shares, which had recovered a little by the end of 1977, he bought stakes in various quoted companies and sold them on for cash at a profit, usually over quite a short period. The first deals included a holding in Bridgewater Estates, sold on to Rothschild Investment Trust, and a 11.5 per cent stake in Property Investment and Finance Limited (PIFL). This was an investment trust, run by merchant bank Kleinwort Benson, which specialized in property shares. Both stakes, built up to 18.8 per cent in the case of PIFL, were sold in the spring of 1978. In the early summer British Land acquired a tiny unquoted property company, Wellingrove, and 15.6 per cent of the quoted Churchbury Estates. These deals added assets and income, especially when the holdings were sold at a profit, to the British Land balance sheet, without adding any debt. The consequence was that these transactions helped to reduce gearing and increase net income. By the end of March 1978 the company was able to report net assets of £62 million, and although borrowings totalled £145 million, that was well down on previous totals and was better financed.

Later in 1978 Ritblat announced the purchase of Kingsmere Investment for £4.2 million, paid for by the issue of 5.4 million shares and £2.35 million cash, (part deferred). Kingsmere was a relic of the 1960s property boom, having been controlled by Felix Fenston, who, with Jack Cotton and Charles Clore, was one of the fabled investors of the post-war period. At the same time British Land took control of the Langham Estate, a collection of properties to the north-east of Oxford Circus, the centre of the London rag trade, which was to prove another well-traded portfolio over the next decade.

The greatest coup in this series of deals was the purchase of 26.22 per cent of City Offices, a venerable company with interests as far afield as Lusaka, Zambia, from the Ellerman family company British & Commonwealth, for £1.52 million cash plus 6.7 million British Land shares, representing 8.67 per cent of the newly enlarged equity of British Land. British & Commonwealth had swopped its near-controlling interest in the solid but rather dull City Offices for a much smaller investment in the more highly geared British Land.

Further purchases brought the stakes in City Offices and Churchbury to 29 per cent and 20 per cent by the end of January 1979. Partly as a consequence of these share deals the company was able to report a return to profit in February 1979. In the half-year to September 1978 British Land made £255,000 against a loss in the equivalent period a year earlier of two million pounds. This was despite £15 million in property asset sales, which had reduced rental income from nearly £7.5 million to £6.8 million. Borrowings were down again to £127 million and profits had been boosted by the contributions from its new acquisitions. In March 1979 British Land sold its 29 per cent of City Offices to Legal & General for £6.6 million against its book cost of £4.57 million and in the next month the Langham Estate was sold to the Water Council pension fund for £9 million, and the holding in Churchbury to London Trust for £1.2 million.

One of the distinguishing features of British Land in the 1970s was its ownership of several trading companies. Between 1970 and 1990 the company has owned such diverse businesses as Dorothy Perkins, the High Street women's clothing store group, and Gripperrods, who make patented carpet-laying grips. The stockbroker analysts could never understand why Ritblat should be involved in areas which they could not analyse and in which they feared there might be some potential risk. Ritblat asserts that it was a perfectly simple theory. 'We bought companies at below asset value, managed the assets and kept them until the markets went up. Then we sold them on a high price-earnings multiple [a ratio between company value and profits which is the normal basis for valuing companies]. We made £50 million net out of our industries.'

Dorothy Perkins was sold in September 1979 to the Burton Group for just under £5 million in cash plus 74 properties valued at £10.5 million. 'We tripled our money on Dorothy Perkins, and it made £30 million profits while we owned it.' At the same time British Land was building up a share stake in Hepworths, the rather old-fashioned, but asset-rich, tailoring group. 'We should have bid for it, but we didn't fancy a fight. An absolute fortune was made out of the properties.' It was left to others to revive Hepworths, which became the Next Group. 'The market refused to accept that we were good at [these non-property investments]. They didn't like the mix.' John Weston-Smith, Ritblat's right-hand man, describes the questions he suffered: 'What sort of company was it? Was it a property company, was it an industrial company, was it a retailer? They wanted a nice pigeon-hole to slot you into, and so they liked it when we became a pure property company. We were doing in a small way what Hanson does.'

In 1979 John Ritblat suffered a personal tragedy. His wife Isabel was travelling in a private plane, and as it began its landing approach, she fell out of the aircraft to her death. Interviewed in 1990, he confessed that the disaster had affected him deeply. 'When something like that happens it changes your perspective on life, you value your relations more.' He was left with three children, and it may be a symptom of the change in his attitude to life that his two sons are both now working for British Land; he also has a daughter. In 1986, Ritblat remarried.

By the end of 1979 the rehabilitation of British Land was effectively complete. The Australian investments were put into a joint trust with the Post Office Pension Fund and the Australian CRA company's pension fund, leaving British Land with a 24.5 per cent interest and a cash repayment of A$19 million. By February 1980, John Ritblat was able to tell his shareholders to expect a dividend for the year which was to end in March 1980. Net debt had fallen to only £76 million by March 1980, against property assets of £192 million; at its peak level in 1976, British Land owed £152 million against property assets of £305 million. The dividend declared in July was the first since 1974. Ritblat was now in a position from which he could make his company grow again, rather than merely make sure that it survived.

In August 1980, British Land made two bids: for the Corn Exchange and UK Property. The former owned the eponymous building of more than 100,000 square feet in the City which had long since ceased to fulfil its original role; UK Property's prime asset was the Heywood Industrial Estate, now modishly renamed the Heywood Business Park, eight miles north of Manchester. It covers 166 acres with 1.4 million square feet of lettable space and room for a further 1.6 million square feet; this property was sold in 1988. UK Property also owned three engineering companies which could be merged into British Land's W. Crowther susidiary. The cost of the two bids, £32 million, was mostly met from share issues. At the same time British Land announced that 16 of the 74 properties acquired from Burtons on the sale of Dorothy Perkins had been sold for £4.4 million, a million pounds more than the value attributed to them at the time of the purchase.

One of the distinguishing features of British Land has been its approach to financing its portfolio. It has always sought to raise unsecured finance; unlike mortgage debentures, such money is not secured on any particular asset and enables the company to take a much more flexible approach to its portfolio. It has not always proved possible to achieve this sort of financing: the refinancing of the company in 1977 depended crucially on the ability to borrow against the security of Plantation House. In 1981 British Land created another debenture, a 'drop-lock'. The concept of a 'drop-lock' debenture was not new; 'We had seen Birmingham do an issue, but we were not interested in following suit. Birmingham had to draw down the loan straight away. At that time we did not want to draw the money, it was too expensive; what was the good of 14 per cent money? I asked whether we could do this without taking the money, but holding an option to draw. Then we would have the credit. David Milne and Malcom Wilde of Guinness Mahon and Graham Axford of James Capel worked up just such a scheme. We were told that we were paying an eighth of a per cent too much for the money, but the big point was that we had a blue-chip letter of credit and we could tell the banks that they could have a power of attorney over that option and then lend to us at the very finest rates. The Bank of England then spotted that such a scheme would lose them control of the money supply, since they would not know when funds were going to be drawn down; we had a letter from the Bank that said we could do it. It was a marvellous innovation.' The maximum amount to be borrowed is £37 million, to be repaid between 2019 and 2024.

Such financial innovation made British Land an obvious source for Godfrey Bradman when he was setting up the finance for 1 Finsbury Avenue, (described in Chapter 3). Much as Ritblat was able to secure longterm finance when he needed it without actually drawing it down, the provision of a debenture on Bradman's development was the key to achieving short-term finance for that building. In this case the providers of the guaranteed finance, British Land, Globe Investment Trust, Dixons and J Rothschild, were given a 29.9 per cent equity interest in the completed development. In 1987 British Land bought out the other minority share-holders in 1 Finsbury Avenue for £18.7 million, paid for in shares, and in May 1992 Greycoat sold its interest in Finsbury Avenue to Ritblat well below the value attributed to the investment as recently as June 1991.

By the mid-1980s, British Land was again among the leading property companies. In 1983 it acquired a 50 per cent interest in the Euston Centre, two 1960s tower blocks connected by a range of low-rise offices and show rooms between Camden Road and Regent's Park, to the north of London's inner ring road. This development had been the work of Wimpey and Stock Conversion under its prime mover, Joe Levy, and its history is well documented in *The Property Boom*. 'We bought it from Wimpey at an 11 per cent yield on cost. They were being squeezed at the time and were effectively a forced seller.' In 1986 the other half interest was bought from Jeffrey Sterling's P&O; the latter had acquired its interest by taking over Stock Conversion.

By 1984 Plantation House had become worth £116 million and the wisdom of Ritblat's fundamental principles was beginning to be apparent: 'British Land's philosophy is that the freehold is the most favourable condition of ownership, and the most reliable source of revenue and capital growth.' The trick is to be able to finance the portfolio while rents are still unable to cover the cost of money, and reap the benefits as rents inexorably rise, over long periods anyway. In this Ritblat has a lot in common with Geoffrey Wilson of Greycoat, who is one of the subjects of the next chapter.

There were mistakes. British Land's foray into the United States, was, like so many British investments in that country, less than a triumph. In November 1982, British Land bought 90 Broad Street, the street adjoining New York's Wall Street. This is a substantial building of 328,000 square feet. The company also owned the Central Savings Bank Building in Baltimore; this was a succesful investment, and was sold for $24 million, a surplus of $10 million over cost, in 1983. In 1986, Ritblat created a separate quoted vehicle for the American interests, British Land of North America, by reversing his interests into the American group Growth Realty Companies, listed on the New York Stock Exchange. 'We miscalculated. We owned too much of the company, but we had never dreamt that the minority shareholders and the Securities and Exchange Commission would effectively stop us operating the company.' The American authorities were keen to guarantee that outside shareholders were not unfairly disadvantaged. Ritblat sold the public company in 1988. British Land's overseas interests were not confined to North America. In Europe the company had several joint ventures with the Dutch company Wereldhave, which were sold in 1987, and it has developed the St Stephen's Green shopping centre in Dublin, next to the prime, and pedestrianized, shopping thoroughfare, Grafton Street. The company has also been part of the consortium developing the old Customs House in Dublin as the Financial Centre, a tax advantaged zone in Dublin intended to make that city a recognized financial services centre.

The major deal of 1984 was the purchase of Rank City Wall Properties from the Rank Organisation, which was disposing of its peripheral activities at that time. This portfolio brought several shopping centres. many of them in Scotland, to British Land. One of these, the Wester Hailes Centre in Edinburgh, was one of the very first new district, non-High Street covered shopping malls in the United Kingdom. A more idiosyncratic investment was that in the restricted voting shares of Stylo Shoe. This company is controlled by the Ziff family through a share voting structure which favours the family shares. Ritblat, like many before him, had identified the fact that, while the Stylo shoe business was not attractive, the shops from which they operated were often in prime retailing positions and owned freehold by the company. British Land gradually bought up a substantial holding in the restricted voting shares, but was unable to prise control from the Ziff family, and eventually sold them on to Nazmu Virani's Control Securities, a company which seems to have picked up large numbers of unwanted trifles from the tables of the larger property companies in the late 1980s.

1985 was notable for British Land's involvement in the Paternoster Consortium, of which it held 20 per cent, and the parallel investment with Stockley in Dorset Rise, the refurbishment of Unilever's building near Blackfriars Bridge. Perhaps the strongest indication of the company's growing self-confidence was its dabbling in areas other than property. Not only had the industrial interests been augmented in the recent past, but now Ritblat was supporting new ventures. He bankrolled ex-Slater Walker investment man Brian Banks in a new investment management house, Guildhall, and began to finance films. Until the 1984 Finance Act, first year tax allowances against capital expenditure made it possible to avoid corporation tax. Many companies found themselves putting money into the film industry; the results were only partly successful artistically and no success at all financially, but then half the cost was effectively paid for by the taxpayer. Kingsmere Productions, British Land's subsidiary, put money into such artistic and financial successes as *The Sender* and *Top Secret*, neither of which registered on public consciousness. The last venture was different: *The Mission*, produced by Goldcrest Films, directed by Roland Joffe who had directed The *Killing Fields*, and starring Jeremy Irons, was a critical success and won the Palme d'Or at the 1986 Cannes Film Festival. It did not prove a box-office winner. The 1984 Finance Act has dissuaded British Land from continuing this interesting excursion into the arts.

In the two years leading to the peak in the market in 1988, British Land was comparatively conservative in its ventures. Purchases were largely confined to the high-yielding areas of activity, such as a portfolio bought from 3i, the investment capital group. This portfolio, mostly industrial units, cost £97 million but was to yield 11.25 per cent after only two years. Shares rather than cash were used to pay for the large purchases of the period: the other 50 per cent of Euston Centre, a £93 million portfolio from Legal & General and another property on the island site containing Plantation House. In 1988, Ritblat bought 20 Sainsbury stores on a 9 per cent yield for £90 million, and the giant one million plus square foot MFI distribution centre in Northampton for £35 million. Against these purchases, the French and Dutch interests were sold for £160 million and, in the run-up to the 1987 stock market crash, so were the industrial interests. The Paternoster Consortium was dissolved in May 1988 with Mountleigh taking out the minority partners including British Land for £73 million, which outsiders calculated gave British Land a 100 per cent profit on its three year investment.

The policy of buying only high-yielding, well-let property continued into 1989. One hundred and thirty-five million was spent on nine further Sainsburys stores together with four offices. But the most significant development for British Land was the attempt to restructure the company. In December the management proposed to split the company into two parts: the investment part of British Land, which would own 80 per cent of the group's assets, would gradually realize its portfolio and distribute the proceeds to its shareholders. 'New' British Land would hold the lower valued assets and manage 'old' British Land. The idea was that the group had become too unwieldy to be able to offer significantly rewarding outperformance of the property market as a whole. The shareholders of 'old' British Land would, if they were non-taxpayers such as pension funds or charities, receive the true value of their investment rather than suffer from a share price which stood at a significant discount to that value. The proposals failed to win the support of the institutions which effectively control British Land.

John Ritblat long ago ceased to have a significant shareholding in the company; indeed, many of the investment institutions suspected that this was the true motive behind the proposal. 'New' British Land offered great incentives to its management, which could earn them a nearly 30 per cent holding in the new company. Ritblat is unrepentant about this rebuff. He sees nothing wrong with having tried to secure the future of his sons through the incentives offered. As he points out, to earn the shareholding, the other holders would have had to do very well indeed.

The rebuff has not lessened Ritblat's appetite for the property business. He has been one of the notable contrarians of the 1990/91 bear market in property, buying large properties regularly and being prepared to increase his debt to finance the purchases, the purchase of the Finsbury Avenue development of Rosehaugh Greycoat in 1991 and 1992 being perhaps the most notable coup. It cannot be said that he is not prepared to take decisions or put his company's money where his mouth is. If he is right, which I suspect he will prove to be, he will have created huge profits for his company. It is, as always, a question of timing. If the property market does not recover within two years, the cost of his borrowing will create some unrest. Should yields fall and rental values start to recover while interest rates remain low, the gains will make Ritblat a hero. The markets certainly have a positive view about the future; at the nadir of this property bear market, at the end of 1991, British Land shares were still quoted around 300p, a sharp contrast to their position at the end of the previous recession and to the shares of the new generation of developers; the experience of near disaster in the 1970s was obviously a valuable experience.

Ritblat sees his company as 'the best long-term holders in the business'. Opportunistic? 'I should hope so' says Weston-Smith; 'and how' adds Ritblat. 'We have never had false pride or images or pretensions about holding things. If you've got the money, you can have Plantation House; it's not for sale, but it's available for sale. It now has planning permission for 850,000 square feet of offices along its quarter-mile frontage, but if Mr Nippon Life came along and said "I've got to have the best and most impressive site in London" we'd say "put your cheque down and its yours". You don't know in this business; there's always some Napoleon who comes along and says "I want this asset" and we've got to be ready for him.'

The company has outstanding planning permission for one million square feet of offices for its investments in addition to Plantation House, although it has no intention of exercising it until the economics are right. 'We won't have a building that is not capable of redevelopment. Property has a life; there ought to be depreciation of bricks and mortar in Reports and Accounts. I hate building buildings' says Ritblat. His development of Rank-Xerox House in the Euston Centre has stood vacant for too long since its completion, probably confirming that prejudice.

John Ritblat is philosophical about the fact that property developers are unlikely ever to win popularity polls. Despite his company's support for many charities and the arts, he understands that the public appreciation of developers is not high: 'It's because people relate to it, and we've had huge riches made by lots of people who couldn't actually earn a living doing anything else, who've just been lucky.' Few, if any, would include John Ritblat in that category; his success has been deliberately sought and resolutely carried out. He is a true survivor.

So is his near contemporary, Jeffrey Sterling, ennobled in Margaret Thatcher's resignation honours list. There is a prevailing assumption that Jeffrey Sterling is an East End boy made good, apparently confirmed by his choice of title, Lord Sterling of Plaistow. Yet this Plaistow is a village in Sussex and not the East End district; his birth in Whitechapel was coincidence and 'I think I was in the East End for two days because I was born in a hospital there.' His father was indeed an East Ender, a second generation immigrant whose family had, at some time, changed their name from Steinberg. Sterling is a tall, dome-headed man with immaculate manners and dress. His voice, with a trace of an inability to roll his 'r's, is the only hint that he was not born to the purple. His father, Harry Sterling, built up a leisure business, Sterling and Michaels. Legend has it that Harry Sterling was a bingo hall proprietor, but his son never had to suffer the privations of the self-made father. Brought up in Surrey, he had a grammar school education, was a talented athlete and a serious musician. For two years he studied the violin at the Guildhall School of Music and Drama.

Instead of a career in music, Sterling has had a meteoric rise in the business world, combining a good strategic grasp with an almost Machiavellian ability to manipulate matters to his advantage. Anyone who has suffered his lobbying for a cause will vouch for the charming but determined juggernaut that he becomes. His success has also been linked with the formidable grasp of detail that his low-key partner, Bruce McPhail, has provided. Together they have moved from taking over a moribund investment trust to the management of one of Britain's largest and most venerable companies, The Peninsular & Orient Steam Navigation Company, P&O.

Sterling's initial break was to work for Isaac Wolfson, the founder of Great Universal Stores and notable benefactor to many educational and other causes. 'I worked with Wolfson for a couple of years. He was a very interesting guy, who always discussed his mistakes.' Sterling was then involved in a small property company, Gula Investments, in the 1960s. When Corporation Tax was introduced in 1965, Philip Shelbourne, the merchant banker, worked out that the company was worth more to its shareholders if it was liquidated. The scheme had originally been worked out for Maurice Wohl and his United Real, but 'he decided that he wouldn't, and so we did.' In that period Sterling met up with Oliver Marriott, then the property correspondent of the *Investors Chronicle* (and author of *The Property Boom*), and Bruce McPhail, who was then working at merchant bank Hill Samuel.

'We worked out a property unit trust, split into capital and income units. Then Oliver Jessel [of Jessel Securities] started a property unit trust which drove up the price of property shares.' The project had to be abandoned, although Sterling claims that the companies which Marriott and he had identified as potential investments have mostly gone from strength to strength since then. Bruce McPhail's role was to demonstrate, through complicated calculus, the potential returns on the two classes of share. 'He was a shock-haired youngster, just back from Harvard.'

'We bought control of Consumer Growth Investment Trust, which became Sterling Guarantee Trust, and then we were on our way.' In the late 1960s and early 1970s, the team acquired in quick succession companies which had a strong asset base and were service companies. Companies such as Buck and Hickman, which was a supplier of tools but had a potentially valuable property in East London, and the two London exhibition venues, Earls Court and Olympia. Oliver Marriott, a rather flamboyant figure, partial to a huge overcoat and wide-brimmed hat, went to check out one of these two properties 'incognito', a concept which makes Sterling laugh aloud. Only one of these acquisitions was traded on: Salisburys, the handbag retailer, was sold to Murray Gordon's Combined English Stores Group. The acquisition philosophy developed by Sterling at that time identified two potential weaknesses which he was able to exploit. 'If the management has no shares in the business and you emerge as the largest shareholder. On the other hand, large family shareholdings are not one holding; after several generations, people's needs are different,' something he and Elliott Bernerd were later able to exploit in their take-over of Laing Properties. 'There is very rarely an occasion where you need to make an aggressive take-over bid, because I think there is a price to be negotiated. If you're building companies, not trading them on, (and there is a tremendous difference in my view), the only thing you can say about the price you pay is that it's either far too much or far too little: nobody pays the exactly right price.' He gives an example of what he means: 'Sutcliffe Catering was a teeny subsidiary of Olympia when we bought it, and is now one of the biggest in Europe. If we look back 20 years, whether we paid twice as much for it or another five or ten per cent one way or another, it would have been meaningless. It would have been meaningful only if we wanted to trade it on, a year or so after the event. If you're building something, all that's proven in the long run is whether it has gone successfully as a field of endeavour; in practice, if something goes sadly wrong, it doesn't matter how cheaply you think you bought it, you've overpaid.

'We did not have a property background; it was not the dominant factor. In practice, in the early days we pushed off the real estate side, on the basis that we wanted to concentrate on the acquisition and running of the companies. If you acquired companies with strong assets, first of all, if you make the odd mistake, which all of us make, it's not going to kill you. But if you bought something with an enormous amount of goodwill, you've got nothing.' With these purchases 'you have a combination of positive cash-flow companies building up profits on one side, and you've got strong assets being built up, either as investment portfolios or development, alongside and one feeds t'other. All strategies are found with the benefit of hindsight; it has also turned out by sheer chance that pretty well every company we own is either the leader or a leader in its field.'

It was the purchase of the old Gamages store on the corner of High Holborn and Hatton Garden which linked Sterling to his near nemesis, Town & City Properties. Gamages, remembered by many schoolboys as the publisher of a catalogue over which they could drool, was a victim of changing fashions in retailing. The property was valuable, but as offices. Sterling was not interested, as he says, in being the property developer so he went into partnership with Barry East of Town & City to redevelop both Gamages and parts of the two exhibition company sites.

Town & City had become the second largest UK property company by the end of 1973, having acquired since 1972 Charlwood Alliance, Sovereign Securities, Sterling Land, (Geoffrey Wilson and Stuart Lipton's company), Elliott Bernerd and Stephen Laurie's property interests, David Young's Eldonwall, and, finally and fatally, Central & District property from merchant bank Keyser Ullman, a deal completed on 3 September 1973. Not only had it paid cash for Central & District, but it also had a development programme costing £160 million. Town & City's major funding partner was the Prudential Assurance, and its banker Barclays. Barclays had unusually taken a direct interest in the portfolio of Central & District when it lent Town & City the money to buy that company.

With the collapse of the property market becoming apparent by the end of the first quarter of 1974, David Young and Elliott Bernerd approached Jeffrey Sterling to tell him of the crisis looming for the company of which they were directors. 'It had reached the stage of a rescue operation' says Sterling. Bernerd and Laurie had become convinced that Barry East would have to go, and the non-executives had become more and more involved in 'fire-fighting'. Although Town & City did not actually owe money to Sterling Guarantee at the time, according to Sterling, the health of his group was inextricably bound up with the survival of the larger company. There were discussions between the Prudential, Barclays and the Bank of England before Town & City mounted a bid for Sterling Guarantee in April 1974. This was clearly a reverse take-over, with the Sterling Guarantee team taking over management with the support of the institutions. Barry East resigned in October 1974, one of eleven directors of the company to resign since the bid, leaving only four of the original Town & City directors, including David Young, still in post. 'Talk about angels fear to tread' says Sterling about his role in Town & City, 'we thought it would take about two years to sort out and it took about eight.'

The company had borrowings of £319 million and property assets of £541 million, of which £196 million was in 57 development properties around the world, totalling nine million square feet, on which a further £160 million would have to be spent. The Central & District portfolio, bought with borrowed cash costing 16 per cent, was then heavily reversionary (i.e. it had imminent rent reviews which would raise the income earned substantially), but currently had a yield of only three per cent, leaving an enormous hole in the income account; at the time, the reader will recall from Chapter One, there was a rent freeze and Town & City was unable to realize these rent reviews. Even after the rent freeze was lifted in December 1974, partly at least as a result of effective lobbying by Sterling, Town & City's interest bill was still massively larger than its rental income. The only way to remedy this problem, even partly, was to sell property in enormous amounts, even into an unwilling and weak market. The problem was exacerbated by the fact that Town & City's interest in many properties was not straightforward. Often they had a 'top slice' of the income, whereby the financier of the property was guaranteed a percentage of rental value, whether or not Town & City had actually let the property and were receiving such rents.

Between the end of March 1974 and October, Town & City sold £71 million of property, at only £2 million less than it had been carried in its books; a further £12 million was sold between October 1974 and March 1975, including £3 million to the Prudential itself. The critical support for the group came in May 1975 when Barclays and the Prudential agreed to subscribe £25 million in the form of a Town & City convertible loan stock. The strain on Town & City's finances at the time can be gauged by the size of its net interest bill in the year which ended on 31 March 1975, a sum of £25 million. The selling continued despite the greater security afforded by the long-term funds provided by the two institutions. Between February and September 1976 a further £47 million of property was sold, but even by August 1977, Sterling was still unable to say when the company would emerge from its slough: 'It is impossible to predict how long deficits will continue and how long it will be before a surplus is reached.'

One of the major sales made by Town & City in its recovery period was of Berkeley Square House, the biggest asset in its portfolio at 320,000 square feet of offices, in January 1978. The Prudential were partners in the property, but even so, the sale netted Town & City over £16 million; so large was the deal for the time that the pension funds of two then-nationalized industries bought the property: British Rail and British Airways.

A further important step towards rehabilitation of Town & City was the conversion of the 1975 issue of loan stock to Barclays and the Prudential into a convertible preference share, paying no interest until 1982. The sweetener for the two investors was that the price of Town & City shares at which they could convert their holding was reduced from 40 pence to 20 pence, much nearer the prevailing level. For Town & City there were two critical advantages: the interest charge on the convertible was temporarily removed, and, just as important, whereas the convertible counted as a debt, a preference share counted as equity and the company's hair-raising gearing was dramatically reduced. By the end of the financial year to 31 March 1978, Town & City's pre-tax loss had reduced to £17 million, and borrowings were £255 million against property assets valued at £326 million. Four years into the rescue and Town & City was still hanging on by its finger nails.

In February 1980 it was announced that Jeffrey Sterling was to join the board of P&O as a non-executive director. P&O had been through a difficult period during the secondary banking crisis. In the period prior to the crash, it had made a belated attempt to diversify into secondary banking and contracting. At the end of 1972, it had bid £140 million for the Bovis contracting group, which had itself bought Twentieth Century Banking. The bid failed, but in February 1974 P&O renewed its approach and bought Bovis for the seemingly knock-down price of £25 million. Although Bovis struggled through the following recession, it was Twentieth Century Banking which brought P&O severe problems. By February 1975 it was announced that the bank was making 30 per cent provisions against its lending, a catastrophic order of losses for a bank. In April 1979 Sandy Marshall, the managing director of P&O, resigned.

Town & City emerged from its own nightmare at the end of 1981. In the seven years between 24 March 1974 and 1981, the company had sold property worth £409 million. Its net interest charge, on borrowings reduced to £177 million, was still £29 million a year, and despite the rise in rents on its remaining portfolio, the company still lost £11 million in the 1980/81 year. The final escape from the red ink came through a bid for the quoted Berkeley Hambro company. By using its shares Town & City was able to purchase, for £59 million, an ungeared property company. At the same time it announced the result of a property revaluation which gave a net asset value of around 40 pence. The combination enabled Town & City to repair both its revenue account and its balance sheet. The company had been rescued from the world of the zombie, the walking dead.

By the mid-1980s, Sterling had emerged as one of the most influential businessmen of his generation. P&O took over Sterling Guarantee, which Town & City had renamed itself as a final divorce from its unhappy history. P&O was feeling vulnerable to an unwelcome bid, and considered it necessary to bring Sterling and McPhail on board as executives; Oliver Marriott, by now semi-retired in Yorkshire, joined the board as a non-executive. P&O did indeed receive a bid from Trafalgar House, another diversified company which was headed by an ex-property man of the previous boom, Nigel Broakes. The latter had taken over Cunard, and the two companies had a lot in common: contracting, shipping and property. But with Sterling's help P&O survived intact.

Sterling had by this time developed another string to his bow, that of adviser to government. His old friend David Young, who had run the Manpower Services Commission and been an adviser to Norman Tebbitt, had so captivated Margaret Thatcher with his 'can-do' attitude and business acumen that he had been ennobled and given a seat in the Cabinet. He recommended Sterling as his successor as industrial adviser to the Department. Over the next seven years he became an important figure to successive Secretaries of State, particularly since he was a constant presence while there were seven different holders of the political post in his time as adviser. Sterling soon came to be one of those with access to Margaret Thatcher; as any civil servant or politician will tell you, access is the critical factor in the influence anyone can have with senior decision makers. He still has the ability to request a hearing at 10 Downing Street and be fairly sure of being successful.

As head of a venerable British shipping company, Sterling has taken his responsibilities seriously. He has been President of the British Chamber of Shipping and is now to head the European equivalent. At the end of 1986, P&O bid for European Ferries. This company, built up by the Wickenden brothers, operated the Townsend Thoresen cross-Channel ferries and also had property interests. Only a matter of days after P&O gained control, the *Herald of Free Enterprise* capsized on leaving the port of Zeebrugge, its bow doors having been left open to the seas. Showing a moral courage which should not be dismissed, Sterling immediately went to Zeebrugge and talked to the survivors and relatives of the dead. It was scarcely his fault that the procedures of a company which he had so recently taken over should have been so fatally flawed, but as chairman of the company, he knew his responsibility. He recalls the experience with horror: walking through the temporary morgue and being the object of hate and insults from those who saw him seared his soul.

It was something of a surprise that a man who had spent most of the past ten years distancing himself from the property market should emerge in 1990 as one of the two protagonists in a joint company bidding £440 million for Laing Properties. His partner in the bid was his old colleague on the board of Town & City, Elliott Bernerd, and against most predictions they managed to wrest away the company which, with 40 per cent of its shares owned by the Laing family or its charitable trusts, was thought impregnable. Sterling still remembered one of his two guiding principles about bids. A rights issue to raise £604 million, announced in August 1991, was at least in part intended to raise P&O's overt exposure to property: the Pall Mall joint vehicle with Elliott Bernerd was to be unwound and the assets split between the partner companies.

Today Lord Sterling has moved away from the property world onto the larger stage of business and politics. He is more than a survivor of the 1970s property crash; he is the man who took the opportunity offered to him to make a reputation on which he could build a career altogether more substantial in the public eye.

7

OUT OF THE BACKGROUND

AS WELL AS the two protagonists of the last chapter who had to manage public property companies out of the problems of the 1970s property crash and on to greater success, there are those like the two subjects of this chapter who came to prominence in the 1980s boom, even though they had been active in the 1970s. Neither man was actually responsible for managing a public or high-profile private company during the worst of the earlier crisis. Geoffrey Wilson and Elliott Bernerd did not command the attention of the media during the 1980s boom like many of the characters so far portrayed, yet their companies and activities were central to that story and, unlike some already described, they will certainly be important to the property market in the next ten years.

Geoffrey Wilson was born in February 1934, which makes him one of the senior participants in the property market. His early life followed what is clearly a pattern for several in this book. After school at Haberdashers' Aske's, he joined the agents Hamptons 'as post boy. Harry Hyams, [the central figure of the 1960s boom], was already a rising star there.' After the College of Estate Management, followed by National Service in the Royal Artillery, Wilson spent some years in private practice. One of his clients was Mason Pearson, the hairbrush king, who had a portfolio of properties in the Piccadilly area which he let on three- year leases, a very unusual prodecure in the days of 21 year and more leases. Wilson then started his own practice, based at 33, Haymarket. 'This was a wonderful location but it had Railway Lost Property on one floor and a private drinking club on the next floor, with my office right at the top. You didn't dare let anyone visit you but it was a marvellous address for a letter-head.'

The big step in his career was going to work for Gabriel Harrison at Amalgamated Investment & Property (AIP), which he joined in 1961. 'I answered an advertisement in the *Estates Gazette*.' AIP had been floated on the Stock Exchange as a public company only a year earlier. 'Gabriel introduced me to the world of very good reproduction Queen Anne furniture and plush Celadon green carpets; I suppose I got a taste for that too. Gabriel was a dynamic and charismatic character.' Wilson became a director of AIP in 1960 at the age of 26. 'I have been a director of a public company for 31 years, longer than nearly everyone else.'

In 1961 Peter Olsberg, Harrison's nephew, joined the company from agents Marcus Leaver. Wilson and Olsberg became firm friends and neighbours. 'We were doing quite a lot of business with Michael Gilbert and Stuart Lipton at Anthony Lipton.' In 1971 he and Olsberg teamed up with Gilbert and Lipton to form what became Sterling Land. The sale of Sterling Land to Town & City, described in Chapter Four, was fortuitous: 'there was no prescience' about the market. Sterling Land 'was a good company. Its development phase was over and Town & City sold virtually all its properties at more than they paid us for them; it was the company that kept Town & City afloat.'

Now without an executive role, Wilson sat out the 1974/75 property crash looking after his family interests in Equity Land, which, among other things had built houses in Hampstead, in one of which Wilson still lives. 'I had offices in Curzon Street and Stuart Lipton had the next office, but we had no property interests in common. Eventually we came together on Townsend House, Greycoat Place' which is whence the name of their new venture was derived. Greycoat's next venture, the refurbishment of the Lutyens designed Country Life House, exemplifies Wilson's claim that he has 'always been concerned about quality. We always had to go out to find or create our own opportunities' which included Euston, Cutlers Gardens and the Halcrow building in Hammersmith. 'At that stage everyone had forgotten about Sterling Land, and were confusing our record with that of Sterling Guarantee; Jeffrey Sterling had ended up owning both Sterling Guarantee and Sterling Land, and it was a waste of time explaining this to everybody. Since we didn't have the status, especially with local councils, we formed Greycoat London with McAlpines to give us presence.'

The story of Cutlers Gardens is told in some detail in Chapter Four, but the financing of the project was a critical factor. Geoffrey Wilson gives a lot of credit to Standard Life's Peter Henwood, 'a contra-cyclical investor prepared to back his own judgement. We needed financial resources, not knowing that Standard Life was looking at the project and we came together.' Greycoat's six per cent interest takes the form of one of the smaller buildings in the development, 5 Devonshire Square. Wilson reflects that the long letting period was not surprising to him, even if it concerned the market. He has a view of the larger properties which informs his development plans today. 'In big buildings there is seldom equilibrium between supply and demand; if you are looking for 250,000 square feet to rent as a tenant, there may be five buildings available at any one time. You discover that two are spoken for and, for some reason, the prospective occupier does not like one of the buildings, that leaves a choice between two. That end of the market is quite unlike the rest. I am constantly amazed that occupiers do not plan ahead. They could do very much better transactions, since it is of great advantage to developers to have a pre-letting on a development, but it doesn't turn out that way.'

The Buckingham Palace Road development above Victoria Station was another which took time to let. 'It follows the same pattern in buildings of this size: in the early days you let 20,000 or 40,000 square feet and people say "you've got another 440,000 square feet to let"; once you get to the half-way stage, everyone says "we always knew it was going to be a great success" and it's downhill all the way. You may know that you have the right location and the right building but you may have to wait for the rent to move up over the cycle. Meanwhile you may have to tread water.' Again this comment is still relevant to the attitude Wilson adopts with his developments and is a reason why, as we shall see, his attitude to finance has sought to enable Greycoat to tread water, but keep its developments rather than be forced to sell them on. The letting of the Victoria development was the occasion of a public row between Greycoat and one of its prospective tenants, the oil company, Conoco. 'Conoco was making public pronouncements that we wouldn't take £19 per square foot, which I knew was absurdly low. North American tenants come from an oversupplied market where the tenant can always dictate his terms; they expected like treatment here, not realizing that this is a totally different market where the landlord or owner has a far stronger position.'

Geoffrey Wilson has two prime guiding principles in his strategy. The first is his belief in cities, and the continuing need for offices in cities, rather than the fantasies of office workers being at their homes at the end of computer and fax lines. 'Frank Duffy of DEGW says people need offices as a place of "intellectual exchange". We will all end up like the reading room of the Reform Club [the first atrium building according to Peter Foggo of Arup], with the mechanical implements physically divorced from the humans. Cities are where one intellect is honed on another. It is not the same in Potters Bar or Basingstoke, because in a city, at different times, different businesses and professions become pre-eminent' whereas, Wilson postulates, in smaller towns the local trade can be decimated by a change of fashion or technology.

The second principle which differentiates Greycoat from many other developers is its search for ways to maintain its interest in its projects. In Chapter One it was shown how most merchant developers sought to make their profits: building, letting and then selling to an institution, since the initial rent will not usually cover the interest cost on the development. Wilson feels that this traditional method is faulty, even if a forward sale to an institution is agreed when 'seemingly the risks are small. Your stock-in-trade is your time and skill. You could spend three years on a development; if you were wrong about development costs, I always felt that was your own fault, because those were the skills you ought to be offering as a developer. But if your development came onto the letting market at the wrong time, that was something you could not control. Then you would have six months to lease the building, and if you didn't achieve that, or not at the expected rent, then your equity disappeared. Your partner would say "Well, you're a big boy, you knew what the deal was when you started", but you would have nothing for your time and effort.' Wilson has therefore been keen to build up the financial strength of Greycoat from an early date 'to be better equipped as a borrower.' There is no doubt that Wilson was upset by the combination of Rosehaugh and Lipton's Stanhope in the redevelopment of the Broadgate site. Greycoat and Rosehaugh had previously discussed the possibility of continuing their Finsbury Avenue partnership for the larger project.

The departure of Stuart Lipton was a surprise to Greycoat's investors, but both sides insist that it was a friendly parting. Wilson says that they have different working styles 'but we work very well. I have a great admiration for Stuart, he is the most professional developer. We always were a team, but he was a high-profile character, perhaps because he is taller than everyone else, so it masked the fact that there was a strong team.' After Lipton's departure, Wilson set about fulfilling his goal of being able to keep more of his company's developments. The first step was a bid for the quoted City Offices, an old established but rather sleepy company with interests as far afield as Lusaka, Zambia. Using Greycoat's shares to buy the other company reduced overall gearing.

Greycoat has been active in the US market, with more success than many. Its first investment, bought from the American Prudential Insurance, was an office on 6th Avenue, the Avenue of the Americas in New York. Later investments included a partnership with Sir Robert McAlpine and Lynton Holdings, the latter managed by Wilson's old partner in Sterling Land, Peter Olsberg. In the US it is often possible to cover the interest cost of loans used to buy a property with the income arising from its tenants. The US market has traditionally combined lower interest rates on long-term borrowing, a generous depreciation policy and higher investment yields. What it does not have is a pattern of long leases. The usual lease in the US lasts only three years, and the laxer planning laws, together with the vast size of the land-mass, makes it quite common for rentals to fall dramatically. A new building may spring up across the road from your investment to which your tenants will emigrate at the end of their leases, and there is nothing the landlord can do to prevent it.

In 1984 and 1985 Greycoat saw the completion of 1 Finsbury Avenue and Victoria Plaza. In neither case did the company have full ownership, but at least in the case of Finsbury Avenue, as was noted in Chapter Three, the issue of a long-term debenture enabled Greycoat to maintain its effective 28 per cent interest. Victoria Plaza was financed by Norwich Union and Greycoat London, the 50/50 joint venture between the company and McAlpine, has only a 12 per cent residual interest in the investment.

In 1985 Greycoat launched another bid for a quoted company, in this case two at once. Churchbury Estates had been revitalized by Oliver Marriott and some colleagues backed by London Trust and the Courtaulds Pension Fund. The Churchbury management had then bid for Law Land, another apparently undermanaged company with large holdings of property between Waterloo and Hungerford Bridges on the north side of the Thames. The Churchbury team had not anticipated the persistence of Sir Henry Warner, who had a substantial holding in Law Land. In his view the offer was insufficient and he did not accept the bid, even though Churchbury won acceptance of more than 50 per cent of the holders. Unusually Sir Henry and his allies held more than 10 per cent of the company after the offer finally closed. Under British law this prevented Churchbury from compulsorily acquiring 100 per cent of its victim. Churchbury took over management of the company, bringing in John Evans, a previous manager of the Courtaulds Pension Fund, as Law Land's manager. The outcome was not ideal for Churchbury. It was unable to use Law Land's assets as security for its own plans, and it could not pay all its subsiduary's revenue out to its own shareholders. The offer by Greycoat, at a more generous level for the old Law Land shareholders who had refused to sell out, was a tidy final act to this unusual impasse.

Geoffrey Wilson had identified one particular attraction in the new subsidiaries' portfolios: they owned land and property in Villiers Street, running alongside Charing Cross station. As a result of this ownership, Wilson approached British Rail with a plan to develop a new office in the space over the platforms of the station, which abuts the Thames. The building which has resulted, Embankment Place, is one of architect Terry Farrell's most successful, adding real interest to the waterside. 'I've always been particularly pleased about Charing Cross because I think the concept was mine' says Wilson now. 'There is great advantage in being a landowner. It's almost the seventeenth or eighteenth century concept which enabled wonderful country houses to be built, even if it meant moving villages which were in the way of the view. Embankment Place is an entirely satisfactory building. It is not just liked by the architectural and property circle, but by the public at large. Its scale is right and it has filled the space very effectively indeed. The office building is the commercial centrepiece of a much wider development. There are shops, the Player's Theatre and all the work we did to Embankment Gardens.' Embankment Place is 345,000 square feet of offices, which were pre-let in 1989 to accountants Deloittes for about £45 per square foot. Before taking up occupation Deloittes themselves merged with Coopers & Lybrand and the new partnership was negotiating to lease Rosehaugh Stanhope's Holborn development, but this deal fell through.

The initial income receivable on Embankment Place is not enough to cover the capital cost of the development, thought to be around £162 million (including an initial payment made to British Rail for the long building lease). Many companies would therefore have sought to sell the property and take the developer's profit. This is not the Greycoat style.

The development has been financed by short and medium-term borrowings of £135 million plus a zero coupon bond for the balance. This latter debt, which raised £21.5 million, is repayable in 1995; since it pays no income in the meantime, it puts no strain on the cash-flow of Greycoat during the time the investment it is financing could not meet the full interest cost of normal borrowing in its early years. However, in 1995 Greycoat is due to repay not the £21.5 million it raised, but £50 million, the increase being the reward to the holders of the bond for not receiving any income during its life. Unless the value of the property is above £185 million at that time, Greycoat will have a deficit on its original cost. That could happen only if there is no rental growth between now and then and investment yields remain high. A gross rent of £15 million a year valued at 8 per cent would give a capital value of almost exactly the property's cost and, unless interest rates are much lower in 1995, Greycoat will merely have postponed its financing problem.

In March of 1986 the company further increased its resources through a rights issue raising £37 million to take its market value to £175 million. Wilson then made one of his few obvious mistakes: he bid for and failed to win control of Property Holdings Investment Trust (PHIT). This medium sized property investment company was not, like the pre-Churchbury Law Land, run by property entrepreneurs but by conservative property investors; in one of the circulars sent out during the bid by Greycoat, Wilson observed that the PHIT's board, until a recent change, had an average age of 63. The two companies had been in discussions but they broke down. Wilson protests that 'I had never planned it to be a hostile bid; I have a great aversion to hostile bids. It was an eleventh hour breakdown [in the friendly bid talks], about the role of management more than anything else. All our horses were champing at the bit and someone said "charge".' The debate over the relative merits of the two companies centred on Greycoat's financing methods and accounting practices, which enabled PHIT to take the attack to the aggressor. Since PHIT managed to retain the support of its two major shareholders, Pearl Assurance and Foreign and Colonial Investment Trust, and Greycoat refused to increase its bid, the battle turned out to be a relatively bloodless victory for the intended victim, and only a temporary reprieve for the victors, since PHIT eventually fell to another bid.

Greycoat moved away from its avowed speciality of central London offices through the acquisition in 1985 of Merevale Estates. Through this new subsidiary the company developed shopping centres, but unlike the offices, there has been no attempt to keep these in the investment portfolio; the securing of institutional financing has been important. The major schemes undertaken include the Alhambra Centre in Barnsley, financed by Eagle Star, The Chilterns in High Wycombe, funded by the Crown Estate, West Gate in Stevenage, backed by Norwich Union, and the Crawley development funded by Friends Provident. The last-named insurance company now has its investment headquarters in a building on

Holborn Viaduct which was originally a hotel and had featured in Geoffrey Wilson's younger life. At that stage, when he was still an agent, the old hotel was being refurbished to become offices; Wilson had noticed that the attractive original door furniture was still in place and was going to be scrapped. He determined to save it from the scrap heap and add it to his own fittings, and set off early one Saturday morning to liberate it. To his chagrin he found that someone else had already had the same idea. It is a good indication of Geoffrey Wilson's character that he can good-humouredly confirm this story, even though it embarrasses him still.

The retail development which embroiled the company for several years was the Town Hall site in Wimbledon. Greycoat made planning applications in 1986 for both that site and another nearby which they had acquired through Merevale. Although local residents and conservationists preferred the Greycoat scheme for the Town Hall, the local council, Merton, favoured the Speyhawk scheme, and granted them planning consent. This permission was thrown into confusion by the spot-listing of the Town Hall by the Department of the Environment. A public enquiry was then convened, in the course of which the local Conservative Party lost control of the council. The planning inspector found in favour of Greycoat's scheme, master-minded by Terry Farrell, and the Secretary of State, Nicholas Ridley, announced that he was 'minded' to refuse permission for the revised Speyhawk scheme, which now retained the listed Town Hall. In July 1988, Ridley finally came out in favour of both Greycoat's plans. This was not the end of the story, since Speyhawk resubmitted plans which were approved by the Council in March 1989, and Greycoat finally announced its withdrawal of its application in June of that year.

The story is a sorry indictment of the British planning process. Speyhawk were first given an option over the Town Hall site in late 1984. Their plan was approved by the Council in April 1986; the Department of Environment set up their enquiry in June 1986, which reported in September 1987. Not until June 1989 was certainty established. Defenders of the system will maintain rightly that the final Speyhawk plan is much more acceptable to the conservation lobby, but the costs involved for everyone, the planning blight and the sheer time elapsed cannot be defended. What might have been a great economic success had it been completed in 1987 is likely to find times hard as it comes to fruition in a recession.

Wilson is not particularly regretful: 'It's not such a sorry saga in the end. The Town Hall site is being redeveloped in a form which is very much modified; I think a great many of the suggestions that formed part of our planning application have been incorporated. We still have our land, [the other site], and in their fulness of time maybe we'll develop it. That's the planning system; it's a democratic system and that's as it should be . . . but it does take a long time.'

In 1987 Greycoat completed two deals which exemplify both strands of its philosophy. It bought the ageing Moor House on London Wall, the infamous Route 11, and issued the zero coupon bond as part of the financing of the Embankment Place development. Moor House is one of the row of dominoes which flank London Wall and is clearly in need of renovation or replacement. Scottish Amicable had bought the property in only 1985 for £19.5 million from the Imperial Tobacco Pension Fund, had negotiated a new 125-year head-lease from the City Corporation and obtained planning permission for a new Farrell designed building of 450,000 square feet of offices and shops. Greycoat paid the insurance company £42.5 million for its interest, which certainly gave the Amicable a substantial profit. Payment was made in the form of Greycoat shares, which enables Greycoat to hold onto the building although its current income is only moderate. Greycoat are in fact asking Terry Farrell, whom in this case they inherited by chance as architect, to submit a completely new design for the new building for, as Wilson says, 'that design is five years out of date and we are looking for more flexible space.' In other words the years of vast open trading floors has, for now at least, passed.

1987 also saw the purchase of what is now Lutyens House on the Moorgate corner of Finsbury Circus in the City. In this instance Greycoat has reverted to its roots in rebuilding a property almost entirely behind its existing facade. This became, in the 1980s, a more acceptable form of development as opinion moved against the excrescences which had often replaced many humdrum but unobjectionable buildings of previous eras. Lutyens House was originally designed in 1925 by Edwin Lutyens as the headquarters of the forerunner of BP, the Anglo-Persian Oil Company. Greycoat had already rebuilt Country Life House, another Lutyens building. Wilson claims that the result 'is a demonstration that you can take an architecturally outstanding building and you can make it an efficient corporate headquarters. You also had the wonderful thing that BP have come back to it again.' BP had recently undergone a thorough purge of its head office staff, which had taken on some of the excesses of the meetings and memos culture which permeates the civil service, and was looking for a smaller corporate centre for itself, removing its staff from the massive Britannic House, a 1960s 'slab'. In 1989 BP agreed to lease Lutyens House's 192,000 square feet at an initial rent of £55 per square foot. The finance of this building is another example of Greycoat's distinctive style. The interim bank finance used to develop the building has been replaced by a stepped interest rate bond with a nominal amount of £150 million, repayable in 2002. The interest on a normal debenture of £150 million would be over £20 million a year at the rates of interest prevailing at the time the loan was raised, which would certainly not have been covered by the initial rent on the building, of under £10 million a year. The answer has been to 'step' the interest rate, like a low-start mortgage on a house. During the first six years of the loan, it carries an interest rate of only 6.25 per cent, rising then to 12.5 per cent; the initial rent now covers the initial interest charge. As a result of the stepped interest rate, the bonds actually raised only £92.5 million for Greycoat, but even so this was more than the total cost of the building.

The *eminence grise* behind Greycoat's financing is Richard Guignard, a figure well known in the City of London, but not by those whose contact with the property world is in the glamorous world of grand architecture. Guignard was originally company secretary of Sterling Land and rejoined Geoffrey Wilson at Greycoat in 1982. A bearded accountant with a stammer and a taste for rose-hip tea, Guignard is the despair of many of the accounting profession to which he belongs, and of property analysts. His view is that property investment is not like other businesses. The cost of interest and specific internal costs such as the work of a development team on a new building are to him capital costs as much as any bricks and mortar; conservative accounting convention has it that these should be treated as charges against the current income of the investment company. 'The purists cannot see the wood for the trees', he protests, 'no company can carry assets above their real value so there is a secondary test: the cost or market value, whichever is the lower. There is no difference between bricks and interest.' He is as firm in his opinions about how property should be treated when it is completed and let. The value at which a property is carried in the balance sheet should reflect any permanent diminution in value. 'Property companies are valued on their assets, whether it's taken above the line [in the profit and loss account] or below the line [through adjustments to reserves]. The deep discount finance enables you to stay in the game. If there is no rental growth over a sustained period of time then there would be other events: the interest environment would be entirely different [reflecting much lower inflationary pressures] and one would refinance. The whole game is to stay in the market and respond. It's the tiller you have to keep twiddling round to get the ship at the sharpest angle.'

Geoffrey Wilson has used this philosophy to enable Greycoat to undertake over £800 million worth of development in central London alone, of which his company is now able to retain much more than the original 10–15 per cent interests it used to have to be content with. Even the second phase of development at Victoria Station, carried out with Sir Robert McAlpine, has not been financed by Norwich Union as was Victoria Plaza. Again, upon letting the property, partly to PA Management Consultants and partly to the Department of Trade and Industry, the bank loans were replaced by £100 million raised from the issue of £125 million of 8.25 per cent deep discount notes. Wilson is quite honest about how the business is structured: 'The whole business is predicated on growth. There will be growth ultimately; you can't say with precision when it will be, but if you think that property has no growth, and is never going to have growth, then you can move on to something else. We are in a particular type of property with a particular type of tenant, and we'll get the best and strongest. The purpose [of the financings] is to allow us to keep the developments – we're there when the building comes into value.

It may come into value when you complete the building, if you've got the right point in the cycle; or it may be coming into value by the time you've reached the first rent review.' This concept of 'coming into value' is an important one for a developer. As we have noted throughout the book, the problem for the developer is that the initial rent on a property almost never covers the interest payable on its capital cost; if, however, the developer can hang on until rents rise to cover any reasonable interest rate cost, then the building has 'come into value'. The alternative is that the building is begun just as rental values are rising fast, in which case the initial rent may indeed match interest costs, but this happens only for short periods before the general inflation drives up building costs.

The Paternoster Square redevelopment is the latest challenge that Greycoat has undertaken. The unhappy story of the site's long subjection to planning blight and indecision is told in Chapter Two, but the financial and business logic of the acquisition from Greycoat's viewpoint is worth mentioning. The site represents one of the three Greycoat megadevelopments for the next cycle: Moor House, together perhaps with Roman House, another building on the Route 11 site (and built where the first German bomb fell in World War Two); the front of Victoria Station (currently the bus station) and Paternoster. Wilson will not start on them until he is satisfied that he has a good chance of completing them in a boom. By the end of 1991 the new wholesale development of Paternoster was thrown into confusion again by two decisions of the City Corporation. They gave support for a building planned for the Sudbury Site, on the north-west corner and not in the ownership of Greycoat and its partners, and sent back the master plan for reconsideration. 'They are the next cycle. A lot of the skill is planning for that. For 123 Buckingham Palace Road we had to tread water for two years, which is not easy to do when you have a partner. You are constantly trying to work out when you can come to the letting market again.'

Paternoster is a very complex development: important parts of it are not owned by the new partners. The cost is likely to be so great that even the ingenuity of Guignard and Wilson could not leave Greycoat as the only owners. The original cost of £160 million has been met by Greycoat in partnership with Park Realty, a New York investor headed by George Klein. Mitsubishi Real Estate joined as a third equal partner in January 1990. The complexity of all this leads Wilson to exclaim that 'sometimes there seem to be more people on the stage than in Iolanthe'; and in this case they are not all either Lords or fairies. In June 1991 Greycoat wrote off its £20 million equity investment in the development.

Geoffrey Wilson is still as enthusiastic about his chosen field as ever.

There's enormous enjoyment in what we do, I count myself lucky. I have to confess I have a love-hate relationship with architects; I say to my wife that I'm totally free of prejudice except against architects. There are not enough good architects to go round; you can name the top half-dozen British architects and you're dealing with some fascinating people. Farrell is a brilliant contexturalist; Rogers' idea of context is a scheme which would have removed Charing Cross – he's Utopian.

You can always be a rational detractor to a developer. You can say 'How will it happen? How will you get planning consent? How will you get possession? How will you let it?' All of them are rational questions, and the only response is: 'I did it last time, and the time before, and the time before, and the time before.' You really have to make things happen, the circumstances may be auspicious or inauspicious, but there's a lot of will-power and persuasion and diplomacy. People have different ways of setting about this but you have to be able to negotiate. That's why there is this fascination.

Where we are different is that we are both the architecture and the finance. They are both enormously interesting in their own rights, and it was a long, long time before it was recognized. Stuart [Lipton] and Godfrey [Bradman] were the ones up in lights.

It is possible to invent a future in which the financing that Greycoat has contracted in order to keep its investments will turn out to be a real burden to the company. Rental growth in central London has fallen back severely since Greycoat achieved the highest-publicized rental in the City for its development on the corner of Cornhill. That letting in 1989 to the Halifax Building Society at £67.50 per square foot of space might now be 50 per cent over what would have been achievable in 1992, so the rental values will have to rise simply to regain those agreed on Lutyens House and Embankment Place. At the same time, it is also possible, just, to see why long-term interest rates might not fall much from current levels. This would prevent Greycoat from refinancing at cheaper cost. But the combination of circumstances would have to be unprecedented. There may be some alarums on the way, but, by 1995, when most of the financing chickens come home to roost, who knows how strong the demand for London offices will be, or the cost of money? Such alarums were raised in December 1991 when Greycoat declared a net £8 million loss for the half-year to September. The share price began to reflect doubts about the ability of rents to rise sufficiently to meet the higher interest bills currently deferred to later years or to refinance the syndicated loans raised on Embankment Place in the bond market, although this latter was achieved in 1992.

Geoffrey Wilson himself underwent heart by-pass surgery in January 1992. The operation was successful, but he is obviously likely to be out of executive action for some time. He must have taken great satisfaction in the announcement at the beginning of January that Embankment Place had been awarded one of the Royal Institute of British Architects' National Awards for 1991.

Elliott Bernerd is another man with a long history of success in the property market in good times and bad. He started early, at 16, in 1961, leaving the educational 'crammer' he had fetched up in after an un-distinguished educational career, to join Dorrington Investment Trust, a small property company, where he was the office junior. The big break for Bernerd came when, at 17, he joined the minuscule partnership of Michael Laurie & Partners, two of whose four employees were the eponymous Michael Laurie and his son Stephen.

Stephen Laurie and Elliott Bernerd became inseparable friends and business partners, in a true business marriage. 'We were exceptionally close' says Bernerd. 'We used to work at either side of a dining room table in matching leather chairs', which Bernerd keeps to this day in his office. By 1970 the two young men decided to 'provide a pension for ourselves and decided that we should find a piece of property. We bought 15 Duke Street, St James's, which housed a tailor named Welsh & Jeffrey. It was an old property which needed either renovation or complete redevelopment. We put a new building on the site, let it and mortgaged it to the Legal & General. Having done it once, we decided to do it again and formed a little company which bought properties in New Bond Street, Oxford Street and Queen Street, Mayfair.'

Through most of his career as a property investor and developer, Elliott Bernerd has also acted as a property agent, advising clients on potential purchases and sales of investments and developments. Was it not possible for these roles to create conflicts of interest between those of the clients and those of Elliott Bernerd? Bernerd was aware of the dangers even in those early days and took care to meet that accusation: 'We bought nothing from any of our clients, they were arms-length transactions. In those days it was pretty frowned upon for a professional adviser to dare to have a position in property of his own. Senior partners of various partnerships had bought reversions on properties for their retirement' but, of the important figures in the market, only John Ritblat was simultaneously building up his property company and his agency. 'We decided that we would have a very up-front policy about this. We'd talk about it. One of the people we talked to was Hambros Bank. They thought about forming a joint company with one of their investment trusts: they provided us with what seemed to us in those days a substantial amount of money. We went off and bought things that we were used to buying except we bought more of them because we had more fire power.' The private company prospered with the property boom of the early 1970s and Bernerd and Laurie were thinking 'very, very seriously' about floating it or reversing it into a small listed company. One of the agency partnership's best clients was Barry East, then managing director of Town & City Properties. 'Following our policy of not being shy about what we were doing', East came to hear of the partners' plans. 'He said "don't do that, instead of going public, you're just what I need here. I'll take over your assets and I want you both to join the board and play whatever role you want within Town & City".' Already on the Town & City board was David, later Lord,

Young, whose company Eldonwall had been sold to Town & City, on whose behalf Stephen Laurie had acted.

Although Bernerd and Laurie joined the board as non-executive directors, they were active in helping Barry East expand Town & City rapidly as the property boom gathered pace. In 1972 Bernerd negotiated the purchases of both Charlwood Alliance and Sovereign Securities, and soon after Town & City bought Sterling Land, Wilson and Lipton's company, and, fatally, Central & District. 'As the problems of 1973 continued into early 1974 it became clear that some management changes were needed: Barry had to go. It had got completely out of hand; our non-executive roles were becoming more executive, largely fire-fighting. It was quite clear that, if anything happened to Town & City, which owed quite a lot of money to Sterling Guarantee Trust, that company would go as well – it was a domino effect.' The result was the reverse take-over of Town & City by Jeffrey Sterling's company, described in the last chapter. 'There were great difficulties that had to be dealt with: the executive duties of Barry East had to be taken away, and most of the board left. We left with a long-term advisory contract with Town & City. It suited us to give up our non-executive roles for which we were not being paid. We became very close advisors to the company in a vigorous campaign to de-gear the company.' Among the deals brokered by Bernerd and Laurie was the sale in 1978 of Berkeley Square House to the British Rail and British Airways pension funds for £37.5 million. In fact by that date the contract with Town & City had expired, but they continued to act for the company as agents.

1979 brought tragedy to Michael Laurie & Partners. On 27 February 1979, Shrove Tuesday, Elliott Bernerd and Stephen Laurie agreed to meet at Wiltons restaurant for the traditional pancakes. 'He didn't turn up but went home with a migraine. I spoke to him that evening and was called over by his wife that night. He went straight into hospital, into a coma on Wednesday and died on Friday of a brain tumour. He was 42 and left three children.' Bernerd was shattered. 'I found it quite horrific, we had worked together across the same table for 17 years. I threw myself into work, but I've never had another partner like him; we had a very special relationship.' The two men had already started buying again by this time, 'the same sort of quality pieces. We had an assortment of property investments limited by what we could walk to; if we had to take a taxi, that was already something which we would have to consider very seriously.'

In the next few years Bernerd's property direct interests were not growing rapidly and he concentrated on rebuilding the agency. As the property market began to pick up again as the 1980s progressed, he began to consider becoming more active on his own account. 'One of the people I had been close to for some time was Jacob [now Lord] Rothschild. He had been trying to persuade me to go public in something for some little while. I remember looking at all sorts of vehicles with him, including the Corn Exchange [later bought by John Ritblat]. Nothing ever really seemed to be right.' In 1983 Trust Securities came into view. Bernerd had met Peter Jones when Stockley Park was still a rubbish dump. He had also, like Stuart Lipton, spent time in the US and had become interested in the concept of the office park. While Trust Securities began its expansion, Bernerd 'took a cursory interest' in it. Then Peter Jones bid for the publicly quoted, but tightly family held Percy Bilton company. 'This was a grave error on Jones' part, and he was slaughtered in the press.' Trust, a small company already engaged in a very speculative and expensive development had tried to buy a large investor/contractor, which, although not the market's favourite company, had at least a reasonable track record.

Following the collapse of the bid for Bilton, Trust Securities began to meet difficulties. The merciless exposure it had been subjected to during the bid had weakened confidence. Elliott Bernerd began a discussion with them about perhaps buying out the Stockley Park project.

> Jacob [Rothschild] had the same interest as I did, and liked the location. As the year went by, Trust Securities' problems became worse and our interest in the London Airport project [at Stockley Park] grew. We decided to bring someone else into the concept. Stuart Lipton had just walked out of Greycoat and had told me he was going on a sabbatical for a year. I asked him to come and look at Stockley Park. To his credit he took an immediate interest. We decided later on that the more sensible approach to adopt was not to go for the site, which was far too complicated, but to take over the company.

The company was recapitalized and the share price moved up from 15p to 40p very rapidly. Roger Seelig of Morgan Grenfell joined the board.

> The work relationship between Stuart and myself went so well. There were acquisitions, joint-ventures, some quite good financings, some interesting developments and the company grew very, very strongly. We had originally hoped to achieve £8 per foot for the new space at Stockley, and now we achieve £32 plus. We did have difficulties with each other, but they were always settled behind closed doors, never publicly and we never had an argument at board meetings.

By 1986 the conflicts of interest between Stockley and Lipton's Stanhope were beginning to create problems in the mind of Bernerd. 'We had managed to avoid all traffic accidents but we instructed Warburgs and Morgan Grenfell to see whether we could achieve either: the acquisition of Stanhope, the removal of European Ferries as a major shareholder or an increase in my shareholding so that Stockley would be my full-time occupation.' At the time neither Lipton nor Bernerd were giving more than 50 per cent of their time to Stockley. In the latter part of 1986 and into 1987 the advisers were deep into investigations which were intended to see whether any of these deals could be consummated. They could not agree. 'I think one of the problems we had was that we were too friendly' says Bernerd. 'I was clearly interested in protecting the Stockley shareholders and Stuart wanted to protect his Stanhope interest.'

The Stockley board then received an approach for the company from the Hong Kong based Jardine Matheson trading house on behalf on its associate, Hong Kong Land. They wanted to make an agreed acquisition and the board of Stockley thought the outside approach might firm up Stuart Lipton's intentions. Jardine instructed their London associates at Robert Fleming and became more and more serious about the deal when 'up pops Tony Clegg, entirely out of the blue.' The fact that Stockley was trying to restructure itself was 'one of worst kept secrets in London', as was the fact that Stanhope and the company had not reached agreement. Tony Clegg felt that it needed a third party to unlock the situation and he was prepared to bid for the whole company. So Stockley was sold in May 1987.

The previous summer Elliott Bernerd had started a small family property company called Chelsfield. Following the sale of Stockley, this became his prime interest. In the period of financial gigantism which culminated in Big Bang in 1986, Morgan Grenfell had bought Michael Laurie & Partners, and Bernerd had been retained on a part-time contract as chairman, and had been allowed to continue with his own property investment interests. The relationship became strained, and when the Guinness take-over scandal overwhelmed Morgan Grenfell and Bernerd's old friend Roger Seelig, Bernerd left.

In December 1991, Bernerd appeared as a witness in the 'Guinness trial' of Seelig. Bernerd had approached a Swiss investor, Victoria Seulberger-Simon, who agreed to buy Guinness shares to support the bidder in its attempt to buy Distillers. She later bought shares in the other participants in the bid war, Distillers itself and Argyll, the rival bidder. When Mrs Seulberger-Simon decided she wanted to sell the shares, Bernerd informed the court, Seelig had asked that they be sold in an orderly fashion by Guinness's brokers, Cazenove, and 'there would be a satisfactory accommodation from her point of view'. According to the *Financial Times* report of the trial, Bernerd understood this to mean that she would be able to sell without loss; he had seen nothing unlawful in Guinness reimbursing Mrs Seulberger-Simon £1.9 million for the loss she sustained by holding on to the shares, or in the invoice for 'financial services'. Bernerd had another connection with the trial: his associate at Chelsfield, George Devlin, formerly a private detective, sat as a 'McKenzie friend' by Seelig's side for much of the trial. Seelig had decided to defend himself, and, in such cases, is entitled to the assistance of a friend who may make suggestions and notes. The trial was stopped after Seelig's health collapsed.

One of the classic deals of the 1980s was the round robin in which Chelsfield featured. Mountleigh had taken over 10/14 Stratton Street,

Mayfair in the United Real portfolio; the property was sold to Chelsfield in early 1987. Chelsfield promptly swapped this property with one in Berkeley Square owned by Eagle Star and sold the resulting acquisition to Mountleigh. This string of deals reveals Bernerd's great ability to see connections where no-one else does. It would have theoretically been possible for Mountleigh to carry out the swap between Stratton Street and Berkeley Square itself; it certainly would have saved that company some commissions. By late 1987 Chelsfield bought several properties from Mountleigh. Bernerd supports Clegg's assertion that the latter had turned cautious by the end of 1987; 'He had decided that he needed to liquidate quite a large part of his portfolio, for whatever reasons he had.' Bernerd took the view that markets would soon improve from their post-crash inertia, and bought 'a lot of properties from everyone' and traded them on.

Chelsfield had one prime object. Bernerd was determined to see how far he could go with a private company.

There was an intellectual challenge. I had more money than I thought that I would ever have in my life, but I wanted to see whether we could run a private company with the total disciplines of a public company. I also wanted the company to take advantage of markets when we thought they were there to be taken advantage of; to be able to hold and buy certain quality pieces of property which were capable of being developed for better purposes. There is an interest on my part in having a corporate team to look at corporate finance. The company expanded through the earlier period quite rapidly without the support of any outside shareholders. In early 1992 Chelsfield announced the introduction of new capital from institutional investors in order to complete the unwinding of the joint venture in Laing Properties with P&O. It now has activities in the UK, Europe and the US, where it has an office.

The group's managing director is Michael Broke, who had been seconded from Jacob Rothschild's activities to become the original managing director of Stockley before the Mountleigh take-over. Now that Chelsfield is part of the consortium which bought back Stockley Park from Mountleigh, he is involved in managing it again.

One rare failure in the Bernerd story was his involvement in Eddie Shah's ill-fated *Post* newspaper venture. It is estimated that Chelsfield lost over £4 million, as did Jacob Rothschild, Shah's other partner. The two deals with which Chelsfield has come to public notice could not have been more different. The first was the acquisition and development of Wentworth Golf Club. This prestigious club, at which the World Match-Play Championship is held every year, had for some years been in the ownership of the contractor AMEC. In August 1988 it was announced that Chelsfield and the quoted Benlox Group, one of the shooting stars of the 1980s bull market, had bought the course for £17.7 million, against the value AMEC had carried the course in its own books at of £2.5 million. The acquisition bought in 800 acres of land in Virginia Water, Surrey, heart of the stockbroker belt, and a further 55 acres were optioned. By the end of the year Bernerd had bought out his partner's 40 per cent for £12.5 million against their cost of only £2.5 million. The total cost to Chelsfield, which, with expenditure on the estate and interest costs amounted to almost £30 million, raised eyebrows. Those disappeared into the hairline when it was announced in 1989 that Chelsfield was intending to sell off 40 one per cent shareholdings at £800,000 per time. These shareholdings would bear some playing privileges and, since the Japanese brokers Nomura Securities were involved in the placing of the shares, it was assumed that this quintessential part of England was to be yet another British asset to fall to the new-found Japanese wealth, with Elliott Bernerd being repaid all his initial investment and left with 60 per cent of the course at nil cost and worth £48 million.

Elliott Bernerd has always been able to charm people, but this was probably his greatest challenge yet. A self-perpetuating group such as the members of Wentworth had always been, were not going to take kindly to some flash London property developer imposing privileged Japanese business members on them and 'destroying the club atmosphere' as the club captain David de Ville was quoted as saying. Bernerd's old colleague from Town & City days, now Lord Young and former Secretary of State for Trade and Industry, came to the rescue: a keen and good golfer, he returned from a trip to Japan with Prime Minister Thatcher with words of encouragement for both Japanese investors and the existing members. The Savoy Hotel invested in three one per cent stakes for its guests. Nevertheless, just before Christmas 1989, Bernerd went to the annual meeting of the club and addressed the hostile audience; it is no surprise to those who know him that he won them over. He reassured the members that their position was secure, and that his intention was to improve further the facilities. On way of showing the earnest of his intentions was the hiring as chief executive of the club of Willy Bauer, previously manager of The Savoy.

Bernerd's second coup of the late 1980s has yet to prove its worth. For some time he had been building up a share holding in Laing Property Holdings. This company, a sister to the contracting business, had substantial investments both in the UK and in the US, but had been assumed to be under the control of the Laing family and its various trusts, which between them owned 40 per cent of the shares. By the time Bernerd was ready to bid, Chelsfield had built up a shareholding in Laing of over 15 per cent. The over £400 million that Laing was worth was beyond the resources of even so resourceful a man as Bernerd, so his solution was to team up with Jeffrey Stirling of P&O, another ex-colleague, in a joint company, Pall Mall, which became the bidding vehicle. In terms of unlocking the existing shareholders, the timing of the bid could not have been better: on the same February day in 1990 on which the bid was made, a contractor/developer J. M. Jones went into receivership and Rosehaugh announced its heavily discounted rights issue. Investors were aware that the property market was no longer a one-way bet, and that risks were at least as great as the previous rewards. After a hard-fought battle, Pall Mall managed to prise away sufficient shares from the Laing trusts and other shareholders to take control. Whether this will prove to be a financial success will only become apparent in the fulness of time. It has certainly not proved possible for Pall Mall to pay off much of the borrowing it took on to bid for the company, as the cycle was by now clearly in its retreat phase. However good a deal Laing may turn out to have been in the long term, the further fall in values since the bid will have put some strain on the relationship with the bankers who financed the deal.

Elliott Bernerd is good at making friends. For a non-musical man, his chairmanship of the trustees of the London Philharmonic Orchestra may seem an anomaly. His enthusiasm and persuasiveness has carried all before him, and he has raised the funding of the orchestra sufficiently for it to bid for and win the residency of the Festival Hall. For a man who left a crammer at 16, he has certainly emerged from the shadows of estate agency into the bright lights of cultural patronage with gusto.

8

THE MERCHANT DEVELOPERS

THE 1980S WERE characterized by a new breed of property company: the merchant developers. In the 1950s and 1960s it was possible for a company to borrow long-term money at a rate of interest below the current yield on a property. It was probable that any rent review would be at least 21 years away, but it enabled the companies to hold portfolios of property. Even in the inflationary early 1970s it was possible for the developers to borrow short-term money at negative real rates, (below the rate of inflation), and let the resulting property at a rent which enabled them to hold onto their creations. By the end of the 1970s, the rigours of monetarism, followed by most of the industrialized world, meant that developers were paying very high real interest rates for long-term money. This made it impossible for developers to hold onto the completed developments. The much lower investment yields on which the completed properties could be sold to the institutions made it possible for a profit to be made by assembling, building and selling a new property. The problem for the developer was that there was no naturally recurring income, any more than Tony Clegg's successful trading in any year made it easier for him to repeat the exercise. Each development was a distinct profit-centre. As soon as one was sold, another would have to be found to take its place. As with Mountleigh, to show a profit progression, the number or size of these developments for onward sale would have to increase year by year.

Two of the largest merchant development companies of the era could not have been more of a contrast, either in their management or, ultimately, in their rewards to shareholders. London & Edinburgh Trust is the only company covered in this book whose management was run by Old Harrovians; the shareholder also benefited from the well-timed sale of the company to a foreign buyer. Speyhawk, on the other hand, was run by a man who had left school at 16, and just failed to be taken over by another foreign buyer, leaving its shareholders to go through the property recession on their own.

John and Peter Beckwith, the Old Harrovians, had each qualified, John as an accountant and Peter as a solicitor, at the end of the 1960s. In 1971 they met Arthur Bergbaum, who had been managing director of City Wall Properties, (later taken over by Rank Organisation and, in turn, by British Land). Together they set up a commercial property development company named Second City Wall; this name had to be changed in due course because everyone would ask 'what happened to First City Wall?' Later Bergbaum and the Beckwiths also formed a second development company, Lyndean. The timing of these ventures could hardly have been worse, since the business barely had time to start before the property crash happened. John Beckwith remembers those days with a wry smile: 'Christ, they were awful. Very quickly we had been up £3 million, then we we were down £3 million. We had to do crazy things. We had a line of credit from Twentieth Century Banking, [one of the leading fringe banks of the period], but they didn't have the money to lend us. We sued them despite the fact that we no longer wanted to do the development. They let us off a great deal of the existing overdraft which was secured on the land for this development.'

The Beckwith brothers had met an ex-patriate Romanian named Ion Ratiu, whom they helped with a property deal in Regent Street. As recompense Ratiu gave the brothers, as they thought, free office space in 54-62 Regent Street. As soon as things became really difficult, Ratiu presented the brothers with bills for the office space and the associated services. 'Instead of fighting him, we gave him shares in our company.' Ion Ratiu had acquired stakes in two other companies, Breakmate, the drink dispenser company, and Nissan UK. This latter was the company which, under its earlier Datsun name, Octav Botnar had set up to import these Japanese cars. At the time the idea that Japanese cars could take a substantial share of the market was as absurd as the thought today that Lada or Skoda might one day do the same. The investments that Ratiu's Regent House Properties made gave Ratiu a substantial fortune. No other property company can claim to have been at least partly responsible for the election campaign of a candidate for the Romanian presidency. In 1990, Ion Ratiu, by now well over 70, returned to his homeland to run as the candidate of the old Peasant's Party. Despite his obviously well-financed campaign, he made little impression.

In the mid-1970s the Beckwiths were forced to turn their hands to anything in order to try to earn a pound or two. 'We bought a lot of UN trucks and sold them to Egypt; we sent engines to Australia. We bought 45,000 pairs of boots from Brazil and opened a letter of credit to sell them to the Nigerian army. We went down to the container depot and opened the first container: they were all left-footed boots. We opened the second container: all left-footed boots. We didn't bother to open any more.' John Beckwith still doesn't know whether their pairs were in the other containers. A few years after this story had been published in a trade magazine, he was nervous enough not to want to find out whether his leg was being pulled when a squash-playing friend told him that a six foot two inch Nigerian army officer was waiting to see him.

The Beckwiths owe their survival over this period to the Bank of Scotland, who stood by them. By 1976 they were able to buy a bonded warehouse in Leith, Edinburgh from British & Commonwealth. The plan was to turn this into a 60,000 square foot office building. They took the plan over from Izzy Walton, whose Glasgow-based Scottish Metropolitan Property could not finance the deal. The Beckwiths persuaded the Scottish Mutual to lend them money at 14 per cent, fixed, and to buy the resulting building, when completed and let, on an investment yield of 10 per cent. This agreement by an institution to finance and then purchase a development, 'forward funding', became commonplace at the end of the 1970s. The Department of Health took the building on a 60 year lease. 'This deal saved our bacon and repaid our borrowings; it was one of the first forward funding deals after the bear market. That's why the company is called London & Edinburgh Trust.'

The developments that London & Edinburgh Trust (LET) carried out over the next few years were mostly of these forward financed developments, often pre-let to major tenants, but by 1979 the company was still a relatively small one, making profits of £600,000 from turnover of under £5 million. John Beckwith is disarmingly frank about the relative inexperience of the two brothers: 'Having not known much about it, we didn't worry too much about the problems. Professional property people used to worry about what was under the ground and survey it too much. They also used to buy the same old crap. By doing something a little bit different, because we hadn't done it before, and by thinking about it' they found success.

The target of their developments soon moved south. 'We did a 50,000 square feet bottling warehouse for Allied-Lyons. They wanted a floor loading [weight capacity] of 2,250 pounds per square foot. It was eventually built for them at 400 pounds per square foot, simply because we got engineers to do tests off-site to prove that they didn't need the higher loading. When an engineer came up with a design and you would say that it was far too expensive, go away and redo it, he would look at you as if you were absolutely mad. The old-style developer would have just accepted it. We used to come up with really crass questions. That, in many ways, is the way to run a business.'

By 1980 the company had discovered a new way to finance the larger developments which on its own resources it could not have espoused. It formed joint companies with two building contractors, London & Metropolitan with Balfour Beatty and Macwall with Tarmac Construction. Balfour Beatty is a subsidiary of the BICC group and its activities had traditionally been based in Scotland. For the joint company Balfour Beatty, under its Chief Executive Bob Rankin, put up most of the cash and guaranteed most of the loans. The first major venture was the Woking Business Park, a site bought from the BTR industrial conglomerate. On this 12-acre site the partners built 250,000 square feet of modern industrial space, which was subsequently sold to the joint Post Office and British Telecom pension fund manager, Postel. With Macwall the first major development was the rebuilding of the old Reckitt & Colman headquarters at Hogarth Roundabout on the Great West Road, Chiswick. This development, with a new business park behind it, was funded by Fleming Property Unit Trust, whose manager at that time was John Newman. In 1985 Newman joined the board of LET as director of retail development.

In November 1983 LET became the second merchant developer to be floated on the stock market. By now the company could show a record of 29 developments completed. Most had been sold on, but the company had managed to hold onto an investment portfolio worth £16 million, of which £7 million was the Ramada Inn in Reading, not the usual basis for a property investment portfolio, as the rent depended to a large degree on the future profits of the hotel. Since the company was to be worth a minimum of £27 million and had borrowings of over £10 million, it was clearly not the asset backing which supported the company's value.

The big carrot held in front of investors in LET was the profit it was going to make out of its developments. In the prospectus profits of £3.25 million were promised for the 1983 calendar year, and from those profits dividends would be paid which would give shareholders a return of 5 per cent per annum at the minimum issue price. With 20 further developments in hand, there was some expectation that the profits might be repeated. The potential home-run was the development of the now-empty Billingsgate Fish Market by the Thames in the City. The old market building and the lorry park beside it were ripe for an imaginative development, but in 1982 when the opportunity came to the Beckwiths the City was still recovering from recession and it was a huge contra-cyclical gamble. What is more LET could not hope to finance the development of 250,000 square feet of modern City office space, expected to cost around £70 million, out of its own resources or facilities. There was substantial risk involved. The tender price which LET had paid to the City Corporation could only be made economic if the new building was rented out at £20 a square foot. Beckwith and his advisers had noted that, since the onset of the mid-1970s crash, only Cutlers Gardens had been developed, and there was a dearth of good new space. However, prime rents in the area were then only £15, and it required courage to assume that rents would rise sufficiently to make the sums add up.

The Beckwiths were introduced to Ephraim Margulies, then the driving force behind S. & W. Berisford, a publicly quoted commodity dealing company. 'Marg' is a small, round, dark man with black-rimmed glasses, a strong contrast with the tall, lean and fair Beckwiths. Margulies and his company hit serious trouble in the late 1980s, with Marg himself being mentioned in the Guinness trial as another businessman who had been approached to support that company's share price. Eventually Marg was forced out of the control of the company which his drive and enthusiasm had done so much to build. John Beckwith and Marg 'hit it off very well, and I'm very sorry what's happened. Marg was very gung-ho about property' and Billingsgate in particular. Being a commodity man, Margulies knew well the area between the Thames and the traditional City locations to the north of Eastcheap and Cannon Street. Berisford had recently entered the major league of property investment by buying another office block along the road from Billingsgate for £18 million. In the first few years of the 1980s, this represented an exceptionally large deal.

The negotiations between the two men took a strange form: Margulies suggested that the company should be split on the basis of how many children each man had fathered. Beckwith could come up with only three but Margulies told him with a laugh that he had 11 children. The original deal was for the venture to be 50–50, but when it came to financing, even that was too high for LET, and the property company eventually took a one-third interest, limiting its equity investment to £6.7 million.

The design of the new building constructed on the old lorry park was controversial for such a prominent site on the Thames. Restricted by the need to avoid overwhelming the old market building, Covell, Matthews Wheatley planned two connected blue-windowed offices stepping back from the old market building, which was itself to be converted into a trading floor of considerable size. The old fish market's walls and floor had to be coated with special material to seal in the smell arising from decades of fresh fish being deposited upon them. It was said that, even then, it might take ten years for the old smell to be dissipated. The new block did not break any particularly new ground in style, and Stuart Lipton of Stanhope is rather dismissive of it. The entrance hall is in the form of an atrium, the bank of lifts rising through that space, which narrows as the building rises. In the original artist's impressions there was the clear intention to drape the external ledges created by the stepping-back with plants, but this has not been followed through. The occupants, the merchant bank arm of the Midland Bank, seem content enough with the result. John Beckwith does not believe that many of the buildings created specifically for the City's 'Big Bang' work any more; the irony is that the renovated market building remains empty. This was not because the Billingsgate group failed to let it. Citicorp took the building for its stockbroking acquisition, Scrimgeour Vickers, but before the building was ready for occupation, the US parent had changed its mind about the shape and size of its British capital market subsidiary, which has been run down. Citicorp is still trying to find someone else to take the old market off its hands.

The financing of the Billingsgate development broke new ground. Even before Godfrey Bradman had discovered its joys, LET and its partner had arranged to borrow £47.5 million from a syndicate of banks headed by County and Chase Manhattan on a non-recourse basis. In fact this finance was never drawn down, since, armed with the facility, Margulies was then able to borrow on more favourable terms on a normal short-term loan from his bank. The commitment fee on the non-recourse loan was £1 million, for money that was, in the event, never borrowed. The financing idea was similar to that used later by Godfrey Bradman on 1 Finsbury Avenue. Beckwith is sceptical about how non-recourse such finance truly is. Does he believe that a company can walk away from such a liability? 'You can as a very small player, but I don't think we can. A lot of these so-called non-recourse loans are really limited-recourse [whereby the lender has some limited further claim on the other funds of the borrower beyond the asset on which the loan is made]. The penalties for walking away are pretty harsh.'

The property was let at £27.50 a foot to Samuel Montagu, which had earlier considered doing the development itself. Both Beckwith and Margulies then needed to find a way of realizing the profit on the building, which was by now worth over £100 million; the number of buyers of individual buildings of that value was small indeed. For both parties, trading profits were an important ingredient. The US investment bank Goldman Sachs, familiar with such challenges in its home market, was retained to find a solution. The ultimate idea was the creation of a single property investment company, whose only asset would be the development. LET had already sold its minority in the joint company back to Berisford. 'Marg thought he could get a darn sight more than on my basis, so he bought us out on my valuation. At the time it made sense for us to take a profit.' In fact two potential buyers for the whole property were found, but Berisford persevered with its plan, selling equity in the development to a wide spread of institutions. In due course, Berisford bought out these partners too and sold the property to Samuel Montagu.

The public issue of LET was not a great success. Investors were not confident they knew how to value these new-style property companies. They feared that LET might find it impossible to repeat its undoubted success on a larger and larger scale every year, yet, on the profits forecast the shares looked cheap. In 1983 there was only Speyhawk to use as a comparator. One of LET's clearing bankers swore that if the issue was less than a triumph he would eat his hat. The issue was barely subscribed at the minimum tender price. Five years later, at a celebration to mark LET's anniversary as a public company, Beckwith commissioned a cake in the shape of a hat and put it in front of his banker.

The second large City development that the group undertook in its early years as a public company was in Ropemaker Street. Granada Group, the TV contractor and rental company, was the controlling shareholder of Barranquilla Investments; the major asset of this latter company was a rather dated office building, Britannic House North, tucked uneasily between the Barbican to its west and the BP head office complex of Britannic House itself to the south. Through London & Metropolitan, LET's joint company with Balfour Beatty, the property was purchased with the intention of knocking it down and replacing it with a totally new building. At the same time it was decided to turn the entrance and orientation of the building, away from fronting the off-pitch Chiswell Street, so that it would now face towards Moorgate station, a much more commercial prospect.

The Ropemaker property was funded by Norwich Union, which had been frustrated in its attempt to be appointed as developer of British Rail's Broad Street station site (now Broadgate). The offices were rented to Merrill Lynch, the American 'Thundering Herd' stockbrokers, and London & Metropolitan (L&M) made a substantial profit on the scheme. In November 1986 L&M was floated on the Stock Exchange as a clone of LET, managed by Rankin and his team. Stock Exchange rules are that a quotation is not granted to two companies where the management is the same and the value of the companies is based principally on the same assets. Since a good portion of LET's assets were in L&M, the Beckwiths had to give up management control, although both they and Balfour Beatty still owned 20.5 per cent each of L&M, worth over £10 million to each company in addition to the £17 million they had taken from the new investors on the issue. L&M was as aggressive in its plans as had been its erstwhile parent: developments were planned for St James's Square, three offices in Uxbridge and the complete internal rebuilding of the faded Whiteleys Department Store in a cosmopolitan part of west London.

L&M was solely and simply a trader of developments. The company preferred to identify the exciting sites, obtain planning permission and gauge potential letting demand. The building contract would often be arranged before the project was sold on. The company would thus avoid the highest risk phase, when the construction was under way but before a tenant had been signed up. It did not eliminate all the risks, since the sites it purchased were often producing little income, if any at all.

The Whiteleys store redevelopment, like the Ropemaker Street one, was indeed successfully funded, this time by a sale to Standard Life. The company shares moved up sharply from their initial price of 145p, so that, by September 1987 it was able to raise a further £26.6 million through a rights issue at 275p per share. Neither Balfour Beatty nor LET took up their entitlement, and their shareholdings fell to 16.4 per cent of the company each. LET sold its remaining interest in 1988 at 200p, which looked modest against the recently prevailing levels, to two investment institutions.

By the time of this last sale, L&M had, in July 1988, entered into the transaction which well-nigh ended the company's life. The Thatcher government had abolished London's upper tier of local government, the Greater London Council, and charged the London Residual Body to conduct an orderly disposal of its assets. Prime among these was County Hall, a fine example of Council Classical architecture, on the South Bank of the Thames, kitty-corner to the House of Commons across

Westminster Bridge. The County Hall Development Corporation, consisting of L&M, Lazards (the merchant bank), Touche Remnant Property Investment Trust, and New England Properties, was thought to have paid £200 million for the existing buildings. For its money, the consortium hoped to win planning permission for about 1.5 million square feet of offices, a hotel and flats.

If a month can be said to mark the peak of the 1980s boom, July 1988 would be a strong candidate. From the end of 1988, as interest rates rose and the bloom came off the economic growth rate, L&M found that its calculations were going awry. Although the consortium paid the deposit on the purchase of County Hall, the partners decided that payment of the balance owing would be throwing good money after bad; the consortium company thus defaulted. Although the involvement was relatively small beer for most of the partners, L&M's loss on the project was enough to damage its balance sheet and credibility severely. In one of the earliest examples of the desperate measures required to keep property companies from the hands of the receiver, L&M's bankers converted some of their loans to equity, and the shares are still quoted.

The Beckwiths had meanwhile been concentrating on building new profit opportunities after their coup in Billingsgate. In the 1980s they were among the first British companies to make a foray onto the Continent, a graveyard for most British investors in the 1970s. Two important buildings in Amsterdam were followed by a development on Boulevard Malesherbes in Paris. John Beckwith rationalizes the move because, by 1985, 'there was a hell of a lot of rivalry between ourselves and Godfrey [Bradman] and Speyhawk, so we decided we ought to do something about that and go into new markets. The reason why people had not made a big success out of continental Europe in the 1970s is that they went in totally blind. Some of the British agents and lawyers from that period stayed on, so the quality of advice was very good. Richard Ellis, for example, are the biggest practice in Spain.'

The French redevelopment of the old headquarters of Empain Schneider was undertaken on the basis of a capital value of FF2,100 per metre, and the last phase was sold for FF4,600 a metre. 'We shouldn't have sold them, but we needed the profits, we were a trader/developer.'

In an effort to avoid the compounding problems of the merchant developer, always having to find bigger and bigger projects to beat last year's profits, LET invented its own solution. It launched a company named LETINVEST in 1987. This company was to be a vehicle through which LET could build up an interest in a long-term investment portfolio, financed by other people's money. The company's share capital was divided between ordinary shares, all owned by LET, and preference shares, mostly owned by investment institutions. The preference shares took 40 per cent of any capital gains, as well as a net dividend of just under five per cent a year. This was cheap capital for an investment company, and enabled LETINVEST to make a profit in its first year.

161

LET also picked up several other ancillary interests. It bought controlling interests in Kellock (renamed Rutland) Trust, a factoring company, and a quoted property company in Hong Kong. In 1988 the company acquired Owen Owen, the Liverpool based department store group from the Ward White Group for £35 million. The deal was property driven, but 'the idea behind it was that, when the property market did turn down we would have other profit centres, and if they could be property related, then so much the better.' Owen Owen had lost its independence to Ward White in the mid-1980s, and had rather lost its way in the department store market. LET sold the stores in Shrewsbury, Bath and Chester, thereby recouping all the purchase price, leaving 16 freehold shops still in hand.

One of the most notorious eyesores of the 1960s development boom is the Bull Ring Centre in Birmingham. Compared with the bustling street market to be seen in old photographs, this windswept, concrete island in the road system has long been deemed a failure. LET bought the property from Laing Property in 1987. There have been 33 designs for the redevelopment of the site, but none have yet been undertaken. LET is looking a few years into the future for the project, into which it intends to bring partners; meanwhile it is a high-yielding investment.

The other major development by which LET will be finally judged is Spitalfields. The old fruit market on the east side of Bishopsgate has now closed, and the competition to redevelop it was fierce in the height of the property boom. The two major competitors were groups headed by LET and one for which Godfrey Bradman of Rosehaugh acted as spokesman. Spitalfields has an extraordinary mix of residents. In some of the old Huguenot weavers' houses are bankers and the artists Gilbert and George. In the roads which flank the market there are the Bangladeshi immigrants who have taken over the old haunts of the Jewish immigrants of the turn of this century. The competitors for the Corporation of London's nod as developers were keen to be seen to be consulting the local residents and several public meetings were held. There is a story, no doubt apocryphal, that at one of these Godfrey Bradman rose to address the gathering: 'I was born in this area – like you. I went to school around here – like you. I am like you.' When it came to Peter Beckwith's turn to speak, he said: 'I was born in a terraced house – in Eaton Square, I was educated at the local school – Harrow; I am not like you at all.'

Whatever the truth of this, it made no difference to the Corporation's decision. In 1987, LET's Spitalfields Development Group was selected as the developer of the 11-acre site. LET's two partners are County & District, a subsidiary of the Costain construction group, and Balfour Beatty, LET's old partners in L&M. As mentioned in Chapter Two, the developer's most recent plans have involved Benjamin Thompson as master planner. This is likely to create a more classical centre to the site, with modern offices like a canyon on the western edge facing Broadgate. LET plan to start development on the project with an eye on the next potential period of shortage of office space in the City area. Beckwith says that 'detailed research suggests that there will be a balance of supply and demand in 1995.' That may be optimistic, but, like Geoffrey Wilson of Greycoat, LET is thinking contra-cyclically, and it is likely to be around to benefit when rents do finally rise again.

The reason why that statement can be made with such confidence is because the Beckwith brothers executed one of the great coups of the 1980s property market: they sold their company at the peak of the market. John Beckwith tells how it happens: 'In October or November 1989, we had asked Lazards, [the merchant bank], to do an exercise to see whether it would be better to break LET down into different companies, or to find a very large shareholder. We had already been approached by Japanese companies. At the same time, SPP had asked Lazards to do a complete review of the London quoted property scene, because they had "x" amount of money which they wanted to put into continental property.' SPP is a Swedish mutual life assurance company with assets of over £12 billion; it is the largest provider of private pensions in Sweden. As described in Chapter Ten, Sweden relaxed its exchange controls in 1989, and Swedish institutions made the most of the opportunity. Lazards reported back to the Swedes that the only company they should buy was LET, because of its spread of European developments.

According to Beckwith, 'the Swedes said: "let's get on with it", but Lazards pointed out that they were already acting for us.' The bid was therefore made by Baring Brothers on behalf of SPP in April 1990, valuing the ordinary share capital of LET at £491 million, and each Beckwith brother's personal holding at about £40 million. The share price of 220p represented an almost ten-fold increase over the narrowly successful tender price of the equivalent of 24p in December 1983: the brothers had timed both their entrance and their exit impeccably. They still manage the company for SPP, and the quality of their developments and investments is certainly unquestioned. Whether the company would command the same price today is altogether a different proposition. In April 1992 LET announced losses of £138 million, caused largely by a £121 million write-down of such investments as the Birmingham Bull Ring and Spitalfields.

The contrast between the Old Harrovian Beckwith brothers and Trevor Osborne of Speyhawk could hardly be greater. Osborne's father was a toolmaker who came from Northern England in the 1930s, and Osborne himself was determined to leave school at 16, in 1959. 'I didn't know what I wanted to do, and I hadn't reached any conclusion when my father saw me reading the local newspaper. "What are you reading?" he asked. "I'm just looking at the houses for sale". "You know you do that every week, don't you?" It was the first realization that I found property interesting, quite by accident. "Why don't you be an estate agent or valuer?" '.

The young Osborne promptly rang up to find out about the chartered surveyors. 'I found it quite difficult to get a job in property unless you were either from a public school or Jewish; you didn't have to be very bright. I didn't have too many offers from the private sector, who were not impressed with my seven "O" levels.' His first job was with Middlesex County Council. 'I remember feeling that the public sector was a good place to train, and there wasn't a finer place to train than Middlesex.' Osborne found it easy to progress. 'Local government was being reorganized, and Middlesex folded in 1965. For the two years prior to that, many of the officers, concerned about their future or not wanting to work for the new GLC, began to seek other jobs. 'All I had to do was to find out who was going for interviews, then go off to see the boss. I'd tell him that I'd learned so much from working for Mr Jones, but now I would like to get experience of acquisitions or management of factories, and the person I would really like to assist is so-and-so, knowing full well that in three months he'd be off.' By being in the right place at the right time, Osborne would succeed to the post, if not the grade, of the pre-identified leavers. 'By the age of 20, I was South Area Estate Manager; the youngest anyone had been anything like that before was 38.'

Three days after his 21st birthday in July 1964, Osborne formed his first property venture. The first investment was a property backing on to the railway in Hounslow, owned by British Rail. It was a perfect place to build four maisonettes, but he bought it with planning permission for only a single house. At that moment a young man named Jeremy Denham, who had been seconded to the antediluvian Osborne at Middlesex, asked him whether he should buy some lock-up garages in Staines with the modest inheritance from his stockbroker father. Osborne suggested instead that his assistant's £5,000 would be better spent on his Hounslow project, splitting the profits. 'The art of development is to develop on someone else's site using someone else's money.' The off-the-shelf company used in this transaction, Glenglebe, was changed to Denborne, eliding parts of each principal's name. Even before the Hounslow deal was set, Osborne found the £5,000 burning a hole in his pocket. He bought a parcel of five freehold ground rents in Twickenham for £4,500. 'Before we actually exchanged contracts, I had set up the sale of three of them to the lessees for £5,000, so on our first deal we ended up with two properties and £500, less a few costs.'

The deal with British Rail in Hounslow was then consummated, and Osborne was successful in obtaining the much more valuable planning permission for four maisonettes. Having sold that on, the Denborne team bought a shop at auction for £6,000. The only problem with this was that there was only £2,500 in their account at Midland Bank, Carlos Place, Mayfair, and although that would cover the deposit, the balance was due in 30 days and there were no funds to meet it. 'I wrote a request for a loan and delivered it by hand the evening of the auction. To my surprise I didn't get a reply the next day, not even a phone call. The day after that there was still no reply, so I rang the bank manager. I wasn't even put through to him. After six phone calls and a week had passed and I had still heard nothing at all, I realized that I had to do something about it.'

By this time Osborne had left Middlesex, and was working for Aviation Property Consultants, a company set up by Ken Joiner as a project manager for airports. Osborne's office was at Heathrow Airport, and in some desperation he went to see APC's bank manager at Barclays.

'Mr Fox, I have another business; would you like the account?'

'Yes, I would.'

'You've just got to lend me £5,000.'

'When have I got to do that?'

'I need the money in two and a half weeks.'

'I'll have to get approval for this. Can you give me more details?'

As Trevor Osborne walked back into his office at APC, the receptionist was answering the phone:

'Yes, Mr Osborne has just come in. It's Mr Fox for you, Mr Osborne.'

'I've got approval for your loan; when can we have the account?'

'When can I have the money?'

'Now?'

'Absolutely fine.'

Osborne did not even take his coat off but walked straight back, signed the papers and moved the account. 'I still bank with Barclays today.'

After Osborne had been at APC a year, Ken Joiner was re-recruited by BOAC, which he had left to form the company, and he asked Osborne to take a 30 per cent stake and build the company up. 'It was interesting, but was not what I wanted to do. After six months Osborne left. The next five years were spent in transacting relatively small deals in Denborne, but in 1973 the partnership with Jeremy Denham broke up. Osborne had bid Denham £1,030,000 for his half-share, (a reasonable return on his father's £5,000 legacy), but Denham insisted on a break-up of the company. At that moment the 1970s property collapse hit home. Osborne spent a fairly miserable three years building out the development sites he had acquired.

In 1974 Osborne bought the contractors, Tellings, which managed projects for other companies. One of the projects on which Tellings was employed was for Fortress Estates, a company supported by the ill-starred London & County bank; its managing director was Derek Parkes. Soon after Tellings had been bought by Osborne, Fortress went into liquidation and Derek Parkes started on his own, building houses in South London. His main contractor failed and when Osborne visited him one day, Parkes was acting as general site agent. When Osborne suggested lunch, Parkes retorted that he couldn't, as he was laying bricks. Osborne had a better idea: 'Let Tellings complete this for you at cost and join me.' By 1977, Osborne had perceived his way forward: 'There was definitely a move by pension funds into property, particularly by supporting developers. I knew more than the funds did. Whenever I talked to these pension funds, they'd had enough of the property chaps with mahogany desks in St James's, a telephone and a Gucci belt but who didn't know which way up the bricks go. I knew about building and could manage construction. But the funds were worried that every company had skeletons in its cupboard from the crash, so I suggested that we start a £100 company with no history but a lot of experience. So that was Speyhawk.'

The first two years of Speyhawk's history, to 30 September 1978, is dominated by the activity of Tellings, but, thereafter, the Speyhawk development programme built up rapidly. At that moment, Speyhawk had a negative net worth, being in the process of developing some sites, but not having taken any profits from them. As a result, the company was in no position to hold onto the completed developments. Derek Parkes' role was to liaise with the banks and help find funds which would buy the completed and let developments. This deliberate strategy was distinct from that of, say Mountleigh, which rarely took a development through from site acquisition to completion and letting. Osborne saw his strengths as being a developer with an eye for a good prospect and the ability to build it to time and budget, for selling to a longer-term investor. The first deals were relatively small, among them 8,000 square foot offices in Teddington and Twickenham, parts of Osborne's old fiefdom as a Middlesex surveyor. Crown House, Windsor, one of two developments in that town, is a good example of these deals. The site was bought from the United Reform Church and planning permission obtained for a three-storey office building as well as a new church and offices for the vendors. The 11,000-square foot building was let to the Property Services Agency, still often the developer's friend, and sold to the Nestlé Pension Fund.

Speyhawk was among the first of the new generation of merchant developers to become a public company, in December 1981. The prospectus contains a list of 21 development projects on which the company was by now engaged. The largest, and most important, of these was the redevelopment of a bomb site in Jewry Street on the eastern fringe of the City of London. Speyhawk had negotiated the deal with the site's vendors, the Sir John Cass Foundation, and was under pressure to sign up, but 'we couldn't because we didn't have the cash.' The merchant bank, Kleinwort Benson, who managed the property portfolios of several pension funds, was introduced to Speyhawk. Tony Mortimer, who was responsible for this side of Kleinwort's investment business at the time, was well matched with Osborne. Another man born without a silver spoon in the family, let alone near his mouth, Mortimer had made his own way, and now cut a rather dashing Edwardian figure, with prominent side-burns and three-piece suits, from the waistcoat of which hung a gold watch-chain. Osborne, who is a similarly snappy dresser, was told that Mortimer was certainly interested in financing the development on reasonable terms, but needed to see some of the developments Speyhawk had already completed. Osborne remembers: 'He came to lunch and we were getting on quite well.' Osborne exuded confidence:

'Could we just have a little chat about the deal?' (implying that it was more or less agreed, which, at that moment it certainly was not). 'We're very keen to do it with you, Tony. Are you broadly happy with the terms? Is the proposed yield all right?'

'Yes, I think we could do it at that yield.'

'Fine. Can I ask you when the next meeting of trustees of the fund is?'

'You've just missed one last Wednesday.'

'Oh, I see. Do you meet monthly?'

'No, quarterly.'

Osborne's face dropped at this news, since he had undertaken to exchange on the deal rather sooner. He explained the position to Mortimer: 'I think if I don't sign within two weeks, they will do it with someone else.'

'Two weeks is a pretty short time, but I think we could cope with that.'

'How can you do that, you won't have trustees' approval.'

'It's my decision.'

Osborne warmed to Mortimer at this news: 'You can take that decision?'

'Yes it's down to me' said Mortimer, adding realistically 'they take it rather badly if I make a mistake.'

'How does this deal rank in terms of the size of transactions you normally put the fund into?'

'This is the biggest they've ever done, the biggest I've ever done.'

Osborne grasped Mortimer's hand and shook it: 'It's the biggest thing I've ever done too, so we'll both better be sure not to make a mistake.' On such relationships are deals agreed. As a result Speyhawk built a 36,400-square foot office building costing £9 million, which was let to Thos. R. Miller, insurance brokers, for £20 a square foot.

Speyhawk soon had a loyal group of pension funds which financed most of the company's developments. Findus and Nestlé both financed more than one project and other blue chip names such as Boots, Pilkington and Hoover pension funds were also involved. Like other companies, to keep the profit flow rising, Speyhawk had to increase the size of its projects and the risks associated with them. The Wimbledon Town Hall site competition with Greycoat has been covered earlier, but, with McAlpines, Speyhawk was also one of the consortia which bid for the right to redevelop the hinterland of Kings Cross station; that failure cost the partners £1.5 million in design and planning fees. The essential nature of Speyhawk did not change, even if the scale of operations did. The company operates from offices in one of its own developments in Old Isleworth by the Thames: Trevor Osborne sticks to his Middlesex training ground.

Among Speyhawk's successful developments during the latter years of the 1980s boom were 108 Cannon Street, and offices in Windsor, both sold to pension funds; the Jubilee Hall market redevelopment in Covent Garden was again financed by Kleinworts. The company's first large-scale incursion into the office park market, the 100-acre Thames Valley

Business Park on the outskirts of Reading, was partly sold to Digital Equipment and to British Gas, for the use of that company's exploration arm. Again Osborne was on home ground here; the development is actually in the Wokingham District Council's area. In the early 1980s Trevor Osborne had been leader of that council, although by the time the development was proposed, he was no longer even a member.

When the property market hit trouble, Speyhawk was still in bullish mode. Its largest development, 285,000 square feet of offices, over Cannon Street station in the City, was already under way, and, although 95,000 square feet of that was pre-let to the London International Financial Futures Exchange, the balance has proved hard to let. The problem was that against an investment portfolio valued at only £70 million in September 1989, there were development properties held worth a notional £140 million, with a further £105 million in joint ventures. Some of these projects were simply plans on the page, rather than buildings on the ground, and most of them were not offering income sufficient to cover their carrying costs. Against these assets was stacked £150 million of debt.

Osborne was not inclined to wait around for something to turn up. 'Nobody would have forecast the depths of this recession or interest staying at 15 per cent for so long. To all these people who have this wonderful, wonderful wisdom of hindsight I say, congratulations. I'm a market man. You have to face up to it: if the only act in town is a circus, you sell peanuts.' Osborne set about selling, not for prices he thought he ought to achieve, but for what the market would offer.

There were several large disposals in the 1990–1991 financial year. One Aldgate was sold to a Dutch pension fund for £45 million and One Hundred Square in Bracknell was bought by Middle East investors for £30 million. These and other disposals were not enough to solve the problem. Speyhawk's other plans, such as a shopping development on Sussex's old county cricket ground in Hastings, were lost by the company's unwillingness to progress in the market environment they faced. Even so, by 30 September 1990, Speyhawk and its joint venture partners had development properties valued at £200 million and borrowings of £150 million. Two development properties were written down in the balance sheet by £6.5 million; one was a West End development with unsatisfactory planning permission and the other was the development of a partly pre-let shopping centre in Weymouth. It would be well-nigh impossible by the date of the valuation to estimate what the 'open market' valuation of such properties was, there was so little appetite for development. In March 1992, Speyhawk announced a pre-tax loss of £217 million for the year to September 1991. Liabilities exceeded assets by £70 million after severe write-downs in the values of the company's empty or only partly let development properties, one of which in St Mary Axe was seriously damaged by the IRA bomb of April 1992.

Trevor Osborne negotiated a restructuring of the company's debt with its 46 banks, including its non-recourse loans. 'I have come to the conclusion that non-recourse debt is a concept rather than a reality' he was reported as saying.

All this misfortune was very nearly avoided for the Speyhawk shareholders, and Trevor Osborne in particular. In June 1990 the Swedish company NCC, part of the Nordstjernen Group, bought a share stake and began talks which were confidently expected to end with a take-over of Speyhawk. By the end of August, the Swedish buyer had withdrawn.

Trevor Osborne is another of the 1980s developer/traders who was simply unable to build up a steady flow of revenue sufficient to carry his company through the drought in the development market unscathed. Being caught on the treadmill of making greater profits on developments every year is not conducive to a comfortable life when the cycle turns against you. Nevertheless, Osborne remains optimistic. 'Property companies and the individual entrepreneur will be the major forces in property investment and trading. All the institutions are concerned with is short-term measurement. Deals being done today are not related to the old criteria; they are related only to the cost of money. The time is right for the predator.'

Although there were many other merchant developers whose fates varied from bankruptcy to survival, two other specific examples give a good illustration of what was possible in the boom years. Helical Bar is not a name which suggests property; its name betrays its original business of steel fabrication and stockholding. By 1984 the company had fallen on hard times. In July of that year Helical announced its move into property through the formation of a joint company with Michael Slade, who was to be the 49 per cent owner of the venture with options to convert that holding into a 29 per cent holding in the quoted parent. The market value of the parent company at that time was around £1 million and the share price had just lifted from its recent low level, equivalent to 3.5p each in their later form.

Slade was no newcomer to the property world. His very first job, in 1965, was selling plots of land in the Bahamas. In an interview in *Management Today* in 1990, Slade described the job as slightly dodgy. He had to pretend to be a rich and idle Brit, offering to act as guide to holidaying Americans. 'After two days they'd buy anything just to get rid of me' he was reported as saying. He learned about serious property development as an assistant to Julian Markham of the private Glengate Property company, whose most notable achievement in the 1980s was the joint development of the old General Post Office in the City with the Japanese contractor, Kumagai Gumi. In the 1970s Slade had then set up a joint company with Equity & Law to invest in Continental property. This venture, Grandvista, found the going rather tough, and by 1983 Slade had resigned as managing director.

After a year acting as President of the British chapter of FIABCI, the international property-owners trade association, Slade took his interest in Helical. If ever a merchant developer made its reputation with one deal, it was Slade and Helical. After two years of relatively modest property trading, Slade hit the jackpot. In April 1986 he bought the site of 48 Chiswell Street, Finsbury, from Whitbread the brewer. Planning permission was obtained for 100,000 square feet of offices in this fringe City location, facing the Barbican residential towers. The development had merchant bankers Lazards as minority partners, and finance was achieved through a non-recourse loan from the Californian bank Security Pacific. The total cost of the development, including site cost, was covered by this £24 million loan, and Helical's total investment was £100,000. The northern fringe of the City was then still considered a low rent area, even though Broadgate is only a quarter of a mile to the east on the same latitude. By November of the same year Helical had exchanged contracts for the sale of the development to BP Properties for a reputed £34 million, giving the company a clear £9 million profit on the project. For a tiny equity base this deal transformed both the profit and asset value of Helical. The share price responded with a rise to the equivalent of over 100p at their 1986 peak, up seven-fold on the year. Michael Slade's reward was a salary of over £1 million.

Helical's problem was then to convince investors that it was not simply another 'one-hit wonder'. The first move was to enter residential development partnerships in West London. On the commercial side Helical bought a £25 million investment portfolio from Allied Dunbar, and lined up developments in, amongst others, Leeds, Woking, Bristol and Cardiff. By this time in 1987, the share price had trebled again, to the equivalent of over 300p, which made Slade's shareholding, now converted into the parent company, worth over £20 million, not bad for an initial personal investment of £49. Slade had eschewed further deals in the City during 1987, preferring instead to diversify into industrial property, but, after the 1987 stock market crash, he showed that he could repeat the Chiswell Street coup.

Slade was in good financial condition at the time of the crash, since, only days before, Helical had secured the issue of £18 million in preference capital. His first two purchases after the stock market collapse were industrial estates, the Aycliffe & Peterlee New Town's portfolio and a property at Biggin Hill airfield in Kent. In June 1988, Helical returned to the fringes of the City of London for its second coup. The company bought, for £11 million, a development site from P&O, facing onto the roundabout where Old Street meets the City Road, well beyond the accepted location even for fringe City offices. The site was to bear offices of 165,000 square feet, but, before much work was done, Helical had sold the property for another remarkable and rapidly earned profit. Again the buyer was BP, which was leaving its base in Britannic House. The price paid by BP was a reputed £62 million, on the basis of the building work being completed. The profit to Helical Bar was £11 million. BP never occupied the building, and, in late 1991, sold it on to Inmarsat for under £50 million.

The proceeds of Helical's deal were reinvested in more industrial property. To complete a hat-trick of deals with parts of BP, Helical Bar bought the South Wales industrial and agricultural properties of Western Ground Rents. This latter company had been acquired by BP's pension fund twenty years earlier, in one of the first forays by a pension fund into the market to buy a complete property company. By early 1989, Helical owned five million square feet of industrial space around the nation.

Even though the property market had by now clearly moved into its recession, there was little sign of it in either Helical's profits or its ambitions. In April 1990, Slade announced that profits of his company, for the year ended on 31 January, had risen to £14.5 million, and net assets had improved by 43 per cent to 429p a share. The company had acquired smart Mayfair offices for its own use, and borrowing had risen to £140 million, 150 per cent of the company's equity. The ambition was to sell enough assets to reduce this level of gearing to a more reasonable, but still high, 100 per cent.

The company proved not to be immune from the recession. Profits in the year to January 1991 fell to only £2.5 million, and net assets of this highly geared company fell by almost one third, leaving the gearing even higher at over 200 per cent. By October 1991, Slade was forced to announced a loss for the half-year to July. Although Slade had previously exuded confidence, claiming, with some justification, that the bottom of markets is the best time to be highly geared, he now blamed high interest rates for the set-back. Continuing asset sales suggested that the gearing of 170 per cent remained uncomfortable, and, despite the rising rent roll coming from the industrial investments, further sales would have to be made.

Helical Bar showed what could be done in the short term with a small, shell property company with some judicious gearing and one or two wonderful deals. There is no reason to suppose that Michael Slade's touch will not provide further stunning profits in a better market; meanwhile his company simply has had to cut its coat according to much less generous amounts of cloth.

Perhaps the most astonishing comet of all those that lit up the property heaven in the late 1980s was Randsworth. Randsworth's origins go back to a tea company named Kotmalie. In 1980 it had been bought into by new controllers who turned the company into a plant-hire group called Jayplant. Its arrival on the infant USM was not followed by great success, and in May 1986 the company had net assets of only £400,000. At that time a new management team arrived: David Holland and Andrew Nichols. Holland is a lawyer who had been involved with the Frost Group of petrol retailers, whereas Nichols had earlier been finance director of the Brixton Estate property investment company. Holland and Nichols sold to Jayplant, now renamed Randsworth, an oil company and some minor property interests from their private portfolios. They toyed with the idea of specializing in the management of nursing homes, but the property development they were involved in, like Helical's Chiswell Street project, dwarfed all their other interests. Randsworth had bought a site in Wilson Street, on the edge of the Broadgate site, for a mere £1.4 million. The combination of achieving planning permission for 60,000 square feet of space, (initially not all of it for offices) and rapidly rising rents, created the sort of surplus which had set Michael Steel's company into orbit. The potential profit when completed and let was estimated to be over £15 million.

Unlike Helical, Randsworth became an aggressive buyer of other companies. In March 1987 Holland launched a bid worth £60 million for London & Provincial Shop Centres (LPSC). At the time Randsworth's own assets were worth only £10 million. LPSC was a company formed in the 1950s, but in recent years it had belied its name and become closely identified with offices in Slough. Much as Tony Clegg had convinced Maurice Wohl that he was the right man to sell to, David Holland learned that control of LPSC might be available from the original partners; Bernard Berrick was, by this time, like Wohl, a tax exile. Holland flew to see him in his retreat in Monte Carlo and convinced Berrick of his ability to underwrite a deal for cash. With the Randsworth shares standing so far above the company's asset value, any addition to assets paid for by shares would increase the bidder's overall asset value per share. This phenomenon was one recognizable to the asset strippers of the 1960s stock market boom. The American bank Chase Manhattan's British investment house underwrote the shares so that LSPC holders could either take cash of 325p a share or Randsworth shares worth a fraction more. Since LSPC's asset value was then 350p, the discount was relatively modest, and a sale was attractive to most holders. Taking Randsworth shares was a more doubtful prospect, since the company's asset value at the time of the bid was only 73p, but its share price was around 150p. The purchase of LPSC almost doubled that net asset value to 134p.

Not content with the LPSC acquisition, Randsworth followed it almost immediately with the purchase of Apex Property, a company firmly in the control of the de Vere Hunt family. In the early 1980s, Courtauld's Pension Fund, which this writer was then running, had built up a modest shareholding in Apex. This was not in fact too prescient a purchase because Apex had not benefited strongly from the property boom. Its major assets were two large office blocks at New Malden, near the Kingston by-pass in south-west London. Parts of these blocks had been untenanted for some time after their refurbishment. Between 1981 and 1986 the share price of Apex had more than halved; despite paying 135p per share, 60p above the low point, Apex cost Randsworth less than £15 million in cash. Randsworth's assets now totalled £60 million.

Randsworth soon used the asset base of LPSC to issue £50 million in long-term debt, giving the company more ammunition for its ambitious targets. In July 1987, the group acquired several properties of that same value, the major asset of which was an office on the northern fringe of the City, between Greycoat's Devonshire Square and the Spitalfield site, for £20 million; the purchase was partly financed by a further issue of shares. By now the company was worth £120 million on the Unlisted Securities Market.

Holland and Nichols signalled their continuing interest in quoted companies by buying an eight per cent stake in Lynton. This stake was later raised to 19 per cent after the 1987 stock market crash. Lynton was eventually acquired by the newly-privatized British Airports Authority, BAA. Randsworth's next big property deal was worth £132 million, the purchase of two portfolios, from Mountleigh and British Land. Among the Mountleigh properties was the Sloane Street one which was now halfway through its six owners in five years. Most of the property was in the West End of London, (in Sackville Street and St Martin's Lane for example) or in Kensington (British Land's old Derry & Toms investment). To pay for this further substantial investment, Randsworth issued another ten million shares at 217p and £50 million of new convertible preference shares, but the total cash raised by this means, just over £70 million, left a gap which was filled by a loan from Chase. What was most striking about these purchases was that the income from the properties by no means covered the cost of the finance raised. Randsworth was thus forcing itself either to sell some of them at a profit fairly quickly, or to raise the rents on the properties.

September 1987 was also a busy month, appropriate for the last month of the great bull market in shares. The good news for Randsworth was that a tenant had been found for its initial coup, the Wilson Street development. In fact the tenant who was supposed to take the space never did so, but Randsworth found the International Stock Exchange was equally eager to take the space at a then record rent for the location, beyond even the purlieus of Broadgate. The property, which cost just over £1 million to buy and a further £12 million to build, was now valued at £40 million, justifying the initial excitement the development generated. By now, of course, Wilson Street was only a small part of Randsworth's assets. A further West End property was acquired when Randsworth spent £15 million buying Prospect House in New Oxford Street from the textile group Lister. The property was let to the Ministry of Defence, but their lease expired in 1990, giving Randsworth hope of either redevelopment or a new lease. Another development site acquired was Gotch House in Farringdon Street, the edge of the Fleet Street area, bought from the *Daily Telegraph* for £7 million.

The results of the frenetic activity undertaken by Holland and Nichols in their year of stewardship were shown in Randsworth's results for the 13 months ending 30 June 1987, announced just over a week before Black Monday. Pre-tax profits rose to £2.15 million from £700,000 and net assets from 110p to 161p. The balance sheet also showed that there was almost

£50 million of debt due to be repaid within 12 months. In January 1988 this problem was relieved to a degree by the arrangement of a £100 million five-year loan, secured on £160 million of the property portfolio.

In the immediate aftermath of the stock market crash, Randsworth continued to buy property. By March 1988 the emphasis of the company's activities had clearly swung towards selling. Some of LPSC's properties in Slough were sold, and at prices below book value. Andrew Nichols was unrepentant: 'When we bought London & Provincial Shop Centres we knew that the portfolio was fully valued.' He defended the purchase as the way in which Randsworth could be transformed rapidly from an asset poor, but high flying small company into a large property market player. Between December and March 1988 Randsworth sold £70 million worth of investments, and in April and May a further £46 million was realized. The group was able to increase its long-term debt still further through another issue of LPSC's debenture stock: £35 million was raised in June. By the end of the company's financial year in June 1988, over £150 million had been raised from property sales over the previous year. Most of the Slough properties of LPSC and all but two of Apex's investments were amongst those disposed of; the investment portfolio was now valued at £307 million. Randsworth's share price had been a notable casualty of 19 October 1987. At one point the shares fell to 80p, against the published net asset value of 215p, but by October 1988, it had recovered to over 180p again. Part of the reason for this recovery was the acquisition of a 5.1 per cent shareholding in the company by another of the decade's new property companies, Markheath.

David Holland then proposed to buy up half the outstanding shares of Randsworth at around the prevailing price. As this was well below the net asset value, every share bought would increase the assets attributable to the remaining shares, a sort of tontine. Unfortunately the purchase would have to be made with borrowed money, increasing both the gearing of the company and the interest burden. The scheme was a short-term psychological boost to the shares, but proved impossible to carry out in the event. Net sales of property seemed to be the only way forward: the Wilson Street development was sold to the Japanese for about £40 million.

By the end of 1988, despite the avowed intention of reducing the debt levels, Randsworth's shares had still proved to be one of the outstanding investments of the pre- and post-crash periods. From a price of 68p at the end of 1986 the shares had now recovered towards their previous high levels, and closed the year at 212p, at which level the company was worth over £125 million. In January 1989 £32 million more was raised through a further issue of LPSC debenture, and this money was soon put to work in an apparent reversal of the previous cautious stance. Randsworth bought St Christopher's Place, a shopping 'village' north of Oxford Street, which had been developed by Imperial Tobacco Pension Fund as an area of chic boutiques and restaurants with offices above them. A property adjoining St Christopher's Place whose façade is on Oxford Street itself was later acquired for £17 million, increasing the possibility of widening the very narrow access currently available into the shopping village from the busy main street. Again the income from the investment, about £2 million a year, by no means covered the interest cost of the capital used. Andrew Nichols asserted that the development was 'quite under-let in our view, and there's quite a bit of redevelopment potential.' This purchase was followed by the acquisition of a fire station in King's Road, Chelsea for £6 million with the intention of developing a shop and office development. These purchases were not offset by a few sales concluded in addition to that of Wilson Street.

By the end of March, Markheath had sold its 10 per cent stake in Randsworth to the Swedish group Reinhold, which, as will be apparent from Chapter Ten, had substantial ambitions in the British property market. A smaller merchant developer, Priest Marians, had also bought a small stake. These new shareholders were greeted by the good news that the Ministry of Defence had agreed to take a new lease on Prospect House, New Oxford Street, at an initial £2.63 million a year, giving a substantial surplus income over the interest cost on the £15 million purchase.

May brought a shock: David Holland, one of the two principal protagonists of the transformation of the company, abruptly resigned for 'personal reasons', thought to be his failure to persuade the board to sell Randsworth to his favoured bidder. The share price of Randsworth had by this time recovered still further to almost £3, giving it a value of over £160 million. Reinhold took the opportunity of this surprise to increase its stake to 16.9 per cent of the company, and Randsworth was now clearly 'in play'. The *coup de grace* was executed in late July with an agreed bid for the company from an American property manager, JMB Realty. In April Randsworth had asked the American investment bank, Goldman Sachs, to search discreetly for a 'white knight', a friendly bidder for the company. 'We didn't want to end up waiting for bids and being raped by a hostile bidder, but wanted to find someone to work with us,' said Andrew Nichols at the time. The total value of the bid was £258 million including the preference shares, and priced the ordinary shares at 325p, almost five times the price at the end of 1986. JMB is a huge Chicago-based property investor, founded in 1968 by Robert Judelson, Judd Malkin and Neil Bluhm. The group was attracted to the UK by its unique lease structure and by the location of the Randsworth portfolio, almost exclusively in London's West End, an area with which most Americans are already familiar.

Randworth's story is one of perfect timing from the point of view of the British investors. The company made big gains when the market was buoyant, and, like LET, was able to attract a foreign buyer at a time, late summer 1989, before interest rates took their last upward lurch and the recession took hold. In March 1992 administrative receivers were appointed to the company which JMB had formed to make the

Randsworth acquisition, and into which the purchaser had injected a further £58 million in early 1991. The comet had fallen back to earth.

David Holland soon resurfaced as the power behind Nash Industries, afterwards renamed Grovewood Securities, in which he hoped to repeat the success of Randsworth. Among his purchases for his new vehicle was Priest Marians, Randsworth's erstwhile investors. Grovewood had bought its initial 23.4 per cent stake in its target at 300p a share, but the balance was bought at a price which valued Priest at only £5 million in November 1990; this rescue bid came after the departure of Priest Marians' chief executive, Simon Fussell, in August 1989, at which stage he had sold his 25 per cent stake to JMB Realty at 375p a share. The final Grovewood bid was worth 36p each. Grovewood also bought Early's of Witney, the manufacturer of blankets and occupier of substantial development sites.

In this company, Holland had overstretched and, by October 1991, receivers had been called in to the company. The shares had already been suspended on the Stock Exchange and the company's borrowings, at over £100 million, had breached its banking covenants. The major problem for Grovewood had been the Priest Marians purchase. Although that company bought with it assets such as the Langham Estate north of Oxford Street, previously in the hands of both British Land and the Water Industry pension funds, it had itself previously bought another company, Local London, for £110 million in March 1989. Local London was one of the first developers to offer serviced office suites to small or new companies. The landlord would provide furniture and equipment for a weekly all-in rent. In the years of the late 1980s, many new companies were being formed and such office space suited the entrepreneurs well; LET had a similar subsidiary. The recession of 1990/91 both made new entrepreneurs a rarity and put many other recent venturers out of business. Local London then began to make substantial losses. Grovewood subsequently issued a claim for £57 million in damages from stockbrokers James Capel, who had advised Priest Marians in its purchase of Local London.

The ability of such merchant venturers as have been described in this chapter to create substantial public companies from empty shells is not unique to the 1980s property boom. This recent cycle was probably more extreme in its creation and destruction of assets even than the mid-1970s, and was certainly more concentrated in time span. There were many other smaller examples of both success and failure, often in the same companies at different moments, but these four examples show what was possible.

9

THE SPACE INVADERS

THE FOCUS OF most of this book has been London. The reason for that is simple: the value of London property, particularly of offices, is so much higher than in any other centre that property investment and development is peculiarly Wencentric. The exception to this general premise is in retailing, where high capital values can be created in provincial cities.

The 1980s saw a revolution in UK retailing, both in the High Street and in the periphery of cities. The High Streets of most cities had been dominated for all the post-war period by the department store chains, Debenhams and House of Fraser being prime among those, and the well-known multiples, with Marks & Spencer and Woolworths to the fore. The old food retailers, such as Home & Colonial and the Co-op, had already lost their position to the 'pile it high and sell it cheap' philosophy of Tesco, and the 'Fifty Shilling Tailor', Burtons, and Hepworths had been overtaken in their markets during the 1960s by the fashion boutiques. The 1980s witnessed a change of attitude among consumers which reflected the growing demand for a recognizable life-style to match their rising aspirations. Burtons and Hepworths fell under the spell of two aggressively expansive retailers, and the newer talents of Terence Conran and Laura Ashley drove style and design even higher in the priority of the shopper.

Although the late 1980s certainly saw a consumer boom, the previous decade as a whole had been a period of rising financial sophistication. While consumer borrowing, most of it against the purchase or remortgage of houses, had exploded in the de-regulated financial market, personal savings also rose dramatically. Many of the problems of 1990/91 recession were a consequence of the fact that these parallel increases were not made in the balance sheets of the same individuals: those who saved were not the same people as those who borrowed. But such an increase in both elements gave a fillip to those companies which acted as intermediaries between saver and borrower. The High Street had already become the victim of the rapid increase in branches opened by the leading building societies during the 1970s, and the trend continued in the 1980s. At the end of 1970 there were 2,016 building society branches; by the end of 1980 this figure had risen to 5,684, and at its peak at the end of 1987 the total reached 6,962. Already in the early 1980s there were complaints that the High Street was turning into a string of financial office outlets, creating no pedestrian traffic of its own. Paul Orchard-Lisle of agents Healey & Baker was often to be found expounding the virtues of a shop investment being on the 'desire line', the most heavily trafficked path, usually between the bus station or car park and the most popular store in the area: in Oxford Street, a shop positioned between Bond Street underground station and Selfridges store was the acme of desirability, and commanded the highest retail rents in the nation in 1980.

By 1978, the retail warehouse was becoming a feature of the edge of towns. In December of that year Harris Queensway was floated on the stock market. Philip Harris had inherited a small carpet retailing business, which he had built up to 129 stores. He had recently purchased Queensway Discount, a furniture retailer, selling from non-high street positions. Queensway had only 23 stores nationwide. In November Associated Dairies, one of the originators of the discount food warehouse with its Asda stores, announced that it was to merge with Allied Retailers, the proprietors of Allied Carpets and Williams furniture stores, both of which had pioneered the same concept in their own areas. The following year Phil Harris rented a large warehouse for his carpet stocks in Swanley, Kent from Haslemere Estates. In April 1979 B&Q became a public company, selling do-it-yourself goods from 26 warehouses, averaging less than 20,000 square feet each.

The scene was set for a developer/investor with enough vision to see that this trend away from the High Street into bigger, edge-of-town units was not a passing fad, and that these properties would eventually be valued more highly by the institutional investor. Peel Holdings was the Lancashire-based textile company which filled that role.

Peel had originally been founded by Sir Robert Peel the elder, father of the Prime Minister of that name. The company had thrived as a calico printer and, at one stage in the early nineteenth century, had employed 15,000 people, but in the more recent past had been in the control of John Whittaker and had fallen upon hard times. Whittaker, who had made his fortune selling gravel for the construction of the M62, now lives on the Isle of Man, where his family's holding company, Largs, was also based. Peel was by no means the only old textile company of which Whittaker, then still farming outside Bury, had taken control. John Bright, another name redolent of nineteenth century politics, and Highams were two others. A third was Clover Croft, which Largs had taken control of in 1973, when John Whittaker was still only 30. There is a rather sad historical note appended to the prospectus issued when this last company was revived. After its take-over by the Whittakers, it was noted that

'Rationalisation of the production facilities followed in an effort to combat the pressures then facing the Company in common with the rest of the Lancashire spinning industry. But even reduced overheads failed to arrest the impact on the Company's business of the inflow of subsidised imported yarn. Diversification into synthetic product lines did not compensate for the decline in production. The Company was obliged to wind down the remainder of its business and sell its assets.' Clover Croft was revived, with John Whittaker on the board, as the ill-fated come-back vehicle for Ron Shuck, erstwhile head of 1970s quoted property company, Cornwall. His new company, Espley-Tyas, was an early casualty of the 1980s.

At the end of March 1980 Peel's total gross assets amounted to only £700,000, and the company made only £41,000 after tax. The company's old mills in Rochdale were being transformed by Whittaker into small industrial units. The initiative for becoming involved in retail warehouse development came in 1981 from Peter Jevans, who had previously worked for food retailer Keymarkets, and Tom Dootson. Dootson and Jevans were principals of Abbeygate, which in the early years of Peel's involvement in developing retail warehouses, 'sheds with shelves', managed all the developments. The first development, in Bury, showed how, by building relatively unsophisticated and cheap warehouses on inexpensive sites, yet achieving rents above that normally agreed on industrial buildings, the company would not only make a potential profit but could afford to hold on to the completed investment. If the building and land in a derelict part of the north-west could be completed for £20 a square foot and let, not at the £1.50 per square foot typical of industrial property in the area at the time, but at over £2, then only a relatively small equity investment enabled the development to show a positive cash-flow. It was still not easy to find an institution willing to take the completed investments. There were two constraints in the minds of fund managers: with what should these sheds be compared for rent review purposes and to what alternative use could the buildings be put? On the first, the solution was often that the rent would bear a fixed relationship to pure industrial warehouse rents, or to the shop rents in the adjacent town; as to the second point, the answer was of course that the building might revert to industrial warehouse use, in which case the premium rents would not be sustainable. The institutions had not understood that this would not be a problem for another seven or so years, since the demand for new space in such developments outstripped supply dramatically over the middle years of the decade.

In 1983 Peel bought out Dootson and Jevan's minority interest in the Abbeygate joint venture, as well as John Bright and other industrial property from Largs, further establishing the Whittaker family control. It is perhaps as well that the original Peel and Bright could never have imagined that their two companies would end up merged, out of textiles and into property development. Jevans was, by this time, gaining a reputation beyond his base in Wimbledon for his ability to pre-let the developments, often before the planning permission on the site was finalized. By the end of March 1984, gross assets of Peel had jumped to £57 million and profit after tax was reported at £1.7 million.

The acquisition of Bridgewater Estates in the winter of 1984 was another example of Whittaker's Autolycus-like collecting of relics of the Industrial Revolution. The Bridgewater Canal, not in Somerset, but in the industrial north-west, connecting Manchester, Liverpool and a local coalfield, was the first commercially successful canal in Britain, built by Brindley for the Duke of Bridgewater between 1760–71. The Estates company was the remnant of the land once owned in the area by the Duke, whose canal had been the monopoly carrier of cotton between Liverpool and Manchester until the arrival of Stephenson's Rocket. Bridgewater Estates still owned 9,000 acres of agricultural land in the area, some of it near enough to the edge of conurbations to hold out the prospect of eventual development; for the rest, sales of the land would provide useful capital for the retail developments.

By the end of 1985, Peel's development programme was such that the company took the opportunity of raising £17 million through a rights issue; at the same time, Whittaker sold some of his family companies' property assets to Peel. In early 1986 Peel raised a further £35 million through the issue of the first debenture stock with an interest coupon in single figures for ten years.

John Whittaker was meanwhile involved in another attempt to buy part of Britain's industrial heritage: the Manchester Ship Canal Company (MSCC). This statutory company had an odd voting and board structure so that, although Whittaker controlled 48 per cent of the share capital of MSCC through his personal companies and another quoted vehicle, Highams, it had only 29 per cent of the votes. The MSCC board denied him representation among its number because the statute under which the company operated dictated that the total number of directors should not exceed 21, of which 11 must be representatives of Manchester City Council, and each quota was full.

Whittaker was not interested in the major responsibility of MSCC, keeping the Ship Canal navigable, but saw the potential of the company's extensive land holdings, totalling 6,000 acres. This included 300 acres at the evocatively-named Dumplington, which Whittaker saw as the perfect site for a regional shopping centre to rival Tyneside's Metro Centre and Dudley's Merry Hill. Whittaker made a bid for MSCC with his family money rather than through Peel. Because each shareholder was unable to vote more than a limited number of the shares in each name, it was not enough for Peel to buy or receive acceptances for more than 50 per cent of the votes, which is the normal criterion for control. The methods used by Whittaker's vehicle to overcome this technical drawback were eventually heavily criticized in a Department of Transport inquiry, set up at the behest of some dissenting shareholders, and published in 1989. Nicholas

Berry, the chairman of MSCC, had alleged that Peel had 'unbundled' its shareholding by trawling the council estates of Manchester for people prepared, in exchange for a £1 reward, to act as nominee holders of MSCC shares, who would then vote out the existing board. It was said that 30,000 such signatures were collected in this way. Whatever the method, Whittaker achieved his end and became controlling shareholder of MSCC.

Peter Jevans and Tom Dootson left Peel in 1986. The relations between the two men and Whittaker had deteriorated. On the one hand there was the tangled complexity of the Whittaker family interests mixed with those of Peel and, on the other, Jevan's very high-profile image with investors and the media; some falling out was inevitable. Jevans went on to run a development company, Merlin International, which hit serious trouble in 1991, and was subject to what appeared to be a 'phantom' bid. 1986 was too late to enter and hope to leave the property cycle before it slowed.

At its March 1987 year-end, Peel could boast a profit of over £8 million and a completed retail portfolio of over 1.5 million square feet with total property assets of almost £180 million. In raising a further £24 million through the issue of convertible preference shares, Peel listed all its retail developments with their tenants, which is an unparalleled demonstration of how this sort of retailing was dominated by relatively few retailers in a limited number of sectors:

Location	Size Sq.Ft	Tenant
Completed		
Dundee	45,000	B&Q
Bury II	16,000	Terleys
Lancaster	22,000	B&Q
Larkfield	31,600	B&Q
Blackpool North I	38,500	B&Q
Torquay	34,250	WH Smith Do It All
Crewe I	30,000	B&Q
Crewe II	25,000	MFI
Bradford I	40,000	Harris Queensway
Bradford II	35,000	WH Smith Do It All
Bradford III	10,000	Currys
Bradford IV	6,000	Topps Tiles
Bradford V	4,000	Motor World
Keighley I	36,250	WH Smith Do It All
Keighley II	8,750	Harris Queensway
Bristol I	51,000	MFI
Bristol II	35,000	RMC Homecare
Rawtenstall	55,000	ASDA
Formby	28,000	Payless DIY
Blackburn	36,250	WH Smith Do It All

Paignton	24,200	Payless DIY
Lincoln I	30,139	Allied Carpets
Lincoln II	41,355	Texas Homecare
Lincoln III	12,000	Currys
Lincoln IV	13,000	Halfords
Lincoln V	20,000	Habitat
Ashford	32,000	RMC Homecare
Great Yarmouth	38,500	WH Smith Do It All
Hyndburn III	40,000	Harris Queensway
Hyndburn III	10,000	Wigfalls
Hyndburn III	25,000	Allied Carpets
Mansfield	45,000	MFI
Leicester	59,600	Allied Carpets
Bury I	36,530	WH Smith Do It All
Blackpool South	56,123	WH Smith Do It All
Southport	45,000	WH Smith Do It All
Rochdale	30,270	B&Q
Morden	36,000	Argyll
Morden	15,000	Business Press
Hyndburn I	51,225	MFI
Hyndburn II	36,105	Payless DIY
Folkestone	39,178	Texas Homecare
Bridgewater	25,560	B&Q
Barnsley I	30,053	RMC Homecare
Wolverhampton	39,705	Texas Homecare
Wolverhampton	39,470	MFI
Maidstone	31,200	WH Smith Do It All
Maidstone	36,265	Safeway
Maidstone	15,760	Multi-tenanted
Canterbury	33,500	Texas Homecare
	1,575,338	

Under Construction

Barnsley II	100,000	Under negotiation
Ellesmere Port	40,000	Argyll Stores
Hyndburn IV	30,000	United Co-operatives
Blackpool North II	12,000	Comet
Bradford V	14,000	Under negotiation
Dumfries	70,000	Under negotiation
Guiseley	110,000	Under negotiation
Halifax	47,000	WH Smith Do It All/ Graham Building Services
Lowestoft	36,586	RMC Homecare
Preston	40,000	Under negotiation

Rochdale II	10,000	Under negotiation
Slough	11,702	Halfords
Stockport I	110,007	Under negotiation
	631,295	

Building Commitments

Tonbridge	55,500	Under negotiation
Yeovil	65,000	Under negotiation
Cheetham Hill	25,000	Under negotiation
Bracknell	180,000	Under negotiation
Stockport II	67,250	Under negotiation
Epsom	120,000	Under negotiation
Wolverhampton	75,000	Under negotiation
Armley, Leeds	28,335	Under negotiation
	616,085	

The preponderance of do-it-yourself stores and discount furniture and carpet warehouses is striking. Although most of the covenants were absolutely sound, Harris Queensway, after its leveraged buy-out and change of name to Lowndes Queensway, went into liquidation. Furthermore, in a consolidation of the DIY industry, W. H. Smith and RMC merged their operations. If they are operating in the same towns, while the two lessees are obliged to pay rent throughout the lifetime of the original leases, the growth in rents may be more restricted. There will also be at least one fewer potential tenant to take the space of whichever of the stores is vacated.

Peel was undoubtedly the leader in this form of development and investment, and had spawned some imitators, most notably Citygrove, an early casualty of the later property crash. As so often is the pattern described in these pages, this was not enough, and in November 1988 Peel brought a 20 per cent stake in London Shop, the company which Godfrey Bradman's Rosehaugh had failed to win in 1982, from the British Steel Pension Fund. Within two weeks, Peel had launched a take-over bid which culminated in success for a total sum of £308 million, paid in cash, of which £121 million was raised through another rights issue.

Despite a move to reduce the debt level by selling off properties from both the original Peel and the newly-acquired London Shop portfolios, Peel had made its purchase just as the retail sector began to feel the early draft of recession. John Whittaker's further ambitions for take-over, of the Mersey Docks company and Trafford Park Estates, which owned most of the huge industrial park of that name in Manchester, had to be abandoned and the share stakes sold. The housebuilding activities were closed down, although the land bank was retained. Finally, in May 1991, Whittaker was forced to sell his family holding of Manchester Ship Canal to Peel, which then bought its own holding company, the Isle of Man based Largs, for shares. The deals reduced the company's overall gearing and, according to Peel's managing director, Peter Scott, avoided the danger of breaching some banking covenants.

The company's results for the year ended in March 1991 confirmed how badly it had been affected. There was a pre-tax loss of £8.5 million and a 30 per cent fall in net asset value. Peel has bought itself time by the rejigging of the Whittaker family interests, but it will need a stronger investment market and a run of good rent reviews before it can begin its recovery.

About as far removed from the smooth, urbane image of the property developer as could be imagined are the West Midland's leading lights of the 1980s boom. The Richardson twins, Don and Roy, are Black Country boys from the accents in which they speak to the bootstraps by which they pulled themselves up. Not that they are shooting stars of the most recent property boom. The twins were born in 1930, and their father built up a business selling second-hand military lorries. This developed into a truck distribution chain; such a business had an obvious need of large areas on which to trade. The knowledge gained led Don and Roy to diversify into property, almost all of it industrial estates in the West Midlands, in the 1960s, and they were buyers in the depths and aftermath of the 1970s property crash. Always taking on projects which no-one else would touch, their first industrial development, in the 1960s, was on the site of an old ICI chemical tip, which no-one believed could be cleaned up. A typical investment in an existing property was the purchase, in 1980, of the 530,000-square foot Coventry Central City estate on which Ford were the largest occupiers. The ability to take a contrary view is crucial to all the really successful long-term property investors. Those who confuse a bull market in property with genius tend to be carried away with more and more grandiose schemes at the top of the market. The Richardsons had actually eschewed the possibility of making Richardson Developments a publicly quoted company in the 1960s, a decision they claim never to have regretted; they might well have found the pressures to offer shareholders ever greater projects too much, and, like others in this book, expanded at the peak. It is of course vital to have the resources to be able to take advantage of the depressed market, and this is only possible if they are not all used up in the upswing.

The Richardsons' 1980s coup was based on an assessment of the potential of derelict industrial land. The Conservative government created the concept of Enterprise Zones, the most notable of which was London's Docklands. In the West Midlands a large area in the borough of Dudley was selected for this experiment in 'unplanning'. As the twins were local men, Dudley Borough Council asked them to become involved in the new Enterprise Zone and 'create activity'. At the time, the metal-bashers on whom West Midlands industry so depended were suffering from the worst recession in their industries since the 1930s, but the Richardsons took a cussedly more optimistic long-term view. They developed a 50-acre industrial estate, the Wallows, in the Zone; 'People thought we were mad'. The Round Oak Steelworks, a victim of the recession, began to sell land, also in the Zone, and when the works eventually closed, the Richardsons had accumulated 300 acres of waste land at Merry Hill and Round Oak, described by advisers as the worst site ever seen; 'There were no other buyers around. We were the only people with the courage to acquire the site' Don Richardson has been quoted as saying. The land stood above one of the thickest and most worked coal seams in the country, and ground preparation was an important and time and money-consuming business: 'We spent more below the ground than above it' said Richardson.

The critical inspiration was to believe this could be the site of a regional shopping centre. The catchment area is certainly big enough, with three million people within easy driving distance, and Birmingham has never been able to establish a shopping centre with the local reputation of, say, Nottingham's two main malls. In 1984 the twins commissioned a survey by agents Grimley J. R. Eve and Mason Owen to investigate the potential demand from retailers for such a regional centre on the Merry Hill part of the site. The response was enthusiastic both from the retailers, and, perhaps more important, from the consumers. The first four phases of the development were unexceptional in concept, being a series of warehouse-type retail units, such as Peel had been developing. The first phase was pre-sold to MFI, who took 40,000 square feet for themselves and let the rest to a selection of other, familiar, names: B&Q, Halfords and Queensway among them. Phase Two was the 'anchor' food hypermarket, surrounded by a mall of enclosed units. By 1986 Carrefour had opened, (now occupied by Asda), and the other units were quickly let. The next phase of retail warehouses attracted the largest Texas Homecare unit. Boots' first Children's World superstore and Pizza Hut's first free-standing unit in the UK.

The fifth phase of the Merry Hill development was the critical one which took the scheme out of the ordinary. Supported by the then-Conservative controlled Dudley Borough Council, the Richardsons drew up plans for a 1.2 million-square foot enclosed mall to add to the 600,000 square feet of space in the four earlier phases. This was intended, like Brent Cross, to attract the major High Street department and chain stores. Neighbouring Birmingham and other boroughs were outraged at this threat to their own shopping and tried by every means to thwart the development. Even Dudley council, which in May 1986 changed to Labour control, belatedly changed horses. It was too late: within hours the Secretary of State for the Environment, Nicholas Ridley, had taken the final decision not to 'call in' the plans for a public enquiry. In 1988 Debenhams agreed to lease the largest, 125,000 square foot, unit, and was rapidly followed by Sainsbury's, Littlewoods, BhS and C&A. Among the total of 150 tenants are included Laura Ashley, Etam, Miss Selfridge, Wallis, Dorothy Perkins and the Early Learning Centre. This major phase of the centre opened in November 1989.

By this time the Richardsons had developed plans for the other end of the site, by the local canal. Here they planned an office, industrial warehouse and leisure complex, linked to the retail centre by a monorail. There were even plans for the tallest building in the world to be built, exceeding the height of Toronto's CN Tower. Merry Hill has become a local phenomenon. It has parking for 10,000 cars, there is a mini-bus service for shoppers within a ten-mile radius, a courtesy bus on the site and free wheel-chair loans. With a ten-screen cinema and a 350-seat food court, Merry Hill has developed as a place to spend a whole day, not just the average shopping expedition. There are even coach tours arranged to visit the development.

What was not known was that between October 1987 and October 1990, the Richardsons had been selling the giant Phase Five of the scheme piecemeal to Mountleigh. Only those properties in which the retailers themselves held the equity interest remained outside Mountleigh's control. Soon after, Mountleigh acquired Phases Two, Three and Four, ending up with what director John Watson was quoted as claiming as 'between 80 and 90 per cent of the value of the development.' Ironically, as described in Chapter Five, Mountleigh needed to sell assets to survive, and agreed the sale of Merry Hill to an investment consortium including American interests, but the sale was held up by doubts about the quality of the ground on which it stood, triggering that company's liquidation.

Although the Richardsons had shown great imagination and courage to develop both the industrial and retail elements within the Enterprise Zones, they too proved vulnerable to the bull market madness of the late 1980s. Having remained as a private company with their main interests, they bought control of the Belfast-based group Regentcrest in July 1985, for only just over £4 million. Regentcrest was to be their public vehicle, but it was not a marked success. In March 1990 the brothers came to the rescue of the company again with a £6.3 million bid, but this was simply throwing good money after bad. By October 1990, Regentcrest had £50 million in debts. Among the creditor banks was Den Norske Bank's London branch, one of many foreign banks which had joined in the fashion of lending on British property. Their loan for £8.75 million was secured on a property in Soho, owned by a Regentcrest subsidiary, Opecland, and said to be worth nearly £14 million. At the beginning of October, the bank appointed a receiver to the property on which they were secured, triggering off a partial guarantee from the parent company. A trade creditor of Regentcrest, reportedly the property agents Herring Son & Daw, then petitioned for the winding up of the parent company. The bank and the Richardson brothers proceeded to give their own sides of the story to the *Birmingham Post*. Brian Hudson, the Managing Director of Den Norske, London, stung by the

Richardsons' blaming his bank for the company's demise, wrote an open letter to the newspaper:

> We had a loan of £8.75 million which was due to be repaid in January [1990]. Regentcrest were unable to pay and asked for an extension. We readily complied and it was agreed that we would receive six payments of £500,000 following which the remaining loan of £5.75 million would be put on to a long-term basis with no further principal instalments.
>
> Five of the six instalments were paid, one of them in the form of a collateral deposit from one of the Richardsons' private companies. . . . They were negotiating to sell the building . . . for nearly £14 million, which would have given them a big profit over the amount of the loan.
>
> Unfortunately, the sale fell through. After that their attitude to the bank changed. They contacted us in mid-September to say that no further payments would be made to us, even though the loan was within only £500,000 of the level at which it would be converted into a long-term commitment. They said that interest for the next 18 months should be rolled up, failing which they would walk away and leave us with the property. . . .
>
> Despite the hard line taken by the Richardsons, Den Norske Bank was still willing to negotiate. My letter to them of September 28 made it clear that the bank would look willingly at a compromise involving, for example, a deferment of the last instalment of £500,000 while the affairs of Regentcrest were sorted out. . . .
>
> The olive branch we offered was rejected. I was told on October 2 that the Regentcrest board had no response to make to my letter and that their position remained exactly as before – not a penny more in principal to the bank, not a penny more in interest. This left us with no choice but to appoint a receiver to the property. . . .
>
> The truth is that if Regentcrest fails, this will be the Richardsons' choice and not Den Norske Bank's. I am sorry that they have sought to make the bank the scapegoat for their decisions.

The Richardsons certainly did blame the bank. Roy Richardson complained 'At the meeting of bank creditors [on 10 October 1990] the directors felt that, in view of the precipitous action of Den Norske, it was decided to allow the company to be wound up. It will be messy and there will be other banks involved. I am angry with Den Norske. It is all down to them.'

These extracts from a dispute over what was a relatively small company are included since it is very unusual for the mechanics by which a quoted company is put into liquidation to reach the public domain. By the end of 1991, similar angry disagreements over what might or might not have been done to rescue public companies had no doubt taken place, but no such dirty washing has been aired over those cases.

The Richardsons lost £10 million on Regentcrest, but they continue to be the great promoters of the revival of the Black Country. Their project to turn Fort Dunlop, that familiar landmark by the side of the M6 in Birmingham, from a multi-story memorial to a once-great British company into a new business centre is still in the planning stage. At the 1991 Labour and Conservative Party conferences the chambers of commerce of Dudley, Walsall, Sandwell and Wolverhampton organized a joint lobby to create political support for further government spending on the local infrastructure and environment. It was widely believed that the catalysts behind this unusual co-operation were the Richardson twins.

The third out-of-town entrepreneur who made his name in the 1980s through a huge retail development is John Hall. Hall is a Northumbrian, born in 1932, whose father was a coalminer; he too worked in the coal industry, qualifying as a mining surveyor. His experience in the property industry began at Killingworth Development Corporation, but in the 1960s he went into business on his own. His first venture was taken over by London & Northern Securities, for whom he worked for 11 years. No sooner had he gone out on his own again than the 1970s property crash hit. His bank, the National Westminster, stood by him, building up a relationship and loyalty from its grateful customer reminiscent more of Japan or Germany than the 'transaction related' links typical of the United States or Britain.

Hall's place in the history of retail development in the UK is secured by his realized vision of a huge, American-style regional shopping centre. This has been built, not in the soft south, or even in one of the more prosperous areas of the Midlands, but in Gateshead, across the River Tyne from Newcastle. In the early 1980s, as its traditional industries of steel, shipbuilding and chemicals went through a depression comparable to that of 50 years before, it was considered ridiculous to contemplate a 'greenfield' retail centre in such a depressed area. In fact, as is often the case, the depression on the Tyne was much exaggerated. A local Porsche dealer, symbol of the southern yuppies, was said to be one of the most successful in the country. Newcastle itself already had one of the most successful of the 1970s shopping centres, Eldon Square developed by Capital & Counties and financed by the Shell Pension fund. The very existence of that retailing success brought into question even more starkly whether the area could support more shopping on the scale envisaged by John Hall.

The Thatcher government's introduction of Enterprise Zones could be said to have enabled the Richardson brothers to contemplate the development of Merry Hill, and the same is true for the Gateshead project, which Hall's company dubbed the MetroCentre. The 100-acre site was an ash tip when Hall first looked at it in 1979, waterlogged and with no access. To make the land fit for use would take £8 million, yet the asking price was too high. The area was one of the first to be designated an Enterprise Zone, and, in 1980, John Hall took an option on it.

Hall's company, Cameron Hall, is owned by his family, with the

Cameron half stemming from his wife Mae's maiden name; both she and their son Douglas and daughter Allison are directors of the company. In 1980 the two senior Halls wrote to all the major retailers with their idea for the site and asking for indications of interest. 'None of them wrote back' said Hall. Only the retail warehouse operators, who had supported John Whittaker's Peel Holdings, had any interest in the idea of out-of-town shopping, and then only for their sheds-with-shelves. Hall and his family persevered, and when he opened an exhibition of his plans in the Five Bridges Hotel, Gateshead in 198, '1,000 retailers came to see us.'

The change had come about as the High Street retailers had seen the success of the retail warehouses. The growing mobility of the average Briton, as car ownership spread, meant that most shoppers were no longer confined to what could be walked to or reached on the old bus routes. These shoppers had also travelled, particularly to the United States in the first two years of the 1980s; the strength of sterling had made that the cheapest and most popular destination for British tourists. They had liked what they had seen and demanded a similar standard of quality for their shops at home. Even the most modern of the city centre developments barely compared with the huge US shopping malls, and only out-of-town centres could offer the prospect of anything like the American experience. Many retailers had noted the success of the retail warehouses, with their longer hours and easy parking, and had set up task forces to investigate whether they too should succumb to these new retail trends.

The critical anchor tenant to be signed up for the two million-square foot scheme was Marks & Spencer. M&S had never taken a store out of the High Street; taking 90,000 square feet was a leap in the dark for them particularly since their Eldon Square shop was one of their most successful. Hall has been quoted as saying 'History will say I was in the right place at the right time, and I needed that piece of luck. My difficulties initially were in getting people to understand what I was trying to achieve in shopping and leisure.' The breakthrough of attracting Marks & Spencer was followed rapidly, and by the time the Centre was officially opened on 13 October 1986, there were about 200 tenants, including most of the well-known High Street retailers. In its first weeks, the Centre attracted up to 100,000 shoppers a day. The next phase of the development, opened a year later, includes a multi-screen cinema, cafes and restaurants, and, an idea of Allison Hall's, a fun-fair for children. By 1988 it was estimated that 16 million people had visited the MetroCentre in a year and spent £340 million.

Cameron Hall financed the centre partly through a partnership with the Church Commissioners. The latter were keen to make an investment in a depressed city-centre area, and could scarcely have been presented with a better opportunity of proving that doing good does not necessarily mean losing money. As a consequence of the Commissioners' involvement, the MetroCentre even has a visiting chaplain to add to all its other facilities.

John Hall has often made plans to duplicate the success of the

Gateshead scheme, but, to date, none of these has been completed. He was in competition to build a regional centre in Exeter, and was a putative partner in the proposed development of a competitor to the Richardsons, in the Sandwell Enterprise Zone in the West Midlands. There are also plans for similar developments in continental Europe. The other major scheme which has progressed some way is the plan to turn the grounds of Wynyard Hall, Teeside, into a business park. There is rich irony in the fact that the Hall family bought the 5,000 acre estate with its mansion in 1987. It was previously one of the homes of the Marquess of Londonderry, whose family fortune had been built on the very coal mines in which John Hall's father had worked.

The north-east has become proud of John Hall, the local boy made good. They cheered him on in his successful attempt to change the board of the faded, but still loved, Newcastle United football team. There was pleasure too in the award of a knighthood to Hall in the 1991 Queen's Birthday honours list. He and the other entrepreneurs in this chapter are certainly out of a different mould from many of the urbane property developers from the soft south.

10

THE BUYER OF LAST RESORT

THE BRITISH HAVE never been very sensitive about the ownership of their country by foreigners. Since the nation has been a colonizer for much of its recent history, any such sensitivity would seem hypocritical. What is more, for a country which has run a trade deficit for most of the post-war period, any attempt to prevent foreign ownership would be self-defeating. The simple truth is that, if you are running a deficit on trade, then that shortfall must be made good by capital flows. Either the deficit nation must sell its overseas assets or attract foreign investment. It is true that such inflows of capital do not have to involve any physical assets: many countries have prevented the foreigner from owning property or other real assets, such as companies. In those cases the capital inflows are in the form of borrowing. The problem with borrowing is that the more of it a country does, the more expensive it becomes and eventually the recipient of the capital has to spend so much of its national efforts simply paying the interest on the debt that it is unable to break out of the cycle of borrowing. The advantage of selling companies and property to the foreign investor is that he is being promised nothing: if the company fails, he has no claim on the country at large and similarly a poor property investment decision will rebound on the investor, not on the sellers. The problem that foreign purchases of property can bring is a resentment among the local population. In the US the purchase of the Rockefeller Center in New York by Japanese investors brought a storm of protest about selling the nation's heritage. It is actually in the deficit country's interest to try to persuade the foreigner to pay the highest prices possible for local assets, and this might seem the deliberate policy of perfidious Albion in the latter years of the 1980s property boom.

Foreign ownership of British property is not a phenomenon of the 1980s. In the 1970s the oil-rich states had become substantial buyers of British real estate, culminating in the puchase by the Kuwait Investment Office of the St Martins property group for £107 million in September 1974, as the property market fell into its worst depression. Also in 1974 the Shah of Iran was said to be behind Evenrealm, a company which bought Blackfriars House, Manchester, Britannia House, Old Bailey and an office in Rood Lane, London. The Arabs were also big buyers of hotels in London: the Dorchester, before its purchase by the Sultan of Brunei, the Park Tower, and the Chelsea Holiday Inn. This last is the hotel which forms part of the Sloane Street site bought and sold at regular intervals in the late 1980s, (see Chapter Five). Most foreign purchases were restricted to owner-occupation; in 1976 Mobil bought half of the building they occupied in Holborn from London Life, and in the next year the Continental Illinois Bank bought the old home of *The Times* for £7.25 million. The bank sold this building late in the 1980s boom to another foreign buyer, Louis Dreyfus, for about £52 million.

In June 1978 English Property Corporation (EPC), one of the many companies which had struggled to survive the 1974/75 collapse, announced that it was in talks with an unnamed 'continental buyer' about a possible take-over of the British company. Although that approach come to nothing, in December the Dutch company Wereldhave, which had earlier bought the much smaller Midhurst Whites, bid £40 million for EPC. This was part of a bidding war for EPC which involved several important names. The battle became a three-way tussle between Wereldhave and two Canadian investors, Olympia & York, and a company owned by the Bronfmann family, owners of the Seagram distilling empire. Olympia & York (O&Y) eventually emerged victorious, although it sold the company on to the British company, Metropolitan Estates & Property in 1985. The Reichmann involvement in Canary Wharf on the Isle of Dogs in London's Docklands has been described in Chapter Two, but the Reichmann story is such an extraordinary one that it merits further attention.

The three Hungarian-born Reichmann brothers, Paul, Albert and Ralph, together with their father Samuel and formidable mother Renee, were refugees from Vienna at the outbreak of the Second World War. Their property empire really only became significant in the mid-1970s. The company, Olympia & York, evolved out of the Olympia Tile company which the young Ralph Reichmann set up in the mid 1950s, and York Developments, a warehouse developer in Toronto which Albert and Paul built up in the 1960s. The early investments were bought from the legendary New York developer 'Big Bill' Zeckendorf, who went bankrupt in mid-decade. The Reichmanns' prime Toronto development, First Canadian Place, was completed in 1975. The purchase of the rump of the Uris empire in New York occurred in 1977, but their major coup in that city was the creation and development of the modestly named World Financial Center on the south-western tip of Manhattan in 1980. The Reichmanns developed this group of buildings on hard-core infill, said to be from the bomb sites of Bristol, in the Hudson River. It lies across the road from the equally reticent twin towers of the World Trade Center. This latter development was already thought to be a little 'off-pitch' for the financial district, but the Financial Center is even more out on a limb. The great success of this massive development of eight millon square feet of offices was achieved through O&Y creating a critical mass of tenants and creating its own location. To do this the Reichmanns offered potential tenants either rent-free periods or concessionary rents in the new buildings while, in many cases, (and more importantly), buying or taking over the leases of the buildings some of their tenants already occupied. For the tenants the immediate boost to their cash-flows was very attractive and it enabled O&Y to let substantial proportions of the development, against the expectations of all New York's wiseacres. Norwich Union and Mountleigh used the same avenue to fill their Beaufort House development, buying office space in Austin Friars from C. S. Buckminster and Moore, and in Lovat Lane from Lloyd Thompson, both of which took space in the new office block.

It is estimated that the gross property assets of O&Y are worth more than $15 billion. What has only recently become clear is what portion of that wealth is owned by the Reichmanns and what is owed to the banks. They also control the Canadian paper company, Abitibi-Price, Gulf Canada, an energy group, and they refinanced the North American store empire of fellow-Canadian Robert Campeau just before it sought protection from its creditors in the courts. The simultaneous collapse in the property markets of Canada, New York and London proved too much for the Reichmann empire. In May 1992, Canary Wharf was put into administration, following the moves taken in Canada and the US to protect O&Y from its creditors. The O&Y empire has fallen, and only time will tell whether the Reichmanns and their bankers will salvage anything from the ruins.

The UK was not considered a prime target for property investment by foreign investors until well into the 1980s. A Labour government which had imposed strict development criteria and taxes and exchange controls were hardly conducive to foreign confidence. The South African Union Corporation was an exception in its gradual accumulation of a large stake in the convalescent Capital & Counties, but then the political situation in its home base was even worse. The first foreign bid of the 1980s was that by St Martins, the Kuwaiti owned company, for The Proprietors of Hay's Wharf, a relic of the days when the Pool of London was the centre of world trade. Hay's Wharf owned most of the south bank of the Thames between Tower and London Bridges and had been the object of redevelopment plans during the 1970s boom.

These early players in the property boom were in time to benefit from the rise in values between 1987 and 1989. Most of the foreign buyers have not been in that fortunate position, since the great invasion of foreign property buyers really started only during this period and was itself a substantial cause of the rise in value. Among the earliest deals done by foreigners were the first two significant purchases by Japanese buyers of UK property in 1985. Mitsubishi Estate bought Atlas House in the City for £34 million and the construction group Kumagai Gumi, in partnership with Glengate Holdings, bought both the old GPO headquarters in St Martins-le-Grand and the Bourne & Hollingsworth store in west Oxford Street; they redeveloped the former building as the new headquarters of the giant securities house Nomura. The official opening of the new building was one of the first public engagements undertaken by John Major in the week after he became Prime Minister in November 1990. Bourne & Hollingsworth has been translated into The Plaza shopping centre.

In 1985 the South-African controlled TransAtlantic Insurance took control of the still-quoted Capital & Counties group, whose net assets now amount to about £700 million; in August 1991, TransAtlantic agreed to inject a further £80 million into the company when it raised over £100 million in a rights issue. The Union Bank of Switzerland were also early participants with the purchase in 1985 of the P&O Building in Leadenhall Street, across the wind-swept paved precinct from the Commercial Union building and built in the same style.

The real explosion of foreign interest in British property came as the expectation and fact of a third Thatcher victory developed. In early 1986 the Dutch property investors, Rodamco, part of the giant Robeco investment group based in Rotterdam, (hence the 'Ro' prefix to its funds), bought the quoted Haslemere Estates. Haslemere had become synonymous in the property world with the refurbishment and redevelopment of old buildings; 'doing a Haslemere' was the expression used to describe such activity. The driving force of the company for many years had been Fred Cleary, who had been instrumental in preserving many of the small gardens which dot the City. His retirement allowed the Dutch the opportunity to buy the company, which cost them £245 million, but bought them control of £350 millions of real estate.

In 1987 there was the largest single transaction to date. Obayashi Gumi, another Japanese construction company, bought the *Financial Times* building in Cannon Street, Bracken House, for £143 million, with the intention of completely redeveloping the site. Only weeks after the transaction the Department of the Enviroment listed the building and it became impossible for the redeveloper to knock down its distinctive red-brick facade. The new building rising behind the old facade is designed by Michael Hopkins, the creator of the highly popular new Mound Stand at Lord's Cricket Ground. Another purchase of an abandoned newspaper building that year was that of the *Daily Telegraph* headquarters in Fleet Street by the American investment bank Goldman Sachs; this was later sold on to Meiji Life of Japan for a reported £200 million.

The buyers of British property in the late 1980s came from all three major investment areas: Japan, North America and Europe. The Japanese buyers included both developer/constructors (such as Kumagai, Obayashi, Kajima and Shimizu), institutional buyers, particularly the life assurance companies, and the speculative traders. Between 1988 and 1990 there were substantial purchases by Sumitomo Life, which bought Angel

Court, just by the Stock Exchange, for £81 million; it later followed this by buying, for £220 million, 53 per cent of the building which J. P. Morgan, the American bank, was developing on the site of the old City of London School for Boys on the Thames Embankment. Yasuda Life bought River Plate House in Finsbury Circus for £140 million; Asahi Life bought a lease on Leadenhall Court on the corner of Leadenhall Street and Bishopsgate for £118.75 million. It is confidently asserted that Nippon Life, the largest of all the Japanese mutual life assurance companies, was the buyer in August 1991 of 50 per cent of Wimpey's Little Britain development at the end of London Wall, (Route 11), for £110 million. Expectations have been raised that Dai-Ichi Mutual is to buy 50 per cent of the Prudential Group's pitched-roof extravaganza, Minster Court, for £200 million, and invest a further £150–200 million in buying 50 per cent of Milton Keynes' covered shopping centre. This would be in addition to its earlier purchase of Randsworth's Wilson Street development for £40 million in early 1989.

The Japanese construction companies have often preferred to develop in association with local experts. Shimizu Construction has invested jointly with Godfrey Bradman's Rosehaugh in a redevelopment in Chiswell Street, and has a share in the development of 1 America Square, as well as an eight per cent stake in Stockley Park. It is also the redeveloper of a property on the corner of Bond Street and Piccadilly, and has ventured into residential development with a very expensive conversion of apartments in Belgravia. Kajima Construction has been a partner of Stuart Lipton, with investments in Euston Square and London Wall, both of which were intended as future redevelopments, but on which the shadow of the property collapse has fallen. The partnership did complete and sell one highly successful development, in Red Lion Square, which realized a profit of more than £8 million.

Kumagai Gumi, being among the first into the British market, has been more adventurous than some others in its solo efforts. It went so far as to buy a small developer, Ranelagh, as well as developing the old *News of the World* building in Fleet Street, for which it paid £72 million in 1987. The resulting investment is now known as Whitefriars and is let to solicitors Freshfields. In the same year Kumagai bought a development site, now being completed, in Lower Thames Street, from Eagle Star; the new building, on the site of the old Vintry car park, has been dubbed Thames Exchange, a 185,000 square foot office. Also in the final stage of redevelopment is the old Hambros Bank headquarters in Bishopsgate, which will provide another 190,000 square foot investment. Kumagai's interest in this prime City position is enhanced by its purchase, for £145 million, of the new head office of Standard Chartered Bank, almost directly opposite the erstwhile Hambros building in Bishopsgate. Standard Chartered had become one of the worst casualties of poor lending both overseas and in the UK, and one way of restoring its reserve ratios was through the sale of some of its freehold offices. Among the jewels in the portfolio were offices in the Far East which were the subject of much speculation when the bank put them up for sale. The spanking new headquarters in Bishopgate, with its indoor trees and fountains, were too spacious and valuable for a bank faced with retrenching its activities, so the sale to Kumagai was a welcome relief. The bank has now taken much more modest space in Aldermanbury Square. The Japanese company was also the redevelopers of the Moss Bros site in Covent Garden and the Distillers Group's old head office on the corner of Pall Mall and St James's Square. Kumagai did not restrict its activities to London: in a joint venture it is involved in a substantial project at Broomielaw, Glasgow.

Many other Japanese companies have been large buyers of selected British property; not all of them were household names for prudence in their own country. The top companies were involved: Mitsui Real Estate paid £135 million for 20, Old Bailey. Kowa Real Estate bought 50 per cent interests in Austral House and 55 Basinghall Street, to the south of London Wall, from Wates City offices, and paid £150 million for Gallus House. Sumitomo Real Estate bought a share of Wates City Offices' Vintners Place development, just yards west of the Kumagai development in Lower Thames Street. The Japanese trading houses have also participated: C. Itoh were partners with Guardian Royal Exchange in buying properties in Fleet Street and Austin Friars; Mitsui partnered Taylor Woodrow in modest refurbishments in Grays Inn Road; Marubeni bought 120 Moorgate from P&O for £45 million as late as the end of 1989; Sogo Sosha bought a 50 per cent interest in one of Mountleigh's few developments to reach completion, the new block on the Criterion site in Piccadilly Circus; Nissho Iwai was involved in two joint developments with Imry Merchant Developers, one on the Isle of Dogs in Docklands and the other off Fleet Street. Daiwa Securities bought a site for its future headquarters in Wood Street for £100 million only to suffer the same fate as Obayashi when the building was listed by the Department of the Environment. Kato Kogaku bought Bush House, the home of the BBC World Service, for £130 million in late 1989, and around the same time, EIE bought West Britannic House, a 446,000 square foot office investment, for £200 million. EIE is now being supported by the Japanese banks, and its venture into British real estate cannot have helped its overall position.

This bald list of investments made by the Japanese over a relatively short period is by no means exhaustive. Property owners are not forced, as are shareholders, to reveal their beneficial ownership, and can hide behind offshore vehicles or nominee companies. Such a list does, however, give some feel for the sheer size of the buying. The properties listed certainly cost more than £2.5 billion, almost matching the total investment made by UK institutions in the two years 1988/89. Also excluded are the purchases of the businesses, and property assets, of two prestige British clothing retailers: Aquascutum of Regent Street and Daks-Simpson of Piccadilly by Japanese investors.

Of the Europeans, perhaps the least likely potential candidates for substantial investment in British property might have been the Swedes. The Social Democratic government which has ruled the country for most of the last 40 years took a very restricted view of capital freedom for individuals, let alone the great investment institutions, and until the end of the 1980s, there were absolute rules against the export of portfolio capital. When Finance Minister Kjell-Olof Feldt removed some of these limitations, first in November 1987 for property companies, and in 1988 and 1989 for other investors, the rush for the exit was headlong. As in the UK after the removal of much less strict exchange controls in 1979, investors embraced with abandon this new freedom to invest abroad, and the results have so far been fairly appalling for the Swedes. The UK property market, then in the last phase of its bull market, seemed to be a low-risk choice for the investors, and the subsequent investment was very substantial.

The first major deal was the joint purchase by Wasa and Windborne of Proctor House in High Holborn for £50 million in September 1989; an anonymous Scandinavian consortium bought Stockley's Dorset Rise development for £65 million. Perhaps the most aggressive buyer of the period was the Skanska property group which developed, either alone or in partnership, Thomas More Square, east of the Tower of London, and a new office above Monument Tube station. Thomas More Square has six office blocks making up 550,000 square feet of space. This has proved one of the slower developments to let, and by the middle of 1991 only a fraction of the space had been taken. Skandia, the insurance group, bought an office development behind Canada House off Trafalgar Square and 146 Queen Victoria Street in the City for a reported £95 million. Another Swedish insurance company, Trygg Hansa, bought 77 Shaftesbury Avenue for £40 million. A Swedish-owned vehicle, Central London Securities, bought the *Times* building in the Grays Inn Road from Elliott Bernerd for £42 million and 1 Drummond Gate SW1 for a further £28.5 million; Pleiad, another Swedish investor, bought Rosehaugh's head office in Marylebone Lane, sold in May 1990 as part of Godfrey Bradman's search for liquidity, for £23.5 million; Arcona bought 14/15 Stanhope Gate W1 for £32 million, the £40 million International Press Centre just off Fleet Street and a development in South Audley Street, Mayfair which it sold in early 1992 for £37.5 million to clients of Citibank; it also jointly undertook the £18 million redevelopment of 14/17 Great Marlborough Street W1. The grand-sounding Scandinavian Investment Property Holdings company bought Wellington House in the Strand for £12 million and Facta Fastigeheter paid £14 million for the Cripplegate Institute, north of the Barbican, for redevelopment.

This partial list, which totals over £500 million, shows how important the Swedes were as buyers in the short period between 1988 and 1990 during which they were active. There were immediately unsuccessful Swedish forays too. A Swedish-controlled company exchanged contracts on the purchase of Dorset House, SE1 for £24 million, but failed to complete, sacrificing its deposit, and Accura Real Estate took over the quoted City Gate Estates in March 1990 for £22 million; by mid-1991, City Gate was in liquidation. The largest Swedish purchase was that of London & Edinburgh Trust by the pension fund SPP, described in Chapter Eight, for £500 million, about the value of the underlying assets, in April 1990. That such a small nation, with a population of under eight and a half million, should have spent over £1 billion on British property in under three years is truly remarkable.

The Dutch, like the other major European maritime and colonial power, Britain, have always been large international portfolio investors. Their interest in British property is relatively long-standing. As mentioned above, the Rotterdam-based investment company, Rodamco, had taken over Haslemere Estates as early as 1986. In December 1988 the fund returned to the UK market with a contested bid for the much larger Hammerson Property company, run by the veteran Sydney Mason; Hammerson's assets were valued during the bid at almost £2.5 billion. The company still has a split share capital, with most of the votes being held by the relatively few ordinary shares. These have been issued very carefully by the company over the years, with the express intention of being able to maintain close control. The major holders of voting shares are Mrs Sue Hammerson, a patron of the arts and widow of the founder, and Standard Life Assurance, the huge Edinburgh mutual company. Standard has been a strong supporter and financing partner of Hammerson over the years, (notably on Brent Cross), and had no truck with the bid, which failed; during the bid, Standard Life increased its voting power to 28 per cent of the company through purchases in the market.

The other large Dutch property investor, Wereldhave, bid £281 million in October 1988 in a successful attempt to buy Peachey Property, a company finally restored in reputation after the Eric Miller scandal of the previous crash. Peachey's most noted properties were in the streets to the east of Regent Street, including the 1960s centre of swinging London, Carnaby Street. A more entrepreneurial view was taken by the Dutch company Noro, which bought effective control of New Cavendish Estates. The Dutch insurance and pension funds were also active: 1 Aldgate was sold to ABP for £50 million, and 120, Old Broad Street for £26.6 million to a subsidiary of the State employee's pension fund, which also bought an interest in Almack House, St James's, for an undisclosed sum from London & Edinburgh Trust. The multi-national insurer Nationale-Nederlanden bought Reed House off Curzon Street for £48.5 million; it is currently developing a £100 million investment in Henrietta Place behind Debenham's Oxford Street store, in a joint-venture with Lynton Holdings. After the market had fallen sharply, ABP returned in partnership with insurers Aegon to buy, in mid-1991, Aldwych House from AB Ports subsidiary, Grosvenor Square Properties, for £75.2 million.

The French, German and Swiss institutions were somewhat behind their continental colleagues, but were also part of the invasion. Credit Foncier bought into developments in Birchin Court in the City for £40 million and in a project in Knightsbridge, again with London & Edinburgh as partners. Zurich Insurance purchased P&O's development at 90, Fenchurch Street for £50 million; Gertler Properties bought Kings Cross House in the Pentonville Road from Speyhawk for £50 million, as well as the Welbeck Street headquarters of Debenhams.

Two of the largest individual foreign transactions were among those where the purchasers were a closely guarded secret. The £250 million spent by an anonymous 'Far East' buyer, widely thought to be the Sultan of Brunei, on the acquisition of Lansdowne House, Berkeley Square, was perhaps the quintessential purchase of the late 1980s property boom. The price was a fabulous one, and the major tenants included Saatchi & Saatchi, a creature which both blossomed and faded with the decade, and Stuart Lipton's Stanhope. Almost matching that deal was the purchase by 'Middle Eastern' investors, of the Adelphi, overlooking the Thames from behind The Strand, for £200 million. A Middle-Eastern company, named Culverpalm, was also active, buying in Berwick Street in the West End and Mountleigh's 85, Gracechurch Street (for £40 million), as well as selling a property in Norton Folgate, on the northern edge of the City, to Wimpey for £15 million. This last property remains unlet and a burden to its owner.

Two large deals in the summer of 1991 proved that the foreign buyer had not suffered from terminal indigestion from earlier forays. The purchase of 50 per cent of Little Britain by Nippon Life for £110 million from Wimpey helped relieve that company's finances, stretched not only by the unlet Norton Folgate, but also by its refurbished but equally empty building by the elevated section of the M4 motorway to the west of London. Similar relief was given to the Rosehaugh Stanhope joint company by the sale, to a fund managed by the US Prudential Insurance, of Bishopsgate Exchange, part of the Broadgate development, for £180 million. To demonstrate that the continuing attraction of such trophy buildings was not the only magnet, in September 1991 the British investment and development company, MEPC, sold a partly let, 40,000 square feet, office in Chancery Lane, Holborn to Deutsche Gesellschaft Fur Immobilienfonds for £18.7 million.

The plethora of foreign deals demonstrates how international the British, and, particularly, the London, property market has become. These deals have been listed in this rather dry way simply because such a laundry list shows how pervasive foreign ownership of prime London offices is; and the list is by no means exhaustive. Many foreign investors were attracted to so-called 'trophy buildings', those that they could point to with pride as being theirs and which had some special cachet. Agents Debenham Tewson & Chinnocks calculated that foreign investment in British property between 1987 and 1990 totalled more than £8 billion, excluding the purchases of whole companies. When this is put in the context of total UK institutions' net property investment in the same period of around £6 billion, it is clear that the foreigner played the unintended role of buyer of last resort for the British industry. Statistics are now published by the government of the number of transactions in property, derived from the forms delivered to the Inland Revenue for the payment of Stamp Duty. These show that the number of deals in individual, non-residential, properties for the whole UK in any year peaked at 117,000 in 1988. With so few transactions, it is no surprise that the foreign investor was the market in those years.

11

DOWN THE SNAKES AGAIN

THE END OF the 1980s property boom was foreshadowed on 19 October 1987. On that day the stock markets of the world fell by a quarter and the phrase 'Black Monday' was to enter the vocabulary of every financier. The boom had been sustained by a combination of extra-ordinary economic growth and institutional change together with gradual reductions in interest rates. The immediate consequences of Black Monday were two-fold: a reduction in demand for office space but, more important in the short term, a reduction in interest rates. After two years of economic growth at more than three per cent, the signs of incipient over-heating in the British economy were becoming apparent. While property developers sunned themselves on the beaches in August 1987, Nigel Lawson had signalled his concern by increasing interest rates by a full one per cent. A gradual tightening of monetary policy would have cooled the economy and the property market, with the probable avoidance of the excesses, both upward and downward, experienced in the following four years.

The stock market crash elicited predictions from many quarters of a repeat of the 1930s. The fall in share values was symptomatic of a deep economic malaise in the world economy and would also have an effect on consumers through the reduction in their wealth; they would become more cautious in their spending plans. As a consequence almost all the monetary authorities in the world, determined to avoid the mistakes of 1929, pumped funds into their economies by reducing interest rates. Britain was no exception. Interest rates, which had risen to ten per cent on 7 August, were cut to 9.5 per cent on 26 October, and further to 8.5 per cent by 4 December. At that stage the concern of the authorities to avoid a liquidity crunch was beginning to moderate, as there was little sign of consumer angst, except in the sales of BMWs in upstate New York. Unfortunately for the British economy there then emerged a dispute between Nos. 10 and 11 Downing Street about the proper level of the pound sterling against the German mark. As a result British interest rates were lowered again, augmenting the already strong underlying trends in the economy. These reductions, which culminated in a bank base rate of seven and a half per cent for a few weeks in May 1988, were gradually reversed as the year progressed further. The damage had been done, however, and the economy was growing so fast that salutary action had to be taken to cool it down. This took ever higher interest rates, culminating in the imposition of a rate of 15 per cent on 5 October just before the 1989 Conservative Party Conference.

The property market brushed aside the stock market crash. Indeed 1987 was the first year since 1979 that property assets had outperformed British equity shares. Rents were accelerating as the inflation rate began to pick up and the new supply of space had not yet reached the market. In 1988 and early 1989 there followed the climactic of the boom. With institutional investors seeking to rebuild their long-neglected property portfolios, foreign investors searching for both trophy buildings and whole companies to buy and rents rising rapidly, returns on property assets outpaced anything seen over the previous seven years. The problem was that this final convulsion was built on very weak foundations. With higher interest rates, the completion of the more deregulated development market's products and the reduction in occupier demand, only the relatively low valuation of property against other investments was a potential support as 1989 progressed.

'Big Bang' in the City of London in November 1986 was a classic example of the effects of new capacity being introduced to a market with ultimately limited demand. For nearly 80 years the London Stock Exchange had protected itself from outside or, worse still, foreign ownership of the brokers. There was an historic compromise agreed between Trade and Industry Secretary Cecil Parkinson and the then-Chairman of the Stock Exchange, Sir Nicholas Goodison, ironically for this book one of the leading property company analysts in the late 1960s, and a man who taught this writer a lot as a young beginner. The government dropped its threat to refer Stock Exchange restrictive practices to the Office of Fair Trading. In return the Exchange promised to open up its membership to outsiders and a removal of the distinction between the brokers, who solicited orders, and the jobbers, who supplied the shares. The result was that, in the period around Big Bang, many new and wealthy institutions were drawn into ownership of securities firms. Almost every major British merchant and US bank, together with participants from France, Switzerland and Hong Kong, took over one of the leading British brokerage houses. The 1980s had seen an explosion in 'securitization': companies, instead of simply borrowing from their banks, had been offered sophisticated means of raising capital from the world's institutional savers, the insurance companies and pension funds, by-passing the banks altogether. It was widely accepted that, to be a major bank in the 1990s, each institution would need an international ability to create, distribute and trade both these new instruments and more old-fashioned ones such as shares and long-term debt. London had long been a centre of innovation in these markets and dominated the European time-zone in financial markets. It was considered a centre in which, along with New York and Tokyo, every world player must have a representation in the securities market.

The new owners of these firms were often surprised to find that very profitable and prestigious businesses were operating from 1960s slab blocks with inadequate cabling for the new technology. Worse still, there was insufficient clear space for the giant trading floors which were to become a feature of the new integrated securities markets. As a result, the old brokers were showered with cash and told to upgrade their facilities. What had been ignored by the new owners was that there were very good reasons for the low overhead operations of the old partnerships. The partners had relied on bonuses for their rewards, attempting to keep their inevitable overheads of office and salaries to a minimum; they remembered the dark days of 1974 when, far from taking bonuses, most partners were called upon to make capital contributions. Now that they were merely salaried employees of banks which had apparently bottomless pockets, they were not going to stand in the way of this quantum improvement in their working conditions. Many of the glass and marble palaces built by the developers were let to those securities houses: Salomon took Greycoat's Victoria Plaza, Shearson Lehman one of the Broadgate buildings and UBS Philips & Drew another, and Citicorp the old Billingsgate fish market building. This last has yet to be occupied, and Citicorp are trying to sell their lease. James Capel, another of the leading houses, was on the brink of taking another Broadgate building when Black Monday came along. They settled instead for cramming themselves into their existing building.

The rash of new building which followed Big Bang was not complete by the time of the stock market crash in October 1987. At that time there was still deemed to be a shortage of space suitable for the financial supermarkets and their suppliers, the lawyers and accountants. Rents on new office property peaked at over £60 a square foot, with 62–64 Cornhill, developed by Greycoat and let to the Halifax Building Society in 1987, said to mark the absolute zenith in London City rents, and similar rents being achieved in the West End. The British economy was still growing at over four per cent in 1988, and rental growth in most sectors was sufficient to drive the value of property up.

According to analysts at Salomon Brothers, the amount of office space in the core of the City had remained at around 56 million square feet for twenty years before the relaxation of the City's planning constraints in 1986. As a result of that change, a further 20 million square feet was perhaps going to be built, with tens of millions more at Canary Wharf and, eventually, Kings Cross. The new supply really only began to reach the market-place towards the end of 1989. Agents Richard Ellis estimated that demand for new space, which had peaked at almost five million square feet a year, was diminishing rapidly. In the last six months of 1989, 2.2 million square feet had been let, and another 1.6 million in the first quarter of 1990, but, by the second quarter, that had fallen to only 0.8 million square feet. At the same time, new space coming onto the market had risen from 3.4 million square feet in the second half of 1989 to 2.2 million in the first quarter of 1990 and 3 million in the second quarter. As a result, the vacancy rate, of unlet property to the total stock, was rising into double figures for the first time in years.

For well-financed companies with strong rental flows, this would have proved an embarrassment but not a disaster. They could wait until the rental market picked up again, either on the take-up of the surplus space, or as inflation drove economic rents to higher levels. However, as we have seen, much of the construction of the late 1980s was carried out by new companies, or those with a need to offer higher and higher profits, generated by trading or development. They did not have a continuing stream of income and their ventures were almost always financed by banks.

It was the rise in interest rates which caused mayhem and disarray amongst these participants. The gradual rise from the middle of 1988 initially had little effect, even though both the housing and car industries gave early warnings that the best was past. The killer blow was the rise in interest rates to 15 per cent in October 1989, one of the last acts of Nigel Lawson's Chancellorship before his resignation at the end of that month.

Although many merchant developers and traders had assumed that interest rates would not always be as low as the salad days of late 1987/ early 1988, none believed that short-term rates would regain the levels in the 'teens previously experienced in the 1980s recession. Because high short-term rates are normally a symptom of accelerating inflation, being the only effective way of controlling that phenomenon, there had been an assumption that such high rates would never again be needed, since inflation had been under four per cent throughout 1986 and 1987. A combination of the excess growth in the economy during 1987 and 1988, together with self-inflicted wounds such as the Community Charge, pushed inflation to seven per cent in 1989, and, after a pause, to almost eleven per cent in late summer 1990.

The recession which followed was of quite a different nature to that of the early 1980s. Only the English-speaking nations were affected initially, and financial services, which as an industry had grown throughout the 1980s, suddenly felt the cold winds for the first time. Although those in the north and Scotland were relatively sheltered from the effects of the 1990 recession, and they would claim that their areas had not fully recovered from the earlier set-back anyway, most of the property value was concentrated in the south and, particularly, London.

The great financial conglomerates created in the 1980s suddenly found all their certainties challenged. For instance the inexorable rise in residential property prices, which had attracted many companies into buying estate agents, reversed; the huge cash-flows of the pension funds dried up as the funds took advantage of their accumulated surpluses to institute contribution holidays. The overheads and spanking new head offices remained, and action had to be taken to adjust the cost base to the new revenue levels. Ambitious plans for expansion were shelved, just as the newly developed space began to reach the market. The seeds of collapse may indeed have been sown, but in 1988 and 1989 a collective Masque of the Red Death was enacted: outside there might be the threat of an end to the good times, but, within the property market itself, things could hardly have looked better.

Rents in 1988 and 1989 grew at a faster rate than at any time since the agent's formal analyses of the market had begun in the late 1970s. There was continuing demand for modern office space, as the newly capitalized investment banks expanded in the expectation of a return to the high volume levels experienced up to the stock market crash in October 1987. The British consumer took spending to new record levels, as interest rates fell and increases in the value of houses were released through remortgages. In the industrial sector, an investment boom finally led to an increase in the demand for factory and warehouse space. Jones Lang Wootton's Property Index showed substantial rental growth in both 1988 and 1989. For offices, the rises were 23 per cent and 17 per cent; for shops, 32 per cent and 12 per cent; for industrial property 18 per cent and 28 per cent.

The rise in rental values also drove up capital values. As we have seen in previous chapters, these were the years of the most frantic turnover in the property market. The sole factor missing from the favourable environment was a fall in property yields. Only industrial property yields fell at all in these two years, and those only by one per cent between the ends of 1987 and 1989. As a result total capital values rose by about the same percentages as rents, and provided property investors with their best returns for a decade. According to the World Markets Company's analysis, the average return achieved by UK pension funds in their UK property portfolios in 1987, 1988 and 1989 were 19.4 per cent, 32.8 per cent and 18.2 per cent respectively. Nothing like those returns had been seen since the three year period 1977–1979; 1987 and 1988 were also the first years in which property had outperformed the UK equity market since 1979.

The enthusiasm for property infected companies which had only been involved via their occupation of buildings in the normal course of business. The first of these was Associated British Ports, the privatized dock company. As the method of transporting sea-going cargoes had changed, so the size and location of the docks changed, and AB Ports had found itself with acres of under-used land. In 1986 the company paid £15 million for the £7 million of published assets and the £100 million development programme of Grosvenor Square Properties, with the intention of using the management of that company to oversee all their property assets. In May 1988 BAA (the privatized British Airports

Authority) paid £165 million in cash for Lynton. Again the logic was that the airports had a large land endowment which needed active management. The largest and last of these incursions from outside was by British Aerospace, which paid £278 million in convertible preference shares for Arlington, the developers of Aztec West, the office park outside Bristol. All three companies have had to suffer the consequences of the poor timing of their purchases, although initially the AB Ports acquisition looked as though it would be very rewarding. By the end of the summer of 1991 British Aerospace was forced to raise over £400 million in new equity as cash continued to flow out of the company; Arlington was quoted as one of the culprits. It is ironic that these property company purchases were intended to be counter-cyclical, but, in the event, this property cycle was coincident with the downturn in the general economy.

The outsiders were not alone in making acquisitions which they learned to regret. The 1980s were the years of creative finance: the leveraged buy-out, whereby a predator was able to raise large amounts of bank borrowing to finance the purchase of a company, crossed from the United States at the end of the decade. In March 1988 a consortium used a vehicle named Giltvote to buy out Estates Property Investment Company for £73 million; the consortium was headed by Stephen Wingate, a survivor of the 1970s crash who had sold his family company to Wimpey, retaining some assets as a private investor. He was joined by institutions such as Eagle Star, Mercury Asset Management and Kleinwort Benson; his most prestigious partner was the London-educated Hungaro-American George Soros. Soros had built up the famous Quantum Fund by taking large positions, through both buying long and selling short, of shares, bonds and currencies.

The purchase of Imry Merchant Developers, itself a merger between its two constituents in March 1988, was initiated by another company set up for the purpose, Marketchief, for £314 million in July 1989. The partners in this company again included Stephen Wingate, (although only to the extent of £1.25 million), partnered by Eagle Star (again), the US investment bank, Prudential Bache, and a Swiss-Canadian investor, Wolfgang Stolzenberg. Already by the summer of 1990, one of the two leaders of the old Imry Merchants, Martin Landau, had left; the company then had to be refinanced by the lead bank, Barclays, since the planned sales of assets had not been sufficient to enable Marketchief to service its reported £200 million debt; Barclays agreed to provide longer-term finance.

This initial refinancing proved insufficient; in June Barclays backed the take-over of Marketchief and Imry by Stolzenberg. The portfolio would continue to be managed by Imry's Martin Myers, and a new joint-venture was set up between Myers, Marketchief and Barclays, which put equity money into the project, a very unusual departure for a British bank. An alternative might have been to put Marketchief into receivership; in this case the bank would be certain to make substantial losses, since the property would be put onto an unwilling market in which the buyers could name their own price. The Marketchief deal marked the zenith of the leveraged purchase, although the Pall Mall bid for Laing was larger and just as dependent on borrowing; the difference there was that there were existing companies onto which the bid was bolted. It was the stand-alone leveraged purchase which was vulnerable.

Between 1988 and 1990 there were over fifty bids for or by quoted property companies. Most of largest of them have been described in these pages, and many of them have ended in tears. Several of the participants have been under serious pressure and five have gone into receivership.

The banks were falling over themselves to lend secured on property assets in the late 1980s. A new generation of lending officers who had not experienced the 1970s, and an influx of foreign banks anxious to buy market share saw the total of bank lending on property rise to £40 billion by the February 1991. This represented about 12 per cent of all commercial lending, well below the 20 per cent level reached in 1974, but still enough to create unpleasant holes in any bank's balance sheet. The critical fact was that half the lending done between 1987 and 1990 was by foreign banks, with Japanese banks increasing their share of outstanding property loans from 2 per cent to 11 per cent over the period, and the other foreign (non-American) banks from 22 per cent to 26 per cent; in 1980 the share of these, mostly European banks had been only 11 per cent. The Americans might thank their recent experience in their home market for the fact that they actually reduced market share over the period from ten per cent to 6.5 per cent. With interest rates on a strong uptrend, both borrowers and lenders found that these easily arranged, secure loans soon turned into rapidly compounding debt millstones.

It was not long before the inevitable consequences of a recession, high interest rates and a flood of newly built space coming onto the market undermined the misplaced optimism. The critical question was whether a company had sufficient cash-flow to meet its interest payments and debt repayment schedules. Those particularly vulnerable also had new unlet developments. Sheraton Securities was a typical victim of the period, with no access to long-term finance and a development programme coming to fruition. Despite its well-respected management and an initial attempt at refinancing from the investment managers Mercury, part of the Warburg Group, in which Sheraton's broker Warburg Securities also operated, the rescue did not prove sufficient. By early 1991, several substantial companies, both quoted and unquoted, had gone broke: from the more residential development area Rush & Tompkins, Kentish Property (which specialised in the Docklands), and Declan Kelly; from the ranks of the commercial developers and traders, Sibec, Broadwell Land, Citygrove, Land & Property Trust and Rockfort were all in the hands of the corporate undertakers. As the reader will have learned from earlier chapters, most of the substantial stars of the 1980s were struggling to make ends meet.

Why did experienced property investors make mistakes which seem so obvious in retrospect? There is a substantial literature about popular delusions and the psychology of crowds. It applies to all markets from time to time, and suggests that there are times when rationality is thrown out of the window in the excitement of the moment. Whether it is the Dutch bulb market of the seventeenth century or the South Sea Bubble, the participants convince themselves that the current environment will continue indefinitely. Outsiders may point out that the interaction of supply and demand will eventually have an effect on rents or vacancy rates, but they are dismissed as ignorant amateurs. In fact the 1990/91 property recession was not as severe as that in the mid-1970s for most mature companies. The rise in yields in the earlier period was much more dramatic, partly because they had not fallen in the bull phase of the late 1980s.

The area of greatest self-delusion of the 1980s property market was that the words 'non-recourse' or 'partial recourse' were a guarantee that the parent company would survive any mishap in a subsidiary. It seems to have come as a surprise to many participants that the banks took a dim view of any company which was prepared to walk away from these liabilities. The same banks would almost certainly have a relationship with some other part of the group, and could prove very awkward when those facilities came up for renewal. On the other hand, the move from relationship to transaction banking meant that some of the newer banks, particularly overseas ones, had less compunction about pulling the rug from a company where they had only one asset against which they had lent. The weakening of the old 'London Rules' of banking, whereby no individual bank would act without the tacit approval of the Bank of England, even if perfectly entitled to do so, probably brought more companies down than at an equivalent stage of the previous cycle. There was less systemic risk to the British banking system in 1990 and 1991 than there had been in 1974/75, so that the Bank of England's need to read the riot act to participants was much reduced.

Will the property market recover? The answer to that is a clear yes. But, as with any economic forecast, the timing of that recovery is much more difficult to predict. Yields have already begun to move down, so that fully let property which is not rented at above current market rates, will begin to increase in value. Should inflation remain low, then the current yields against which property is measured, of bonds and shares, will fall, and property yields would seem astonishing value. Rents are still falling, as the modest economic recovery meets the flood of new space still hitting the market. I believe that this will move into reverse sooner than most observers currently think, although the recovery in rental values will be very patchy, and is unlikely to begin anywhere before 1993. The City of London office market is the one with the greatest uncertainty and overhang. No-one believes that this market will recover before 1995.

Whenever the recovery starts, there will be new participants, who will be less constrained by the experience of this recession than those who lived through it. They will repeat many of the mistakes of the 1980s, as many of the companies repeated the mistakes of the 1970s. The market will then be driven to levels which will prove unsustainable. The market will discover again that no bricks can stand when assembled by mere mortals and built upon foundations of sand.

BIBLIOGRAPHY

Binney, M (1991) *Palace on the River* London: Wordsearch Publishing
Corporation of London, (1984) *Continuity and Change – Building in the City of London 1834–1984*
Duffy, F. and Henney, E. (1989) *The Changing City*, London: The Bulstrode Press
Duffy, F. and Chandor, M. (1983) *Orbit 1*, London: DEGW and EOSYS
Esher, L. (1981) *A Broken Wave: the Rebuilding of England 1940–1980*, London: Allen Lane
Glancey, J (1989) *New British Architecture* London: Thames & Hudson
Green, S. (1986) *Who Owns London?* London: Weidenfeld & Nicolson
Marriott, O. (1967) The Property Boom, Abingdon Publishing
Plender, J (n.d.) *That's the Way the Money Goes*
Reid, M. (1982) *The Secondary Banking Crisis,* London: Macmillan Press
Robinson, J. (1987) *Minus Millionaires,* London: Unwin Hyman
RIBA (1990) *Buildings and Health – The Rosehaugh Guide to the Design, Construction, Use and Management of Buildings*
Tutt, N. (1989) *The History of Tax Avoidance*, Wiseden
Wales, HRH the Prince of, (1989) *A Vision of Britain*, London: Doubleday
Whimster, S. and Budd, L., eds (1991) *Global Finance and Urban Living: the Case of London*, London: Routledge
Williams, S. (1990) *Docklands*, Architecture Design and Technology Press

INDEX